E-COMMERCE ACTIVATED

*The Ultimate Playbook To Building A
Successful E-Commerce Business.*

BY DAMIEN COUGHLAN

Foreword: Kevin Harrington

DC Global Marketing LLC
20235 North Cave Creek Road Suite 104-167
Phoenix, Arizona 85024
USA

Print ISBN: 978-1-7370324-0-3
E-Book ISBN: 978-1-7370324-1-0
Audiobook ISBN: 978-1-7370324-2-7

April 2021 Self Published By Damien Coughlan

Cover Photo by Vali Alina, Firfirica Studio

Disclaimer: The author make no guarantees concerning the level of success you may experience by following the advice and strategies contained in this book, and you accept the risk that results will differ for each individual. The testimonials and examples provided in this book show exceptional results, which may not apply to the average reader, and are not intended to represent or guarantee that you will achieve the same or similar results.

DEDICATION

To my father Gerard, for being a perfect role model, giving me an incredible work ethic, and showing me what true entrepreneurship was all about growing up on the farm. To my mother Mary, for your support, focus on education, and for literally doing everything and anything to make me the person I am today. To my brothers and sisters, Joanne, Louise, Fergal, and Gearoid, for always being there for me, whenever I needed a helping hand.

TABLE OF CONTENTS

"Don't wish it was easier, wish you were better. Don't wish for less problems, wish for more skills. Don't wish for less challenge, wish for more wisdom." - Jim Rohn

FOREWORD

By Kevin Harrington

I have been a successful entrepreneur for over 40 years, and I've met a lot of bright and intelligent people on my travels, none more so than Damien. As you can imagine, when Damien asked me to write the Foreword to his book, I was naturally thrilled and excited.

I first discovered Damien when we connected on a Zoom call during a business startup that we were both working on. He was sharp, enthusiastic, and had a nice southern Irish accent.

I subsequently met Damien a year later in person at a high-level mastermind in Miami, Florida.

Not only does Damien have the experience and qualifications, but he is a master's educator.

This book is the ultimate guide to building a successful e-commerce business.

Damien outlines the book into four key quadrants, each quadrant a steppingstone to success.

The first quadrant describes how to start your business the right way using Damien's exact strategies. He outlines the best platforms and models to use, and the content within is useful for beginners who want to start an online business or established businesses that are trying to scale to new levels.

The second quadrant outlines how to find the right products to sell. I have launched over 20 businesses that have grown to over $100 million in sales each. I can tell you that having a great product to sell is one of the major keys to a successful company.

The third quadrant outlines how to scale your winning product. Today, companies are swapping billboards, newspaper, and radio ads for digital marketing.

The final quadrant is to systemize. This quadrant teaches you about systems, people, processes, and technology and how to remove yourself from the business so that you can work on your business and not in your business.

Now more than ever, people are shopping online. And if you are someone looking to take advantage of a trillion-dollar industry, this book will give you the exact strategies needed to start and scale a successful e-commerce business.

So, if you are someone looking for a book on e-commerce, this is it. Damien has outlined in great detail the exact strategies that he used when he saw a gap in the market and started selling dog products online to people all over the world.

Finally, I want to thank Damien for writing this book and congratulate you for reading it. As I said to Damien a few years ago when I met him, whatever you vividly imagine, ardently desire, sincerely believe, you must enthusiastically act upon it, and then it will inevitably come to pass.

Kevin Harrington – Original "Shark" on the Emmy-winning TV show, "Shark Tank," Inventor of the Infomercial, As Seen on TV Pioneer, Co-Founder of the Electronic Retailers Association (ERA), and Co-Founding board member of the Entrepreneurs' Organization (EO).

INTRODUCTION

EMBRACING OPPORTUNITY

I'd like to begin this book with a quick story; the story of how it all started and how I made the transition to e-commerce. People love stories. As children, we are told stories to develop our imagination. Stories teach us about life, who we are, and about others. I hope this introduction is a powerful means by which I can help influence, teach, and inspire you to begin your own journey and take a chance to unlock your full potential.

It's 7:40am on a cold September morning in San Francisco and the year is 2016. I am in a taxi en route to San Francisco International Airport. Morning routines are big for me; I am eager to finish listening to one of my favorite motivational speakers, Jim Rohn, and a Youtube video by Kevin Harrington as I take the last sip of a delicious green shake.

As we drive down US 101 South, we overtake buses and cars, most of them on the way to work. Some of the biggest companies in the world, like Apple, Google, Facebook, and Genetech transport their workers from San Francisco to their company headquarters in Silicon Valley—an easy 90-minute commute.

The traffic is predictably busy; the energy is high, people are frantically trying to get to work while simultaneously taking their early morning conference calls. It's a race to the office. Arriving on time is never certain with the volume of traffic that exists in California. The luxury private corporate buses with tinted windows transport their employees, each already working on their laptops with high-speed Wi-Fi. This is a real hustle and bustle part of the world.

Competition is at the heart of the Silicon Valley ethos, and as the saying goes, "the early bird catches the worm." This is the typical Bay Area morning routine; and one that I have been doing for almost four years straight.

This morning was different, though, because I wasn't on my way to work. A few days ago, I left my corporate job, and I was considering a major life decision, the kind of decision that almost makes you feel sick with worry with "what if this" and "what if that" scenarios.

I had arrived at a crossroads in my life and I was making the tough decision to take a break from corporate life and pursue a goal of becoming an entrepreneur. Most people said I was crazy and rightly so, but I was going with my gut, and it was something I had in my mind for six to nine months. I was just a farm boy from Ireland with a crazy vision to live the American dream. I had accumulated seven years at one of the biggest companies in the world; I had made incredible connections and worked on the most exciting product launches in history, like the iPhone and iPad.

Why would I throw away the security, the 401k, the stock options, the yearly salary, and the discounted products? Simple, I was burnt out. I could not do it anymore. I had given my heart and soul to corporate life and I needed a change!

For four straight years, I commuted three hours a day to and from work. Add those hours (which can be stressful if you know about commuting) to a typical Silicon Valley sixty-hour work week and that quickly adds up. My life was incredible at times but it seemed like a never-ending rat race. As soon as I reached home at night after a long workday, I was fit for nothing but a bed. There were certain times of the year where I would break out with giant ulcers in my mouth from the stress and lack of sleep. This would mean I couldn't eat for days. Everything in life has positive and negative. I was operating a dream job but at the same time, my body was saying no.

Today though, I was doing something different. I was embarking on a 22-hour flight to attend my first ever private entrepreneurial event in Asia, a continent I had never visited. This event was solely for e-commerce entrepreneurs who were doing six, seven, and eight figures in revenue.

How did I manage to get accepted to an event like this, with no prior experience or results? I guess the answer is having a big vision, not taking no for an answer, and communicating with the organizer and host on a deeper level. I remember having a direct message conversation with the event organizer and wiring him the money thereafter; at the time, it was such a big move for me to invest four figures into myself.

Am I crazy? What will my friends think? What will people at the event think? Am I good enough to be there? Why would I pay four figures for a three-day event? These questions were some of the limiting beliefs that ran through my mind, thoughts that popped into my head since childhood.

As I approached the airport, the taxi driver asks, "what airline"? I say, Cathay Pacific. "Wow, vacation sir," he asks? "No, just business and self-education," I said. The taxi driver was someone just like me, an immigrant to the United States trying to grab the opportunity and realize his full potential. Maybe he has a family he is trying to support, or pay for his rent, or just live in a country that is all about rewarding people for their hard work and ambition. I tipped him $50, his face lights up and he is almost in tears. I just made his day.

I grabbed my small rucksack and stepped out into what was the next big chapter of my life. It felt like my first day of college again, I meant business and I was ready to soak up as much information over the next three to four days. It was GO time, and this crazy Irishman was on a mission.

As I sat on the plane, about to take off, I realize that I should probably have chosen a late-night flight, as I prefer to sleep through a long flight. That is ok though, I used the time to create my masterplan: and map out some of the goals and results that I want to achieve from this event. I also wrote down some of the lessons I learned from my ten years of corporate life. I find journaling as a way to learn and grow by looking back at what worked and what didn't work. As a side note, you'll notice that throughout this book, I reach into my folder archives for old photos and references. Why? Because I treasured those moments on my path to new pastures.

The following day, I arrived in Bali, Indonesia, a little jet-lagged but ready to rock. As I step outside the airport, there are so many taxis to choose from, the cars are a little different from the Western world and it is extremely humid. I quickly grab the villa address and head straight to the meet-and-greet event. This is a gathering for people to get to know one another before the first day of the event mastermind. We stayed at a large, private villa, and I was about to meet people I had never met before. It is daunting, but life challenges us when we take big steps into the unknown and I was ready to grab it with determination and seize the opportunity.

So, what was this event all about? It was an e-commerce specific event where twenty-five of the brightest minds were coming together to learn from one another and seek the knowledge and expertise to take their businesses to the next level. I was a little nervous and sweating as I approached the villa doors. I heard music playing inside and people talking and having fun. Was I at the right place? It sounded like my kind of party, so I got excited.

I opened the door and I was greeted by the host Don Wilson. "How's it going buddy, fancy a cold one? he says with a smile. My first impressions of Don were just like I imagined, friendly, happy, excited, genuine, and there is almost a little Irish to him! I grabbed the cool Bali beer called "Bintang," dropped my bag, and began to introduce myself to the other attendees. Don is the founder and CEO of Gearbubble and is a very successful Internet Marketer. My goal is to model success, figure out what is working and how best to replicate it.

The event was a massive success. Those three to four days were life-changing. I immersed myself fully, kept a notepad and paper with me at all times, and made sure I connected with every single person at the event.

Figure 1 - My first ever self-investment. The final day at the Bali, Indonesia mastermind.

One of my most favorite parts of the event was a roundtable "hot seat." Here, each member had their own chance to speak. It was an opportunity for each person to share some of the struggles they were currently facing and the help that they needed. It was also a chance for people to share what was working well for them. When it came to my turn, I opened up like a fire hose. I started listing out a bunch of questions.

"Hi, I am Damien; I just left my job."

"What is the best niche category to sell in?"

"How do I transition from corporate to entrepreneurial life?"

"What does it take to build a great website?"

"How do I hire virtual employees?"

These were the typical beginner questions and there was nothing wrong with them. That is why I felt good being in the room with people who resonated with my questions and wanted to help. Every question was answered with clarity and detail. This was beginning to feel like the best money I had ever spent. The questions that I had perceived as challenging were solutions that other people had. It's hard to describe, but when you invest in yourself, your self-worth and confidence goes through the roof.

I was finding the right connections, gaining knowledge, learning inside secrets, and building the self-confidence to realize that I was just like everyone else in the room. If they could hit six and seven figures, so could I. I could barely contain my excitement on the trip home. My notepad was full, and I had a lot of work ahead of me. I almost felt like a completely different man. You have to remember there is a big difference between living a structured corporate life and being an entrepreneur. I had been catapulted into the entrepreneurial world headfirst.

A couple of weeks later, I am back in San Francisco working on my event notes. We also have an accountability Facebook group where we give updates. One evening while scrolling through another online e-commerce group, I saw a guy named Lawrence Aponte. He posts a picture of himself by his garage, shipping hundreds of orders from his new e-commerce store.

Figure 2- The photo of Lawrence shipping orders from his basement.

I remember the first time Damien reached out to me...He was so full of energy and very straightforward with his approach."Hey Buddie, I see what you are doing online and I want to learn!" It was from that day that Damien made the decision and stayed extremely committed.

– Lawrence Aponte

This guy seems cool! I thought. I instantly messaged him and he tells me about a free event that is happening in Phoenix, Arizona. There are going to be over 2000 people in attendance. I literally called him on Facebook Messenger seconds later. I was hungry, I wanted it bad, and he must have thought I was crazy.

Lawrence had just started selling products on Shopify. Shopify is an e-commerce platform that was taking the world by storm. It allowed non-technical people to start their own e-commerce business through their incredibly user-friendly interface. As Lawrence and I chatted about e-commerce and the event, I got to know him a bit more. Lawrence tells me his life story, which was incredible, to say the least. I told Lawrence right then that I was in, and before you know it, I was in Phoenix, Arizona, at my second event. At that event, I connected with other suppliers, marketers, agents, and just all-round good people. My circle was beginning to grow fast.

I arrive back in San Francisco after the event and I'm chatting with Lawrence on the phone about what's next. We talk about how awesome the event was and how we could create our own mastermind with the folks we just met: There were a lot of people that were just like me, looking to learn and grow fast. We came up with an idea to host an incubator-style house in Arizona where we could all live, learn, and work together under one roof. The house was later named "Marketer's Mansion," and it was located in the hills of Phoenix, Arizona. Now, I am a minimalistic guy and the only reason we got such a big house was because we had so many people interested, and we were able to divide up the costs, which made sense for everyone.

Instead of it being a short stay, we made plans to rent the house for at least six to twelve months. That would mean temporarily leaving San Francisco to completely immerse myself in learning e-commerce and everything that came with it. Again, the "am I crazy?" thoughts entered my mind. I had built up a solid Irish community in San Francisco and was leaving it behind.

I decided to go with my gut instinct and before you know it, I am driving the 11 hours from San Francisco to Arizona to begin a year-long experiment of living with seven other e-commerce entrepreneurs.

The house was massive, the view was incredible, and the excitement was real. I couldn't wait to start learning. Over the next year, everyone at the house committed to helping one another. We each had our own unique and special skills, which we shared, so everyone was learning from one another. We worked day and night to build our stores to hopefully make them a success.

Within a week, we each had fully built stores, connected supply chains, organic and paid traffic, virtual assistants, and a daily schedule down to a fine art. We were mostly selling physical products in the fitness, jewelry, and pet niches.

We worked hard and partied harder; each success was met with celebration. This was it; the era of making money online with e-commerce was in full flow. Waking up with a bunch of sales "cha-chinging" on our Shopify app, setting up abandonment cart email and SMS sequences asking people why they abandoned their cart, emailing suppliers, and handling customer service was the daily norm.

In about thirty days, I had a fully operational e-commerce store. I hit my first $100,000 in sales at a 25-percent profit and I was selling customized high-top sneakers—a product that I never touched or shipped myself. I could not believe it. This was the transition I needed, and this was my introduction to big-time e-commerce.

Figure 3- "Peetree" serving as a model for my custom high-top sneakers.

Side note: E-Commerce is the activity of electronically buying or selling products through online services over the Internet, and currently, it is thriving in this digital era. In 2019, retail e-commerce sales worldwide amounted to $3.53 trillion US dollars, and e-retail revenues are projected to grow to $6.54 trillion US dollars in 2022.[1]

I had taken a big risk, immersed myself fully, and dedicated my attention for one year to make it work. I had accountability partners, people who were backing me, and I was fully charged and committed to keep going. For once, I began to feel a level of confidence that I had never felt before.

The reason I share this origin story is to give you context on how my journey began. If you really want to succeed fast, you have to take the shortest path to success and the path of least resistance. What has continually spurred me on through the highs and lows of life is a realization that someone else has the solution to your problems and that you have the solution to other people's problems. This is why mentorship and the need to surround yourself with the right people is critical to continued improvement and success.

I hope this short story gave you a good insight into how it all started for me as you may find yourself in the same situation: commuting to work or sitting in a taxi wondering if leaving behind a secure job is worth the risk.

The strategies and techniques that I share inside this book were not designed for any one particular type of person. In fact, e-commerce does not discriminate. It does not matter where you are geographically located, what age you are, what skills you possess, or the experience that you have obtained.

You also don't need to be a coding expert, which was my biggest fear. I leveraged simple platforms to guide me through the website build, almost like a drag and drop process. You don't need to have a massive company or a broad product line. You don't need to have a fancy degree or special qualifications. Sure, I had a marketing and a master's degree, but honestly, a lot of college education becomes outdated fast, and the world today is a much different world than it was when I received my degrees.

Many of my students and clients succeed without a college education. In fact, many of today's brightest minds and visionaries have little to no college education. The education of today is moving online, and there is no better experience than hands-on experience. The best advice is to get started, find a mentor, and learn and adapt as you grow.

You don't need to have huge financial backing. I literally started my first e-commerce business using a drop-shipping method, which we will talk about later. This allowed me to sell products without buying or storing inventory upfront, which was a huge time and cost saver. Stay-at-home moms, busy dads, college students, local shop owners, retired hobbyists, full-time workers—literally anyone can build a successful online business with e-commerce.

Figure 4 - Me speaking at a private event in Scottsdale, Arizona, USA.

Here are some of the categories that have utilized my strategies and techniques:

- People looking to start an online business for the first time.
- People that are looking to earn an additional side income.
- Existing brick and mortar businesses that want to move online.
- Existing e-commerce businesses that want to scale.
- People who have failed in other business ventures.

I often find that the people who have the strongest desire and the greatest work ethic, with a rock-solid mindset, are the ones who succeed. If you are reading this, you have what it takes because if I can do it, you can, too!

More and more businesses are beginning to understand the importance of having an online presence. In 2020, because of COVID-19, traditional brick and mortar businesses that did not have an online presence struggled. With or without this virus, we were heading in the direction of greater adoption of e-commerce. For my students and I who own e-commerce stores, we have seen huge growth and a major shift in consumer spending habits. I really believe that this decade and beyond will be huge for e-commerce store owners. It has also been my busiest year to date, helping brick and mortar businesses move parts of their business online.

A simple online search will highlight some of the giant companies that we all thought were invisible but collapsed because they failed to move swiftly to acknowledge the growth of online spending habits. Some of the companies that were not quick enough to adapt and filed for bankruptcy are: Sears Holdings, J.C. Penney, Forever 21, Pier 1, Toys R Us, and more.[2]

My goal in this book is to give you the best content without the fluff! Human beings are impatient today and I know you want me to keep this book short, so I'll try my best! I am going to pull back the curtain on everything that I have learned and put it into practice successfully so you can do the same. If you follow the secrets inside this book, you will have enough information to achieve anything that you put your mind to.

Finally, there are two main reasons why I wrote this book. One is to help others who might be curious about making money online and realize the potential of e-commerce. Maybe they are tired of their job or feel they can build their own business rather than someone else's. I felt a book was the best way to disseminate the knowledge and information that I have acquired over the course of my entrepreneurial journey, a lot of which was gained through trial and error, and not to mention a lot of costly mistakes.

The other reason for writing this book is to challenge myself. This is my first ever book, I always dreamed of writing a book, but I never knew if or how that opportunity would arise. Research shows that there is a book in all of us, so I hope I inspire you to write your own book someday! As I type the words on this manuscript, I am in the COVID-19 lockdown in Medellín, Colombia. It is intense and strict here: you cannot leave the apartment, so what better way to take my mind off the uncertainty than to write. Every negative can be turned into a positive if you just take a moment to reflect and think.

Figure 5- A beautiful morning in Colombia working on this book.

"If you don't design your own life plan, chances are you'll fall into someone else's plan. And guess what they have planned for you? Not much." – Jim Rohn

MY E-COMMERCE SUCCESS PRINCIPLES

Before we get into the details of the book, let's first start with an overview so you can see how the following success principles are embedded consistently throughout the entire book. This chapter lays out what I believe to be *the most important principles* to ensure e-commerce success. I will go into more detail throughout this book and show you how they integrate.

Through my master's level education, experience in business, working with other clients, and gaining knowledge from my high-level mentors, I believe these are the most critical aspects to success in any e-commerce business. The list is presented here in no particular order.

1. **Know your customer:** Who is your ideal customer and where are they located? What distinguishes them, and how can you speak to or market to them in a way that builds trust, loyalty, and repeated sales. When I started my first e-commerce business, I sold to dog owners. I did not know anything about them, but I did know it was a massive market. I had to learn everything about them. I created a buyer persona with the goal of finding out more about their consumer habits. I needed to know where they hung out, what was the typical age range, their favorite websites, buying motivations, buying concerns, educational levels, and interests. Through a few days of research, I was able to gain a complete picture of who I wanted to market to and how my products would satisfy their needs and wants. One of the free tools that I like to use is Facebook's audience

insights.[3] It's a free tool that you can use to find out more about your niche market or target audience.

2. **Build or source a great product:** Your product is a key component of business success. A great product with average marketing and sales will always outperform a poor product with incredible marketing and sales. One of the best ways to be unique in the marketplace is to create your own product. I have designed and created my own product and it helped me be unique, control the supply chain, and tailor a unique product for my customers. The other option you have is to find products you can sell through other suppliers. I have also done this on a large scale. If you are selling a product you do not have total control over, beware of outside variables that may impact your business. One of the ways to start your business is to first use suppliers to test the validity of your product; then, once you have established that the product works, you can begin to take control of the supply chain, the ingredients, and the other areas that you initially did not own or control. Avoiding risk in the early stages of your e-commerce business is helped by using a dropship model, which essentially allows you to sell other people's products without buying or storing any inventory. If you have a product idea, chances are incredibly high that there is a supplier in your region that can manufacture, source, and ship it.

3. **Optimize your website for conversions:** A customer's shopping experience means everything, one of the biggest mistakes I see is people wasting their marketing efforts on a poorly designed and structured website. An obsession with marketing over a lack of focus on site optimization is where many people go wrong. Visitors to your store want the shopping experience to be easy, informative, and fast. Mobile e-commerce is currently the most popular way to shop online. Optimize your site for the mobile shopper in mind. Luckily for us, platforms like Shopify have plenty of themes that allow us to have different views for desktop, tablet, and mobile in just one solution.[4] If you are getting a lot of traffic to your store but your conversion rate is not where you want it to be, that's a clear sign that you need to work on your site experience. You should also dig deeper into building trust, product pricing, and any other factors which may cause people to be just browsers instead of actual buyers.

4. **Become omnipresent:** We have to keep growing our business! Today, humans have lower attention spans, but we are becoming obsessed with the Internet and social media in general. As a result, we need to master the art of not only attracting customers but ensuring they stay long enough to see or hear our message. It is not a good idea to have your business presence on just one social media platform. For example, Facebook might be the most popular way to market your product right now, but what about potential

customers who do not use Facebook or are more inclined to read blogs, use Twitter and YouTube as an example. It is vital that you branch out into all sales and social media channels or, in other words, become *omnipresent.* Not every potential customer may exist in the channel that you are posting content and advertising in. The channels you are neglecting may prove to be less competitive and produce a greater return on investment (ROI) than your current marketing channels. You need to be constantly looking at ways to find new pockets of customers and leverage the power of organic and paid traffic. The marketers who are willing to test and do more often outperform their competitors. As of the time of writing this book, the two new social media channels that have launched and have a high demand of users and low supply of content is TikTok and Clubhouse. By creating TikTok and Clubhouse accounts for your business, not only are you securing your handle name and account, but you are also moving to where the "new" action and eyeballs exist. If you are unsure about what platform is best for you, the solution is to be present across all channels and let the audience and market decide for you. You'll quickly discover where your ideal customers hang out.

5. **Believe it; content is King**: One of the neglected methods of marketing your products is leveraging SEO (Search Engine Optimization). This is typically because the results are slower than other methods of attracting customers and we

entrepreneurs are a little impatient sometimes. It is true that it takes time to rank high in the search engines for particular keywords, but it is a practice that will reap huge benefits over time. Imagine if your ideal customer would search for a keyword like "dog leashes," and your website would show high up on search results; not only is this great for brand awareness, but you are essentially getting free traffic to your website and building authority. One of the biggest expenses in e-commerce are paid advertisements and by investing time and effort in optimizing your site for SEO, over time, you are going to bring more organic sales as a percentage of total monthly revenue.

6. **Embrace email marketing:** Email marketing has been around forever and is used by every successful e-commerce entrepreneur. The beauty of email marketing is that it allows you to market to your customers and subscribers for free. You have already acquired their email through a subscription or opt-in, or you have acquired them as a customer. Email marketing allows you to create campaigns and flows. A campaign might be a once-off valentine promotion, with a specific goal in mind offering a special 25% discount off your entire store. If you have an email list of 10,000 people, you can quickly see how profitable email marketing becomes. Let's say you earn $15,000 per month with email marketing; now you know each email subscriber is worth $1.50. A flow is a type of email that is automatically sent based on a subscriber's contact information, behavior,

or preferences. This becomes incredibly powerful when you can segment your audience. An example might be a pet store. You sell and market to all types of pet lovers. Imagine having the ability to segment your entire email list so that you can create content, offers, and follow-ups that are targeted to dog buyers rather than generic pet buyers. The reason people do not focus on email marketing is because they put too much attention and focus on acquiring new customers. New customer acquisition is awesome and crucial to your growth, but it is far cheaper and easier to retain existing customers than to find new ones. If you cannot satisfy your current customers, you need to reassess your business and find ways to deliver more value to your customers. Finally, and most importantly, email marketing lists are owned by you, whereas your social media following can vanish at any given time. You are at the mercy of Facebook and the other social media giants. For example, I have seen large Instagram accounts of one million plus lose everything overnight just because Instagram decided that their content was in breach of their terms of service.

7. **Create a lifetime customer:** Selling more to the same customer is every marketer's dream! Two of the most important metrics in e-commerce are *average order value* (AOV) and *lifetime value* (LTV). The AOV is the total revenue divided by the number of orders. Imagine if you could increase the revenue per customer order so that instead of your customers purchasing one product, they

purchase two at a discount, which in turn brings more revenue and profit. Just like a server at McDonalds asks, "would you like fries with that?" The same applies in your business; how do you ensure that you capture more revenue from the same customer, which in turn allows you to spend more money to acquire the same customer. He or she who can spend the most to acquire a customer in paid advertising usually wins. LTV is the average revenue in total that a customer will bring over the lifetime of doing business with you. If for example, you know that a customer is likely to purchase from you every month, you can predict how much that customer is worth to you each year. I had a client who sold a skincare product. The cost to acquire the customer was $40-$50 with Facebook ads. The price of the product was $30, so they were losing money on the initial acquisition, but they knew that if that customer became a loyal customer that they would generate at least $360 per year.($30 x 12 months)

8. **Make the customer experience pleasant:** The next principle flows perfectly from the last. If your customer experience is a pleasant and memorable one, people will buy from you again. If you build a loyal customer base, your customers can become your best marketing tool and refer new customers to you by talking about your products and services. Over-deliver and under-promise are a sure way to delight your customers. One effective method we use is adding a simple "Thank You" card inside our packaging.

Not only is this message personalized to the individual, but we also invite our customers to share a special discount with their family and friends.

9. **Build a powerful team:** You are one piece of the jigsaw and as you grow your business, you will also need to grow your organization. You cannot do everything yourself. Hiring the right people, especially those that align with your vision, will alleviate some of the workload and stress off your shoulders. The goal in quadrant four of my E-Commerce Success Framework (ESF) is to build systems, strategies, find great people, build a strong culture, and leverage technology to really grow and scale, so you work on your business and not in your business. I will speak about my ESF framework shortly. ESF is a graphical representation of how I recommend people to approach e-commerce and identify where they are and what they need help with.

10. **Build a brand:** Most people realize halfway through their business that they are not building a brand. There is no brand congruency; there is no brand identity; there is conflicting social media and marketing efforts, unhappy customers, poor products, and in general inconsistent sales. The long-term vision of any e-commerce owner should be building a brand asset. Everything in your business should be an asset. That includes your email list, social media accounts, proprietary information, software, employees, logo, website, and the list goes on. The reason I was able to

29

sell one of my e-commerce stores was because I built a brand, and I was patient. Investors were attracted not only to the sales but to the assets that I had built. Sure, I could have focused on higher margins and profits but the underlining assets were what really attracted the buyer. Just recently, a few relatively new e-commerce brands have sold for millions of dollars in such a short period of time. The Movado Group acquired the watch startup company MVMT for $100M.[5] I hope my principles were insightful for you; I will be discussing them in greater detail throughout this book.

MY E-COMMERCE SUCCESS FRAMEWORK (ESF)

When consulting with individuals or larger businesses looking to start or scale their e-commerce business, I leverage what I call my "E-Commerce Success Framework" (ESF). This framework helps me decipher what phase or level people are at and what information or action plan they need to reach the next level.

Some people are completely new and have no prior experience, so they start off in quadrant one in the ESF model. They need a particular action plan that will differ from those in the other three quadrants. The goal here is mindset, training, focus, and preparing a plan to reach an end goal.

Quadrant two is where we help our clients sell products and services and start gaining data, sales, experience, and customers.

Quadrant three is where we begin to have our clients focus on what is working and scale that particular business, product, or service.

Quadrant four is where we have our clients build systems, processes, and a great team to systemize the operations and in general, have predictability in the business.

The goal of my ESF framework is for you to eventually reach quadrant four and have you work *on* your business and not *in* your business. Working in your business is one of the most critical mistakes entrepreneurs make when trying to scale their operations. Throughout this book, I will reference this model in more detail.

E-Commerce Success Framework

Quadrant 1 - Start	Quadrant 3 - Scale
• Learning	• Optimization
• Mindset & Focus	• Capital
• Planning	• People
Quadrant 2 - Sell	Quadrant 4 - Systemize
• Testing	• Systems
• Sales	• Processes
• Data	• Technology

Figure 6 - My ESF framework that helps people succeed with e-commerce.

SUCCESS STORIES

Those who have followed my training have not only received what they need to know in order to start or scale their business, but many have become lifelong friends and some business partners.

Most of the more than 800 people who came to visit our house in Arizona are still my friends today; it is the sense of community that exists when everyone is committed to helping one another.

Figure 7- Marketer's Mansion in Phoenix, Arizona, USA.

The people I did not meet face-to-face, but through Zoom and my online training, are still phone calls, video chat, or email away. These connections are what keep me committed and focused on the mission at hand. I am always looking at ways today to connect with more people.

I've added a number of success stories on my website, which you can visit at your leisure. If you are curious about some of the results and happy customers who have implemented our strategies, I've compiled a list of screenshots and videos celebrating their wins.

Feel free to check these out to inspire you towards what's possible at EcommerceActivated.com/success.[6]

Whatever you choose to do, surround yourself with the right people as it makes the journey more refreshing and rewarding. I think without me making a decision, four days after leaving my job, to attend the mastermind in Asia and subsequently finding mentors, I would never have had the courage to go all in.

Remember, not everyone is going to relate to your vision and that is fine, don't take it personally! You must protect and value your time or you'll end up being part of someone else's dreams and not yours. Focus on what inspires you and makes you happy. I hope that by reading this book and following my training, you will become my next student success story.

"All our dreams can come true if we have the courage to pursue them." – Walt Disney

SECTION ONE

CHOOSING YOUR MODEL

CHOOSING A MODEL TO GET STARTED

Quadrant one of my E-Commerce Success Framework (ESF) is about choosing the right e-commerce model for you. I suspect many of you reading this book may be looking for new opportunities and have a similar background story to mine. Maybe you've always wanted to start your own business, live life on your terms, and build a brand you can be proud of. I get it, I have been in your shoes and it's hard to know where to begin, who to follow and trust, and how to quickly learn what you need to learn in order to be successful.

The other problem is information overload, as it often causes people to become frustrated, hinders them from taking action or often giving up too early. Yes, the Internet is revolutionary and has an abundance of information, but it is scattered, disorganized, and can be overwhelming. One of the goals of this book is to organize and structure the most valuable and critical information in 350 pages or less. Stick with me throughout as I plan to reveal each one of my golden nuggets to help you position yourself for success. By the end of this section, you'll get a complete overview of the different types of e-commerce models that are actionable today. If you need any help deciding, feel free to reach out. As always, I am here to help.

I'll begin with the time we were all living together in Arizona, where each one of us was in the process of launching our first e-commerce businesses. Let's go back to that Monday morning in 2016. I was sitting out on our artificial grass overlooking the vast hills of Phoenix, Arizona. Nothing much grows here where the warmest month of July can average 106.1°F. Coyotes can be heard barking down in the valley while they scavenge for food.

It's a far cry from the fresh green fields of Ireland, where I was born and raised, but these are the adventures and challenges I sought out when I immigrated to the United States. As my father said, "you can't have butter on both sides of your bread."

It was also difficult adjusting to a new way of living without the busy structured corporate life of Silicon Valley and the Bay Area commute. Lack of routine and structure is one of the biggest differences you face when you become an entrepreneur: you have the freedom, and you are accountable only to yourself. You decide how your day runs.

As everyone in the house wakes up and ventures out front to begin their morning routines, we reflect back on a fantastic first weekend where we took the time to get to know one another, have some fun, and talk about how we all could work together and benefit from each other's specialized knowledge.

For me, I was a marketing expert, Lawrence Aponte was a growth hacker, Jonathan Foltz was superb at human behavior and sales, Gerardo Tafolla was a high-level connector, Aaron Burton was an ad expert, Ruslan Bezuglyy was a conversion rate optimization specialist, and so forth.

Figure 8- Jonathan Foltz teaching Axiology at the Marketer's Mansion.

Since this is an "incubator style" living, the goal is to find the skills that we are each proficient in, so we can help one another in the areas where we lack. I am really laser focused on what I need to achieve. Here, we will spend the next few months learning what e-commerce is all about and hoping to help one another crack the code.

As I embarked on this entrepreneurial journey, I thought about my corporate managers and the decisions they made at some of the biggest companies in the world. Every day, decisions were made that would impact millions of dollars, a workforce, processes, technology, and systems. I am proud of my corporate achievements, but everything had to be ultimately approved by executive management. It was very rare for anyone to make a change in the company without management approval.

Now, for the first time, I was about to make a few decisions on my own as an entrepreneur, and they were pretty big. In my corporate days, one particular factor to having projects or ideas approved was if the solution or model was simple and easy to understand. If something was difficult to explain or had too many risks with little upside, it was very rarely approved. What did get approved had to be something simple, easy to understand, make financial sense, and could be created with minimal costs and impact to the business.

So, taking this experience, I turned to a decision I had to make. What model of e-commerce could I choose that would have the lowest risk possible, is easy to explain, simple to implement, gives me maximum return for the lowest investment, and can be run from the comfort of a home with the help of virtual assistants?

We chatted at length amongst each other and decided to go with the model that had very little risk and was proving to be successful amongst Shopify sellers and made the most sense for us: drop-shipping. As an aside, the model you choose should be based on how involved you want to be in the business, the level of investment you have, and the resources at your disposal. For beginners, I think drop-shipping makes the most sense, while for established companies with their own products, you may prefer to find expert fulfillment companies or fulfill your products in-house.

I'll explain the beauty of drop-shipping shortly but one of the biggest benefits is that you do not have to invest any upfront capital in purchasing inventory. You simply find a suitable third-party supplier to supply and ship products to your customers. Having said that, not everyone reading this book will be beginners, so I will talk about other options available later. Lastly, as I learned later, do not feel pressured to pick and stick with one model. The beauty of building an online business is that it is a lot easier to pivot than it was many years ago when the Internet did not exist.

DROP-SHIPPING

As mentioned previously, drop-shipping was the e-commerce model I started with in 2016. Looking back, as someone new to the world of entrepreneurship, this was the best and correct option for me to take. It is also the model of choice for many of today's first-time sellers. You may have seen and still today, a lot of the younger generation post screenshots of their online store sales; a lot of them leveraged that same dropship model.

Most people who launch their online business do so while also maintaining a "day job," so it makes sense in terms of managing workload and mitigating risk. I know many students who make a commitment to work on their business at night as soon as their nine-to-five is finished. The aim for most is to reach a level where the income earned from their side hustle is greater than that of their monthly salary. This is a great way to step into entrepreneurship because most people want to be entrepreneurs but often aren't willing to make the sacrifice.

Drop-shipping is when someone purchases a product on your website, but you pass the order details to a supplier, who then ships the product directly to your customer. The biggest benefit is that you do not need to buy upfront inventory, own a large warehouse, design or manufacture the product, or deal with the actual shipping of the orders. Essentially, the entire supply chain and production are outsourced to a third party, leaving you to manage the website, marketing, and customer service.

Figure 9 - The dropship model explained.

The main benefit is you only pay your supplier once an order is placed by a customer on your website. In the example above, a customer places an order for $40 on your website. You send the order to your supplier and they charge you $10 for the product and shipping. You keep the $30 profit less any expenses such as marketing. This allows you to list products on your website without having to purchase anything upfront. The added cherry on top is that orders are synced via your supplier's application programming interface (API), so communication on payment, tracking numbers, and customer information is in sync and accurate.

You can drop-ship from different websites like Ali Express, Alibaba, eBay, Etsy, Amazon, Walmart, Spocket, CJdropshipping, Banggood, and much more. These companies have such a large database of suppliers and products that you can literally source any type of product. Ali Express and Alibaba were the most common websites to drop-ship from in the early boom of e-commerce drop-shipping. The beauty is you can use apps like Oberlo[7] and Dropified[8] to manage the connection between some of these suppliers so that order processing and product management is much easier. I offer a free PDF on my website that goes into greater detail and lists all one hundred plus drop-shipping companies for a wide variety of products. You can also find it in the resources EcommerceActivated.com/resources section of this book.

Steps to Creating a Drop-shipping Business:
- Select a niche or audience, such as the dog niche, fitness niche, health niche, etc.
- Perform research on what products are selling in each niche.
- Find a supplier you can trust to source and ship your products to your end customer.
- Build your store using an easy platform like Shopify.
- Create a marketing plan with a focus on organic and paid traffic strategies.
- Analyze and optimize your site for conversions.
- Build a brand by delivering high-quality and in-demand products with a great customer experience.

Benefits of Drop-Shipping:
- **Lower capital requirement:** With drop-shipping, you don't need to store thousands of dollars' worth of inventory. Instead, you only purchase a product once you receive an

order from your store. You are also buying the product at wholesale prices and selling at retail prices.

- **Wide product selection:** When you don't need to stock your items, it allows you to offer a wide variety of products in your store. E.g., You can list as many dog products as you wish on your website and give your customer as much choice as possible.

- **Low risk:** If things don't work out, you aren't stuck with thousands in inventory that you have to sell at a loss. You can also literally start an e-commerce store for under a hundred dollars. A monthly $29 subscription which has a 14-day free trial, and a domain name which will cost about $11. I'll have all these links in the resources section of the book.

- **Location independence:** Because you don't have to worry about fulfillment or running a warehouse, it's possible to run a drop-shipping business from anywhere in the world with a laptop and Internet connection. As I was writing this book and managing my stores, I was in Medellín, Colombia.

- **Highly scalable:** There is a huge opportunity to scale what works! With social media and paid online ads, you can scale a product to millions of dollars in a short period of time.

Drawbacks of Drop-Shipping:

- **Lower barriers to entry**: More people dropship, which increases competition because of the low capital requirements and speed of setup without stock requirements. If a product proves popular and it is seen to be going viral, other marketers will jump on the trend and that will naturally increase competition for the same customers. A perfect example: The fidget spinner craze.

- **Lower margins:** More competition in the marketplace means margins for drop-shipping stores are usually lower; typically, dropshipping stores operate between 20-25% profit margins. This makes it harder to grow in the initial stages as a beginner if you cannot find the right products and the correct percentage of the cost of goods sold. Once you learn how to increase the average order value (AOV) and lifetime value (LTV), things become a lot easier.

If you are a business owner who is trying to grow online or someone who is building a business for the first time, I hope this chapter gives you an insight into how e-commerce drop-shipping works. If you are still a little confused, don't worry, as you will pick it up as you go through the book. I will focus on a few business models rather than all of them, as I suspect that many of you reading are either launching your first-ever business, scaling an existing business, or taking a brick-and-mortar business online. Either way, the information in this book will cater to you.

PRINT-ON-DEMAND

The next model available to you is Print-on-demand (POD). POD is where you create your own custom designs and place those designs on other products like mugs, t-shirts, hoodies, blankets, socks, leggings, phone cases, and so on.

POD is drop-shipping but with customized items. A big trend today is allowing customers to personalize their products. You might have seen couples in public wearing shirts that have funny slogans like "I don't need Google, my husband knows everything" or "Looking at my wife, I think DAMN, she's a lucky woman." Those types of shirts that you regularly see are print-on-demand products that we marketers create. The big opportunity today is allowing people to personalize those items with names and catch phrases. The world is really moving towards a personalized customer experience.

You can leverage companies like Teespring, Customcat, Gearbubble, Teelaunch, Printful, Pillow Profits, Viralstyle, and Shineon to upload your own designs on their products and have these companies ship the final product to your end customer.

The following is a recent example of a print-on-demand jewelry product on one of my stores that generated over $100,000 in sales. What really sold this item was the actual message card insert behind the jewelry piece. This message emotionally connects with the buyer (husband), who is giving the necklace as a gift to his wife. Also, with Facebook "hyper-targeting" ads, I was able to easily target men who were married, and were over 45 years of age, and showed an interest in custom jewelry.

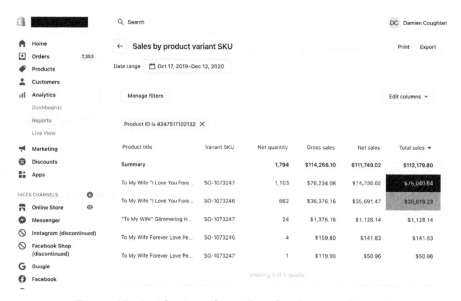

Figure 10 - Inside view of my Shopify admin dashboard.

Figure 11- One of my best-selling custom jewelry products.

The reason why these categories of products sell so well is because print-on-demand products are unique. Online Shoppers's have never seen anything like these types of products in any traditional retail stores. Some people buy on emotion and if you can show someone a product that they really want but never knew they needed, you are on to a winner. Obviously, competitors emerge as time goes by, so it's important to take advantage while you have a winning formula.

You can imagine when you combine a product that most women wear, in this case, jewelry, with a passionate and loving message, you get a lot of viral likes, comments, shares, inquiries, and ultimately sales.

Simple Steps To Launch A Print-On-Demand Business

- _Select a niche and product. (e.g., dog lovers, t-shirts)_
- _Find what is trending by performing a simple search._
- _Create your designs using Canva or Photoshop._
- _Choose the print provider. (e.g., Printful)_
- _Add designs into your store._
- _Market and promote your products._
- _If you see something that works, replicate it for other niches._
- _Spend time perfecting your designs._
- _Have fun._

Figure 12 - Steps to launching a print-on-demand business.

PRIVATE LABELING & MANUFACTURING

Let's move to another very popular model for e-commerce sellers. A private label product is manufactured by a contract or third-party manufacturer and sold under a retailer's brand name. As the buyer, you specify everything about the product – what goes into it, how it's packaged, what the label looks like. This is usually the next step that most people who enter the world of e-commerce choose after drop-shipping.

Benefits Of Private Labeling

- *The product is to your specifications*

- *You control the packaging*

- *You get brand recognition*

- *You can charge a higher price*

- *Greater market stability*

Figure 13 - Benefits of private labeling.

A simple example of a private label product that you may or may not have seen over the past few years is a company called Blendjet.[9] They started off as a drop-shipping company. Blendjet's slogan is "Be Anywhere, Blend Anywhere." They sell a blender that is USB chargeable, self-cleaning, lightweight, powerful, and portable. Think of your favorite water bottle with a blender on the bottom. You can crush ice, mix protein powder, or even create your favorite cocktails on the go.

Blendjet found a need in the marketplace, and it was a perfect solution for those people who have busy lifestyles, perhaps a professional who is health-conscious and wants to be able to have their shakes at work or right after the gym.

Blendjet started off just like a regular drop-shipping store, where they were testing different products and shipping directly from China to their initial customers, without any logos or fancy packaging. As soon as they discovered that the blender was a hit, they started to private label the product with logos and customized packaging and reduced their shipping times by having warehouses in the US. As you scale a product, you cannot keep drop-shipping. By private labeling their product, they were able to charge a premium price, build brand loyalty, keep customers happy, and attract large influencers in the fitness space like Jen Selter.

This is just one of many examples of how people start with drop-shipping by finding products that have an X factor, appeal to a mass market, and can be instantly branded once the demand is proven.

The below is a photo example from the website Alibaba, which produces almost identical products to Blendjet but is served only for demonstration purposes. I took a Chinese supplier that I know of and showed you the process involved in making one of these units. I showed you Blendjet's product in the same image as a way to illustrate how private labeling works. Blendjet now has its own manufacturing and supply chain in the USA.

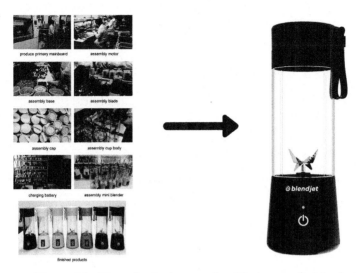

Figure 14 - Hypothetical example of factory to finished product.

WHITE LABELING

White labeling refers to a product or service purchased by a reseller who then rebrands the product or service to give the impression that the new owner created it. The difference between white label and private labeling is that in the case of private labeling the product is created to be sold exclusively by a single reseller.

I have a client in the fitness industry who has a large social media following. One of his long-standing goals was to build his own e-commerce supplement brand. For years, he promoted other people's products as an affiliate. He was essentially getting paid a percentage of every sale he referred. Some of the companies he worked with were large protein and pre-workout brands that wanted to leverage his loyal and large social media following.

He was earning on average 15% every time he referred a new customer. The problem, though, was that he was not building his brand but someone else's. Every sale he referred was building equity for someone else. Within a few months, I was able to leverage my network and help him create his own line of products, over which he now has complete control and ownership. Instead of 15% of the revenue, he now gets 100% of the revenue.

As my client is a specialist in fitness and not product creation, it makes sense for him to choose the white label option. That way, he can stay focused on what he is good at and truly passionate about. My client literally took the white label suppliers, tried and tested formulas and implemented them into his business as if they were his own. This is such a huge benefit and takes complete responsibility off of his shoulders.

Some of the Benefits of White Label are:
- You don't have to be an expert.
- You don't have to have a design/recipe.
- Often less expensive than private labeling.
- You get brand recognition.

If you've ever bought supplements online, I bet if you check, you'll find the same ingredients across a number of similar brands. The only difference is the marketing and packaging.

It's not just supplements. You can white label services, products, websites, funnels, and much more. There is always a solution for your needs and that's why in quadrant one of ESF, we go through your available options.

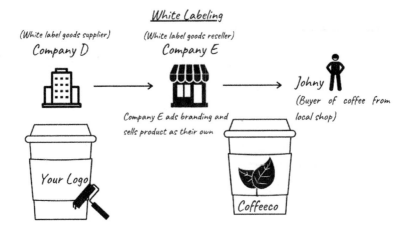

Figure 15 - White labeling model explained.

WHOLESALING

Wholesaling is often a good middle ground between manufacturing and retailing. Wholesaling means you (the wholesaler) are buying in bulk at discounted prices from your manufacturer. In this scenario, you might have forecasted future demand, or you may have a number of retailers willing to stock and sell your product. You can create a wholesale-only section on your store where people can register to create accounts to sell your products if they qualify. Margins are typically smaller with this model, but if you can mass produce items that are in demand, it can be a fantastic model to get to market quickly. When it comes to wholesaling, relationships are everything. A *note of caution:* There is a greater risk involved and more chance of failure because you are dealing with a larger movement of goods.

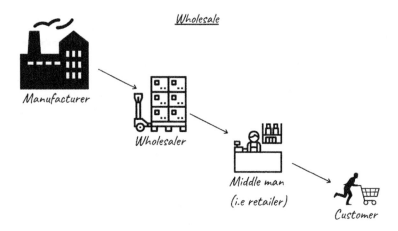

Figure 16 - Wholesale model explained.

IN-HOUSE FULFILMENT

In-house fulfillment is when you handle the entire order fulfillment process yourself. Usually, fulfillment can be handled at your home or office or, depending on the scale of your operations, a nearby warehouse. It involves having a team of operators with an available supply of products on hand that can select, pack, and ship orders as they come through on your website.

As you can imagine, it requires the business to take on a whole new level of responsibility and costs to ensure the customer gets the right product delivered, to the right destination, at the right time. It is almost in itself a second business, tied into your existing online operations.

For the in-house fulfillment model to work, you'll need to consider purchasing or renting warehouse space, employing and training staff, buying equipment, investing in the right software and paying for insurance. As you can imagine, at this level of operations, you will need to hire really good people to support you in your business. We will talk about people later when we perform your self-analysis and how involved you want to be as you scale your business. We'll discuss this in quadrant four. Do not take lightly how difficult in-house fulfillment is if you are not ready or have the resources on hand.

The benefits of in-house fulfillment are that you have more control over the entire supply chain. You'll have a better customer experience with faster shipping times, and you'll have the ability to customize the packaging, along with any personal messaging that you want to include.

You can choose to outsource your fulfillment to a third-party company if you feel your efforts would be best served to marketing and sales, and in general, growing your business. One example that you can is the Dollar Fulfillment company.[10] Again, I will list all references at EcommerceActivated.com/resources.

I remember the first time I tried order fulfillment from our house in Arizona. I launched a second site selling to heavy equipment operators called Dieselmad. It was a huge learning curve for me, albeit on a small scale. I will attach a photo of me shipping out the first orders of a custom-made product that I created for the heavy equipment niche!

Figure 17 - Left: Me in Arizona shipping orders from home.
Right: Happy customer with a photo review.

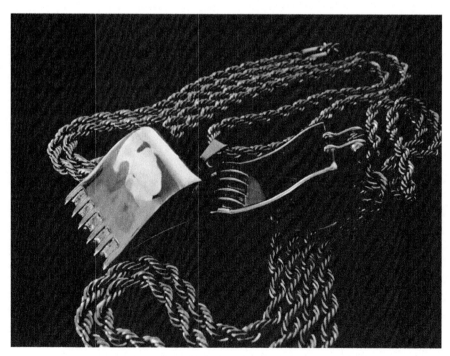

Figure 18 – Closeup photo of the necklace I created,
designed, and manufactured in 2016.

As you can see, I was printing labels using the Shipstation app and a small printing machine. Yes, the riches are in the niches! What this means is success can be found by going deep inside a particular niche and discovering what they want. I surveyed inside my heavy equipment Facebook group that hard-working, mostly male operators, wear jewelry too, so I designed a product that they wanted!

If you're keen on this model, hire an operations manager to manage your people at the fulfillment center. My friend Jonathan has a fulfillment center in Miami, Florida and I can tell you that it is labor-intensive and requires people who are highly skilled at systems and processes. One mistake can cost thousands of dollars, missed opportunities, and unhappy customers.

For me, this would make sense if you were either a) a specialist with a product that only you could manufacture; or b) someone with a lot of capital and a seasoned business owner. Put another way, let's say you are someone who sells unique items like "handcrafted, Irish-made furniture." The unique selling point of your product is that it is "handcrafted and made in Ireland." Most people will want it shipped and handcrafted by you personally. This is a different type of product compared to say, just selling phone cases. You are paying extra for the quality, workmanship, and origin of said material.

SUBSCRIPTION MODEL

Every entrepreneur loves recurring revenue. The subscription model is one of my favorite models and is what I use for students who want help to build predictable monthly revenue. In the case of e-commerce storeowners, the subscription model is where the storeowner provides ongoing products or services on a regular basis in exchange for regular payments from the customer. These payments are usually made monthly and can be cancelled at any time. The subscription model has become very popular over the last few years as it benefits the customer, the seller, and the supplier.

Customers enjoy the convenience of a high-value offer at a low-cost, recurring investment. Companies offering subscriptions can also more easily predict revenues, build deeper relationships, increase lifetime value, and build a bigger brand. It also provides a more accurate prediction of demand, which helps a company keep its production streamlined and enables it to be proactive rather than reactive.

A great example is the supplement brand "Dollar Shave Club." With their model, each month, you receive five replacement cartridges at the advertised cost of just $1 per month, hence the name "Dollar Shave Club."

Two important terms to know and understand are acquisition costs and churn rates: Acquisition cost is the cost to acquire the customer; churn rate is the percentage of your customers who cancel or don't renew their subscriptions during a given time.

Obviously, your goal is to keep the churn rate as low as possible. One way to do this is to constantly survey your customers and ask for feedback while also delivering new and improved products that meet consumer needs.

If you are a new company starting off, a subscription model allows you to predict future revenue and will definitely help you overcome possible cash flow issues. If you know your churn rate and your expenses, it becomes easier to predict monthly profit and loss.

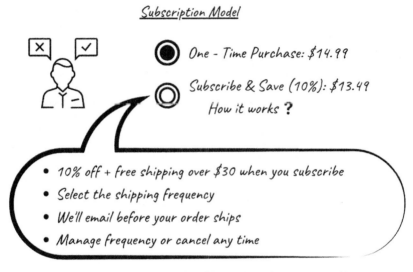

Figure 19 - An example of how the subscription offer looks like on a product page.

I remember the old days when the grocery delivery man used to come to our family house every few days. We paid for the convenient service as it ensured we would have fresh bread, milk, and the newspaper. My sister recently came to me asking for help starting her first fruit and veg business. She lives out in the beautiful countryside of Ireland. The benefits of living in this part of the world are the beautiful green fields, bountiful rainfall, and water you can drink from the stream. She is passionate about healthy living and there's a local food market in a town called Kinsale. My aim is to help her sell online *and* also set up a stall so that she can promote and sell her vegetables to the local community. In these uncertain times, one thing communities are doing is helping local businesses.

My goal for her business is to first turn a profit. The second and most important goal is to bring in predictable revenue through a subscription offer. Imagine if, at the start of each week or new month, she would have eighty to a hundred customers ready to replenish their orders. If you have a great product, people will come back for more, and that is what drives the benefits of a subscription model business! Even more, you'll soon discover your customers referring their friends and family members. Finally, I want you to take inventory of your personal and professional subscriptions. What made you join; what value do those subscriptions bring? I know off the top of my head I have Audible, Dropbox, Google Drive, Netflix, Amazon Prime, and Apple Music, to name just a few.

Now that you've been shown a few different models to help you launch your e-commerce business, it is fair to say that there is something for everyone. If you are still confused or uncertain about which route to take, keep reading. It will make sense with some additional context. I'll also finally mention that choosing the "Drop-shipping" method is always a great choice if you are eager to get started with little to no effort or upfront costs.

The next few chapters in quadrant one will focus on your strengths and weaknesses, how to build a solid mindset, and how to prepare yourself for the road that lies ahead.

SWOT ANALYSIS

Let's now focus on the benefits of performing a Strengths, Weaknesses, Opportunities, and Threats (SWOT) analysis. I've often found a SWOT analysis to be beneficial as it helps you understand you and your business better and may help you in taking action and choosing what's right for you.

The SWOT framework is credited to Albert Humphrey, who developed the approach at the Stanford Research Institute (SRI) back in the 1960s and early 1970s.[11] The first step of creating a SWOT analysis to write down all of your strengths, weaknesses, opportunities, and threats. Be honest with yourself, remove the ego, and try and be as honest and accurate as you can.

- What are you really good at?
- What do others seek your help with?
- What is something you could become better at?
- What is one thing you are told that you could possibly improve on?
- What are the opportunities for growth?
- Is there a resource that is available that you could learn from?
- Could you partner with someone?
- What are some of the threats that exist that may stop you from achieving goals?

Here is an example of the SWOT analysis in action when decided on a new product launch:

Strengths: After one year, you've built a list of five hundred thousand dog lovers across your social media pages. You polled them to ask what products they'd like you to sell. The biggest request was for the ability to upload photos of their dogs onto canvas artwork. Not only are you asking your ideal customers what they want, but you are building a community and brand. Having a large following is a huge asset and strength that you must leverage.

61

Opportunities: Create canvas wall art products where your community can customize their own canvas products using a simple app on your website. Provide incentives to your designers by giving them a percentage of total sales made so they can produce more designs each hour. Your designers are happy because they are getting paid more, and your customers are getting their orders processed faster.

Weaknesses: Since this is a specialized and personalized product, the labor and fulfillment are a little trickier and more time-consuming. Make the product so amazing that it will allow you to charge a premium price for the service. In this type of scenario, for something like a pet portrait, customers will spend more.

Threats: Competitors may enter your market. Allow your customer to become affiliates so they can refer their friends and other dog enthusiasts. Building a strong army is going to increase your chances of becoming the industry leader in personalized dog products. You can also leverage celebrity influencers to become brand ambassadors.

So that's an example of how you perform a SWOT analysis at its most basic level. The goal is to look at the viability from all angles. What are the areas that you excel in and what are the areas you need to improve on or monitor? You can perform this analysis in any life situation, personal or business. Obviously, you would try and list as many benefits and drawbacks as possible to come to the best decision.

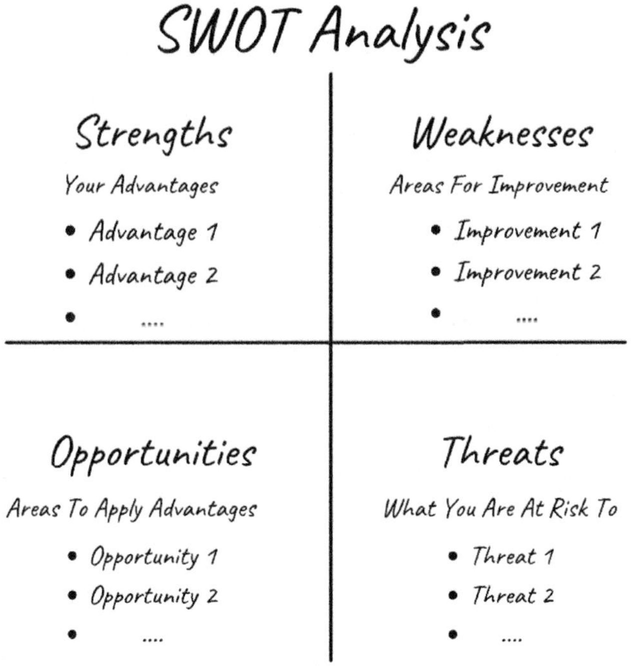

SWOT Analysis

Strengths

Your Advantages

- Advantage 1
- Advantage 2
- ....

Weaknesses

Areas For Improvement

- Improvement 1
- Improvement 2
- ....

Opportunities

Areas To Apply Advantages

- Opportunity 1
- Opportunity 2
- ....

Threats

What You Are At Risk To

- Threat 1
- Threat 2
- ....

Figure 20 - SWOT Framework.

If you are in a position right now to hire more people to help you in your business, then it is important for you to create your SWOT analysis. That way, you can hire the right people to handle the areas of your business where you are less skilled.

When I reached that house in Arizona, I too had to think deeply about my SWOT analysis. Since I was focused on a drop-shipping model that had custom products, I needed to hire a really great designer. If you are a company that sells custom shirts, shoes, etc. then your designer will be the lifeblood of the business.

I knew that if I wanted to scale my custom sneaker sales, I'd have to hire a professional designer. Most of these artists have years of experience and I knew that the cost of me actually trying to learn and create the designs was not a good option. Also, I wasn't inspired or passionate about art; when I looked at my strengths, I realized that my attention would be best served to marketing and trying to get as many customers as possible into my business through paid and organic traffic methods.

Remember, you won't be able to do it all yourself, so it's perfectly fine to delegate and outsource some of the workload. Just because you may see other Entrepreneurs doing everything themselves doesn't mean that they are a) more cost-efficient or b) in more control. It is quite the opposite. When Henry Ford built Ford motor company, he knew he had to hire the brightest minds and experts to compliment his skills.

"The smartest man in the room surrounds himself, in that same room, with people, who are smarter than he." – Henry Ford.

The purpose of this chapter is to get clear on what you are good at, and what you are not so good at, and where you need help. The other question and most important is what inspires you and what do you love to do. The beauty is what you may perceive as challenging or a chore is often fun and exciting to others. You just have to go and find those people who are willing to do what you are not.

I hope this chapter was an eye-opener, so you can go ahead now and start filling out those goals and taking massive action. By creating your master plan, you can move through this book with clarity, purpose, and focus.

SMART ANALYSIS

When setting goals, I encourage you to follow the SMART formula. SMART stands for specific, measurable, attainable, relevant, and timely. It was developed by George Doran, Arthur Miller, and James Cunningham in their 1981 article "There's a S.M.A.R.T. way to write management goals and objectives."[12]

Most people set goals but never accomplish them. Here's another example: As I was proofreading this manuscript, I realized that writing a book is a lot harder than I ever imagined. That is usually the first mistake people make. They set unrealistic goals, and when the going gets tough, they give up. A couple of years ago, I discovered that setting micro-goals is a lot more effective.

Let me give you an example. I knew I had to write a book in 2020. Instead of having this broad goal, I divided it up into smaller milestones. I knew I needed to first think about my broad idea: I needed a title, I needed an outline, then I had to write individual chapters. There were almost eighty deliverables needed to achieve the completion of the book. By dividing the book into deliverables, I was realistic with the level of effort required and accomplishing micro goals. As soon as I completed goal one, it motivated me to move to goal two, and so forth. I challenge you to do the same with any goal, break your goals down and make them more achievable.

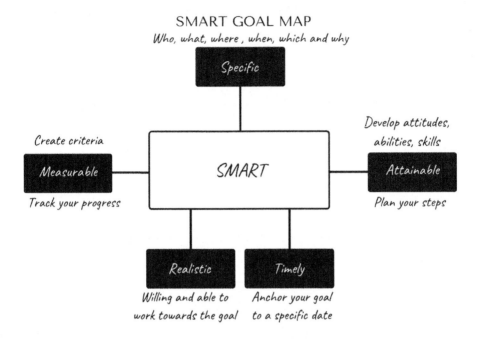

Figure 21 - SMART analysis explained.

Once I identify and write down my goals on paper, I transfer them to Trello. Trello is an organizational software that you download and use on your computer or phone. The world is changing every day and do not feel like you have to stick to your original goals. What I thought were the steps to writing a book at the beginning changed as I learned more about the specifics of writing a book. Heck, there's been times when I get writer's block; I've had to go for a walk or try and revisit writing the following day. Imposter syndrome is another problem, and I, like many others, often question myself if I am really good enough to take on such large challenges.

Too many people stick to goals that they do not value anymore for fear of judgment. I encourage you to revisit goals daily, adjust, improve, and trust the process. Also, slow down and take a break if you need.

I want to share with you how I set, revisit, review, and adjust my goals so I have a strong master plan at all times. Your goals may change over time, this can happen because of internal or external factors and that is perfectly fine! This is why it is important to revisit your goals every week at least and adjust them to meet your long-term objective.

When I first started out in e-commerce, I failed! I actually tested (which means launching a product to the marketplace to estimate demand) a number of different t-shirts and they failed miserably. Remember, just because something fails once does not mean it will continue to fail. "Failure is simply the opportunity to begin again, this time more intelligently." – Henry Ford

I asked myself why they failed and how I could I re-adjust my goals? Luckily with the e-commerce business model I follow, testing can be done quite cheaply and without the need to buy inventory. I had set a target of $1000 in sales in my first week and I sold a big fat zero. I spoke with one of the guys and we walked through some of the adjustments that needed to be made. I adjusted the target from $1000 to $100 in sales. $100 in sales meant I had to sell four t-shirts. It now became a lot clearer to me; the target was more identifiable and manageable. I also hired a part-time remote designer. I focused on what was already working in the marketplace and asked my designer to take inspiration from those designs and make ours better. I didn't copy the exact design, but rather took a concept that was working and improved it.

So, we adjusted the goal by reducing the target, making it more measurable, increasing the visual appeal of the design, and focusing on outsourcing some of the workload so I could get back to what I was good at, which was marketing. That same week I sold six t-shirts! I could not believe it, my heart started to pump fast, and I felt a rush going through my body. For those of you who have made your first sales online, you know what I mean. For those who have not yet experienced the feeling, it is worth the wait.

I took the profit and re-invested it back into my business. I set new goals for the week ahead. As you will see throughout my story, I am constantly adjusting, tweaking, and optimizing for success.

I encourage you right now to take a goal that you have failed at achieving in the past. List every single action that you believe is required for you to hit that goal, big or small. Take those actions and order them in terms of difficulty, one to ten. Next, move them into an order that is needed for you to begin. Look at the difficulty of the first action item and give it a due date. I bet the goal seems a lot easier right now. Then, take immediate action on the first deliverable. Monitor your progress and reward yourself once you have completed action item number one.

HOW TO PUSH THROUGH YOUR WORKLOAD

Before going further, I want to talk about how to push through your workload. These are the core tasks that need to get done, even if they are not high on your values list. As you have probably experienced already, there will times when you will not want to work on particular goals. This is because that specific goal or action does not align with your highest values.

One of the experts I study is Dr. John DeMartini. I met Dr. DeMartini at a Miami conference a couple of years ago. I was blown away by his knowledge of human behavior. In his book *The Values Factor: The Secret to Creating an Inspired and Fulfilling Life,*[13] he provides insights on how to create an extraordinary life. He mentions how people are motivated and inspired by what lies highest on their values. For example, someone who loves data and numbers is going to be more inspired by the accounting and financial aspects of a business as opposed to marketing and sales.

As an entrepreneur, how do you force yourself to complete tasks that need to get done regardless of what you love to do? The reason I say this is because in the initial stages of growth, as the founder and visionary, you may have to wear many different hats in day-to-day operations. When difficult tasks that do not align or inspire you arise, you will need to identify how that task, once completed, helps you achieve a more long-term goal.

Once you identify how tasks that you perceive to be difficult and challenging play a role in reaching bigger goals, your mindset will change, and you will be inspired to push through each struggle and void. Here's one example: By building an e-commerce store, even though you may not like the thought of doing it or you may lack the knowledge, by figuring it out and making it happen, you'll send visitors to your store and acquire your first customers. A simple exercise to try: List the first ten steps that need to happen to get your first sale. List them in order and use them to guide you through each task and reach the end goal of acquiring a customer.

I say this because it happened to me. I procrastinated so many times on launching my e-commerce business, but when I started to break down the tasks into smaller detail and use a "link and stack" method, I was able to push through goals because I always connected the tasks and linked them to the end goal. A lot of these strategies can be found in Dr. DeMartini's book.

Another tip is to start tackling the most difficult tasks earliest in the day. As the day moves on, our discipline wavers, and we start thinking about what we can push off until the next day. I find having a daily routine is key to having a productive day. Planning your day the night before gives you clarity, purpose, and drive. It allows you to notify your team, family, and anyone else, that you are busy and unreachable.

Taking regular breaks is another way to stay fresh and push through the workload. I usually work in two-hour intervals. I might go for a walk in the morning and listen to audio, then I'll work straight for two hours, and then I'll grab another 30-minute break.

Finally, reach out for help. Yes, that's right, if you are stuck, look for someone to help relieve some of the pressure and burden. It might be a family member, friend, employee, or mentor who can lend a helping hand. Trust me; I would not have been able to launch my e-commerce business without the help of Lawrence, Jonathan, my friends, and mentors. We can't let ego get in the way of asking for help.

YOUR BRAND AND MISSION

When you launch your business, you need to have a brand identity and mission statement. That means establishing the building blocks that make your website and other brand assets appealing. Too often, this part of the launch strategy is overlooked. Many people jump into a business launch headfirst, cross their fingers, and hope everything will magically fall into place.

If I mention McDonald's logo, you immediately visualize the red, yellow, and giant "M" symbol in your mind. The same should eventually apply to your business.

Additionally, if you look at any successful company, there is meaning behind what they sell. Again, more and more shoppers are starting to focus on the "why," whereas before making a purchase was solely based on price and utility. I know companies that are crushing it right now because they are selling products that are environmentally friendly. They have built a message around "improving the planet with biodegradable material." Patagonia, a giant outdoor clothing company, has a corporate policy of "100% for the planet." This is in line with their customers' profile: people love spending their time outdoors, whether it is hiking, walking, or enjoying other adventure sports. Their customer is someone who would do anything to protect the great outdoors in which they spend most of their free time in.

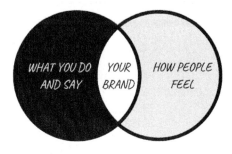

Figure 22 - How a brand is created.

Be consistent by ensuring your employees know the mission, brand ethos, and if they don't, design a brand guidelines document. Your mission statement is an asset and should be unique to you. Here are some key questions to ask yourself about your brand and mission *before* you launch:

- What are your brand guidelines?
- How do you want your brand to be represented?
- What is your mission statement?
- How do you want people to feel when they think about your brand?

Why is this so important? You may be surprised to hear this, but one of the most commonly viewed pages of an e-commerce store is the "About Us" section. This is why you'll see companies, especially those that charge a premium price, focus on being unique or being extraordinary in how they represent their brand in the marketplace.

My question to you is: What makes your company or brand different? Why would someone buy from you as opposed to your competition? What is it that attracts buyers to your products and services, and what do people say about your brand when they mention your name?

In a recent 2021 report, Shopify stated, "Brands must demonstrate authenticity, transparency, and accountability as consumers increasingly support local businesses and sustainable products."[14]

Additionally, the report found:

- 53% of consumers prefer green or sustainable products.
- 49% of consumers respond positively to retailers making a donation to a cause with each purchase.
- 23% of consumers shop at local or independent retailers to reduce their environmental impact.

As this Shopify report reveals, the consumer is doing their part to contribute to a changing world. If you cannot compete on the above, think about the other ways to differentiate yourself from the competition.

Maybe you employ moms that work from home or college kids, or you sell only organic products, or you cut back on packaging to help the environment. Find your unique distinguishing factor that obtains a competitive advantage in the marketplace and be sure to highlight it.

Before I launched my dog brand in 2016, I mapped out the entire vision on a giant whiteboard. I outlined what attributes dog lovers would want from an amazing, new, and innovative dog brand? I knew the market was competitive, so I wanted to be unique and different. I also knew that my marketing skills would give me an advantage. I looked at my time at Apple and started to think about how they have mastered the ability to attract and retain customers.

Before I knew it, I identified the best colors and fonts to use in my store. I created an online community where I could get relevant feedback on products that my ideal audience would want. I added my friends who were dog lovers into a private Facebook group, including Lawrence, who has a Chihuahua named Peetree. Before I knew it, I started to get a feel of how my potential customer acted and thought.

Every day, the community posted pictures and suggestions. I started to map out my brand guidelines and eventually came up with a mission statement. I gave group members access to a preview of my store and took more suggestions. I was finally confident in launching, and a couple of days later, released the site for its grand opening. This goes back to my earlier thoughts on seeking help: You must be open to input from other people if you truly want to deliver a great product.

HOW TO MOVE YOUR EXISTING BUSINESS ONLINE

Usually, there are three types of people I help in the marketplace. The first is looking to build an online business as a complete beginner. The second is someone how has an established business and wants to scale. The third is an established brick-and-mortar retail business owner who wants to create an online presence for their products and services. The people in this final group are who we are going to talk about in this chapter.

An example might be a furniture shop that has a brick-and-mortar presence but wants to start selling online to reach a wider audience, increase the number of products they sell, increase sales, and avail itself of economies of scale. In the case of moving your business online, it is easier than you think.

You've already built a presence offline, acquired customers, built brand loyalty, and now you are ready to replicate your success online. In fact, in the year 2020, I helped a lot of struggling businesses that were suffering because of the restrictions faced by their business due to pandemic lockdowns.

The first step is to create an online store using a platform like Shopify. I will talk more about these steps when we get to the building of your store section. The next step is to set up what is known as "curbside pickup" or "local pickup."

This allows your customers to drive by and pick up the orders they placed online without having to enter the storefront. All they have to do is pay online, wait for the order details and delivery instructions (sent via email or SMS), and drive to the store to pick up their order. This is a great way to reduce your shipping costs and minimize person-to-person interactions without compromising quality, safety, convenience, or flexibility. You can also choose to ship your customer's order via regular post.

One of the best ways to generate cash flow for your new online store is to set up digital gift cards. Once customers purchase gift cards, they are delivered to your customers by email. All active gift cards can be managed and tracked inside your e-commerce store as customers redeem them.

Once you have set up your online store, it is time to notify your customers. One way is to email your existing customers with an announcement of the launch of your online store. In that email, you can let them know that business, as usual, still operates in your physical stores, but you are now launching online to cater to new demand. You may also want to offer a one-time discount to get them in the mood to start purchasing online. Most people may be a little nervous buying online for the first time, so it may be a good idea to have a list of instructions to guide people through the purchasing process.

The next step is to announce your store launch on any social media channels and in the store itself. You can also run local advertisements in magazines or simple Facebook and Google ads using geo-targeting. Add your new website to local community forums, phonebooks, centers, magazines, newspapers, Google itself ("Google My Business"), and any other platform that will allow you to list your website and company details. Finally, you can go old school and hand out flyers to place on cars parked in busy parking lots. I am sure there are also local business associations that can help you promote your products and services.

If you are someone that would like help with this venture, do please reach out to me at damien@damiencoughlan.com or on social media.

CHOOSING YOUR MODEL CLOSING THOUGHTS

As you can see, there are a number of different models that you can avail of to launch an e-commerce business. There are even more in other unrelated categories that I have not listed, and I'm sure as we evolve over time, there will be new models and technological advancements that will change how we do business.

The following link shows you how one of my students launched their online business with e-commerce and grew to over six figures. This is a particularly powerful story and shows you how anyone can launch a successful online business with zero experience and little to no startup costs. Go to EcommerceActivated.com/start[15] to watch it now.

I for sure am excited about how fast we are moving, and how easy it is for us today to launch the business of our dreams. Again, I love drawing the comparison with traditional brick and mortar businesses. They are slow; they take time to build, they need a retail presence, fixtures and fittings, light and heat, and are restricted to a set number of hours per day where they can generate revenue. The biggest problem is acquiring customers; location is such an important determining factor on how much footfall and sales will come to your shop on a daily basis, during a set number of hours. That's why shopping space in Las Vegas, New York, Paris etc. is at a premium.

Today, with an online business, we can sell worldwide, with unlimited capacity to scale, all from the comfort of our computers, and get the support from virtual assistants and suppliers that can help and fulfill on our behalf.

Summary:

- Taking action and choosing a model is the first quadrant of my e-commerce success framework.

- The different models that I like are drop-shipping, print-on-demand, private labeling, white labeling, wholesaling, and subscription model.
- If you are new and want to take action with the highest reward and lowest risk, I recommend going with a drop-shipping model to get started and build confidence.
- If you have a brand and are looking to create a product, then private labeling or white labeling makes the most sense.
- The beauty of building an online business is that you can operate it remotely from anywhere in the world.
- Performing a SWOT analysis on you and your business helps you get clear on what you are good at, what you could work on to improve, what you need to be aware of, and what threats to look out for.
- Setting goals is important in achieving anything in life and you should leverage the SMART framework to get clear on your goals.
- We operate our lives on a set of values, the higher something lies on your values, the more inspired you are to accomplish. Check out Dr. DeMartini's "value determination process" to discover your highest values.
- Moving your brick-and-mortar business online is easier than you think.
- Aim for quick wins in your life; progress is better than perfection.

Action Steps:

- Re-read this section if you need to familiarize yourself with the different e-commerce models.

- Perform a SWOT analysis to determine you and your organization's strengths, weaknesses, opportunities, and threats.

- Write down your goals but make them specific, measurable, realistic, agreeable, and timely.

- If you have a business and want to grow online, feel free to reach out to me so I can help you get off to the right start. Alternatively, go to the resources section of this book. (www.ecommerceactivated.com/resources)

- Write down a list of values that inspire you and identify why.

SECTION TWO

PRODUCT AND SUPPLIER RESEARCH

PRODUCT RESEARCH

One of my favorite activities which a lot of people fail to do consistently is product research. Why do I like it? Because it is the single most impactful and important task that will put you on the path to e-commerce success. Without the activity of product research and looking to discover what is selling in the marketplace, you will never generate any sales or find that new viral selling product.

Yes, it may be boring and a little tedious, but it is the single biggest weekly activity you should be doing to get to your first four, five, or six-figure month. Product research is the activity that very few will be disciplined in, and their lack of results will show. Without a successful product, you have no business.

By the end of this section, you will be able to identify what product research is, how to use a framework to consistently research on a regular basis and get into the mindset of attracting and seeking out winning product ideas. Finding winning products is something that comes with experience and knowledge of your market, so be patient and consistent. Don't freak out if you have not yet mastered it; you eventually will through testing, trial, and error. Be careful though, it is not what you like and think will sell but what the customer wants.

Remember, a niche is a classification of people that share similar interests or have special characteristics in common—fishing, farming, cycling, dog lovers, shoe lovers, cake lovers, etc. We first start by looking inside each niche for clues and trends on what products are selling in the marketplace. This is my simple philosophy of modeling success: Don't copy; take inspiration from what is working from others and make your product and offer better.

If you see a celebrity or influencer wearing a new sports item, or you see that the media or niche blogs are talking about a new line of sports apparel, maybe you need to follow and start researching those trends. A winning product must also have the potential for high demand. If the market is too small, you won't be able to scale. Let's take a random example. If I search on Facebook, it tells me there are about 5,800 Trumpet players in the world that have a Facebook profile that list trumpet player as their occupation. Obviously, if I am looking to scale, I might not be able to generate the number of sales that I want with this small audience. For starters, only a tiny percentage of these people may be buyers. You really want to aim for global audiences of 500,000 and above; that is why I choose to sell products to large audiences like the dog niche and the family niche and so forth.

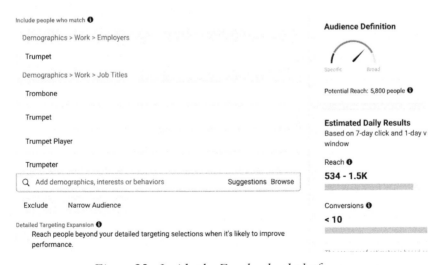

Figure 23 - Inside the Facebook ad platform.

A winning product could also be something that solves a problem. Or maybe the product helps someone feel good about themselves, helps to work in harmony with something else, or appeals to a mass market because of its simplicity. Think skincare products, dog products, hiking boots, cooking utensils, equipment that makes life easier, unique clothing, or cosmetics that enhance beauty.

A winning product has the "IT" or "WOW" factor and grabs your attention. It might have a low supply or is difficult to find or currently not advertised. If you are first to market with a new product, this puts you in the position as a first-mover advantage.

A winning product combined with high-profit margins is a perfect combination as it gives you more room to test and scale as you start to find what works best. I like to go with the 80-20 rule. This means keeping your costs of goods sold (COGS) to 20 percent of your product's selling price. This allows you to spend up to 80 percent on the customer acquisition cost before losing money.

If you are selling a product for $100, and it costs you $20 from your supplier, then you can spend up to $80 to acquire a customer. This is hugely beneficial because it gives you a greater spend threshold to outbid your competitors. I will talk later about online advertising, but he or she who can spend the most to acquire a customer usually wins.

The product is the most important part of your business so spend time identifying what a great product is. I will show you more examples throughout this book. A great product with average marketing and sales has a much higher chance of success than a bad product. Remember: Good marketing cannot solve a bad product!

Before we dive into the strategies of product research, I want to give you a real-life example from back in 2016. This is what I call my ah-ha moment! At this particular time in my life, I became obsessed with finding new ideas and products to sell. I was living in San Francisco and I was heading out for my evening bike ride. I would cycle out to the Golden Gate Bridge any time I needed to take a break from life.

Figure 24 – Bike riding to the Golden Gate Bridge.

On my bike rides, I frequently noticed how many dogs and their owners were out walking. I noticed how many different dog toys and accessories the dogs had. I noticed the different dog breeds and sizes, from miniature to large. Not only that, but the dog owners themselves were kitted out in dog-themed clothing and there was clearly an obsession between the dog owner and their dog. "New research has shown that owners and their pups often share personality traits, too. A paper published in the *Journal of Research in Personality* says a dog's personality reflects the personality of its owner. Just like humans, dogs vary in their personalities. And they can potentially change over time." – Discover Magazine.[16]

It was then it started to click. I started to realize that dog owners pretty much treat their dogs as family and would do anything to keep them happy. My research began and I discovered some incredible statistics. Growing up on a farm, I saw the passion my Dad had for his animals, like cows and sheep. But it was nothing on the level of what I found in dog owners.

In the US, 36 percent of households own a dog (AVMA).[17] Nine in ten households consider their dog part of the family.[18] Dogs are the most popular household pets in the United States. I then decided to start searching for dog products online. I tried my best to use the keywords based on what I commonly saw amongst dog walkers on a daily basis. Could this be a niche that I could make money despite not being a dog owner myself or not having much knowledge of any of the dog breeds?

To re-iterate, product research is required to identify what is selling in the marketplace, what trends exist, and what new innovations in consumer products are on the streets. Product research methods are everywhere, and in this section, I will be going over some of my favorite techniques.

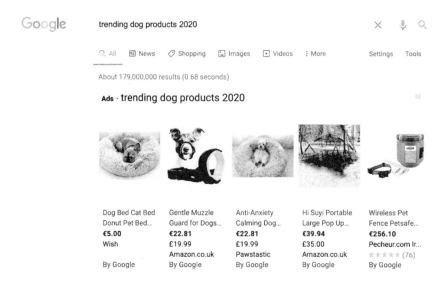

Figure 25- Google Ads displayed below search bar.

A framework for data entry, product research & collection?

First, you need a system to record your product ideas. You need to be able to find the idea, record it, and action it into a launch plan to test. The system can be as easy or as complex as you want. Below is a list of the various ways you can track ideas so you can share or revisit them later:

- Notepad.
- Diary.
- Bookmark tabs.
- Google Sheets/Docs.
- Microsoft Excel spreadsheets and Word Docs.
- Evernote or iPhone notes.
- Send ideas to your virtual assistants.
- Tag your team in posts on social media.
- Save social media videos and articles.

- Highlight chapters of a book.
- Circle magazines and newspaper articles.
- Take photos and create a folder called product research.
- Ask friends or family members to send you their ideas.
- Search your emails and push ideas into a folder.

My favorite method of recording ideas is taking a photo or copying the website URL and adding the link into a giant Google sheet that my team and I will sort through on a weekly basis and pick out the best ideas. Often, we may have over 50 product ideas each week. Not every product idea will work, however. Perhaps one in eight ideas will bring some initial sales and scale to some nice numbers.

Google Sheet column headers:
- Reason for choosing this product idea.
- Product name.
- Product URL.
- Audience niche.
- Idea origination.
- Competitors.
- Image URL.
- Can I source it?
- Supplier name.
- Supplier costs.
- Margins.
- Launch date.
- Notes.

In each of these columns, you'll enter as much information as you can. You may think it is overkill, but as I will discuss later in quadrant four of my ESF model, you'll understand why systems and documentation are crucial.

I hope this chapter laid a foundation for you to start creating your product research framework. If you do not know what to sell, do not worry! Focus on the process and follow the steps. Think about ways that you can get going on product research. Perhaps there is an upcoming event, a season is approaching, or you saw something interesting on social media. Write it down and take action. As you gain experience, you can create a system and train other people to help you find products.

CUSTOMER-CENTRIC VERSUS PRODUCT-CENTRIC

Before we dive into some of the product research strategies like Facebook and Google, I think it is important to give you an overview of two different approaches to bringing products to the marketplace, whether you want to be a product-centric company or a customer-centric company.

A product-centric company is one that is focused on the products it brings to market, rather than the customers who buy those products.

A customer-centric company focuses on the customer needs, wants, and serving those customers at the highest level, with a focus on building long-term relationships.

I prefer the customer-centric approach. Why? First, your customer is king. If they leave, you have no business. Second, it is far cheaper to retain existing customers than to find new ones. In this section, I want you to think about serving the needs of your customers at the highest level: How can your customers benefit; what similar products can you continue to sell to them at a later date; and how can you ensure they don't go elsewhere to find products that you don't sell.

A perfect example of a customer-centric company is Apple. Here are some of the reasons many customers love Apple:

- Simple and easy buying experience.
- Fantastic after-sales service.
- Visual appearance.
- Integration with other Apple products.
- Status symbol.
- Quality products.
- Unique product features.

I must admit that I'm an Apple "fanboy," I first bought an iPod, then an iPhone, then I added a MacBook Air, MacBook Pro, iPad, iMac, Airpods, and who knows what else. What am I worth to Apple? Maybe $10,000 or more. I know Apple is a trillion-dollar company, but I want you to start thinking about your own customer and how you can deliver great products that leave your customers begging for more.

When I launched my dog brand, I knew that my customers would eventually move from buying dog leashes to dog shoes, dog kennels, essentially moving up the value ladder. As they became familiar with my brand and began to gain trust, they spent more money.

Now that we know why product research is so important and have a framework for capturing ideas, let's dive into where we actually go to find those ideas and winning products.

AMAZON RESEARCH

Amazon.com is the largest physical product database online in the West, while Alibaba and AliExpress are its Eastern competitors.

What I love about Amazon research is that I can find what is popular pretty quickly on one of the biggest sites in the world. Amazon even identifies and labels some of the best suppliers as "Amazon's choice."

Amazon usually requires its sellers to purchase inventory upfront, so the sellers have to be certain that the product will sell; otherwise, they will be left with unwanted and costly inventory. If a product is new and is selling well, then there is a good chance you can jump on that trend. There are different categories inside Amazon and five of my favorites are as follows:

- Best sellers.
- New releases.
- Movers & shakers.
- Most wished for.
- Gift ideas.

On individual Amazon product pages, you can check the "Best Sellers Rank" to find out how popular an item is in its category is. With more than two billion sellers selling on Amazon, researching here should not be taken lightly. Those sellers invest thousands in product research before they ship their bulk product to Amazon's warehouses.

The "movers and shakers" section allows you to find products that are gaining traction, something that you can monitor if you are someone who likes to be first to market. In the case of Amazon, you can go ahead and find that same product in China or the US and have it sold on your store within hours using the drop-ship method. If it turns out to be a success, you can invest in faster and cheaper shipping options.

GOOGLE SEARCH

We have all heard of Google. It is another great way to find product ideas for your store. It is of course, a massive search engine, with two trillion search queries per year.

Google Trends uses data from Google search to display how often a particular phrase is searched for. Google Trends can help you discover what's popular amongst consumers over time and throughout different regions.[19]

You can also see what ads are shown for particular keywords. For example, if I search for the keyword "dog beds under $20," it's going to bring me back both organic and paid search results. This is a quick indicator of who is selling what and how well they are performing.

By looking at the Google search results, you can see what is currently being advertised and reverse engineer the brand, the product, and even the amount of traffic that is on their website every month, using the *Similarweb* tool.[20]

The other important division of Google is Google Shopping. There is a specific tab you can click to see the products listed inside the Google shopping catalog.

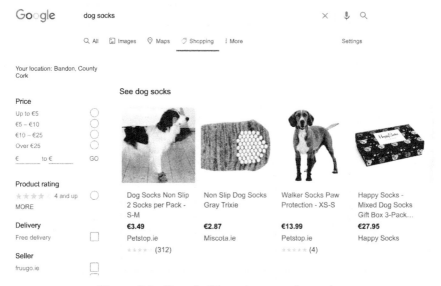

Figure 26 - Google Shopping search results.

FACEBOOK RESEARCH

Over the past few years, Facebook has become one of the most popular research methods by e-commerce entrepreneurs looking to find "viral" products. The keyword here is viral. Think of viral as something that people are going crazy for. It could be a funny advertisement, or a must-have product, or something mysterious that people are drawn to and need to check it out.

For many people starting off that have little to no prior experience, the best way to launch your business is to jump on trending products. Facebook ads have been around for a couple of years now, and with Facebook continuing to grow its audience size,

Facebook ads remain the primary source of website traffic for a lot of e-commerce marketers. Facebook ads are extremely powerful because they allow you to target their two billion users by using attributes like age, gender, location, job, income, and more.

Facebook has data on each and every one of us. What we do, where we live, and what we like? If Facebook is the number one platform right now to sell products with paid ads, then it would make sense that we would use it for product research. There's a Facebook search bar on the top of your Facebook feed, which you can use to search for some of the following keywords. These keywords are usually keyword phrases that marketers like us use in our sales copy when advertising.

Keywords to use:
- Free shipping today.
- Not available in stores.
- 50% off today.
- We will sell out.
- Get it here.
- Get yours.
- OMG, ("Enter your niche" lovers) are going crazy over.
- Almost sold out.
- Grab one for free.
- Buy two or more.
- Buy it here.
- Buy it now.
- Grab yours now.
- Hurry, free shipping today.

- OMG, I need this.
- Shop here.
- Click here.
- Order now.
- Order here.
- Tag a friend.
- Tag someone who needs.

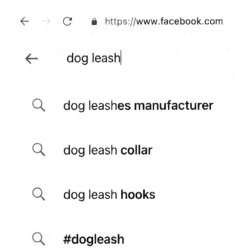

Figure 27 - Typing keywords on the Facebook search bar.

When you type in the keywords listed above, Facebook is going to bring back results that show the most popular videos and images, products that have been shared a lot, and help lead you down a path of research. You may need to scroll down or click through to find the real insights and golden gems. Most marketers will only skim the surface, so I recommend going much deeper into your research; it will pay off in the long run.

You can also narrow your search by month, year, and by filter for pages, groups, and so forth to help you find what is trending this week or month. When Facebook retrieves the search results, look at the engagement on the posts, check to see what people are commenting on and if they are tagging their friends. If people share content, this means the product is resonating with them.

Figure 28 - An example of a viral post with 140,000 comments and 79,000 shares.

As you find product ideas, copy the URL of the Facebook post link into your Google tracker framework. There have been times where I have found a product for my store, and two hours later, that product is launched, and I am sending traffic to the product page. In this case, you are the mouse getting the cheese, as someone else did the majority of the initial testing and validation. Your aim is to now improve on the current offer.

The goal should also be to become an "engaged shopper." You become an "engaged shopper" by clicking on the "Shop Now" button on Facebook ads. By doing this, Facebook shows you more of the same products, as they think you are someone looking to buy. If you click on lots of dog-related ads, Facebook categorizes you as a potential dog buyer.

Follow your competitors, add products to your shopping cart, and proceed to checkout. The more you go through the sales process, the more Facebook will deliver products to you that are selling really well. Facebook is in the business of making money through ads, so if they can find sellers more customers, sellers will spend more money on ads. We will talk more about how Facebook does this later with the Facebook pixel.

I remember the first time I discovered Facebook ads. One day I was scrolling on my Facebook newsfeed and came across an Irish American themed t-shirt. You see, Facebook knew I was Irish and knew I was living in California—based on my Facebook profile—so it served me the impression (or what they call view). When I looked at the image and the text more closely, I discovered the word "sponsored," which was displayed in small writing on the top left corner.

Figure 29 - Irish American themed shirt on Facebook.

Figure 30 - An example of a mobile newsfeed carousel Facebook ad.

I didn't know what it was, but eventually, through trial and error, I discovered it was a targeted Facebook ad. As a result, by clicking through, I was able to find the page, the store name, where they were sourcing the product from, and why I was targeted. This set off a major light bulb for me and was the main driver for me going forward to sell hundreds of thousands of dollars' worth of dog products through Facebook ads.

INSTAGRAM RESEARCH

The next product research method is Instagram. Instagram is a social media platform that emphasizes photo and video sharing via its mobile app, especially popular in the e-commerce world for fitness, health, beauty, and clothing niches.

You can use the hashtag search feature to find trending products on Instagram, for example, #dogtoys #cattoys #beauty #ad #sponsoredpost, etc.

Depending on when you are reading this book, the industry may have changed, so adjust your social media strategy accordingly to what social media platform is trending right now.

Another subset of Instagram is Instagram influencers and promotion pages. An example is Cardi B, a music artist who promotes the big brand Fashionnova.com.[21]

By following large Instagram pages, you'll get to see which products are trending, and you can use it as a signal to identify the current fashion and product trends in the marketplace.

PINTEREST RESEARCH

Pinterest is a social network where its users can find inspiration and ideas for their interests and hobbies.[22] It is a highly passionate platform for enthusiasts to share what they like. I believe it is an underrated platform for you to find creative and winning products.

The first step is to create a free account. Once you create your account, you can perform keyword research to find different pieces of content that may spark your interest.

Let's once again use the example of dogs. By performing a dog-related search, Pinterest will show you content in the form of product pins, videos, and more.

Product Pins are enriched with metadata and formatted to let users know that they're shoppable. They contain pricing info, availability, product title, and description.

The pins will usually lead to an external site such as an e-commerce store that you can then click on and make a purchase. Some of the big niches on Pinterest are pets, beauty, fashion, technology, crafts, home decor, and DIY.

Figure 31- Dog Bowls on Pinterest.

101

ASD MARKETPLACE

One trade show that I recommend you attend is ASD Market Week in Las Vegas. It is a trade show for consumer merchandise that brings the world's widest variety of retail merchandise together in one efficient shopping experience. Since 1961, ASD Market Week Trade Show has been bringing buyers and sellers together to network and build business relationships.

This show will give you an incredible opportunity to find new and innovative products. You will also meet your industry peers and connect with huge Chinese suppliers. The in-person experience enables you to place purchase orders and negotiate better deals. The last time I attended, I met with two incredible suppliers based in Shenzhen, China. One connection can be the gateway to a massive six or seven-figure business. You can go to asdonline.com to find out more.[23]

If you are not in the US, search for local trade show conferences near you. If you want to be different from anyone else, and you want to find the hottest products to sell, you must be willing to do what other sellers are not. Trust me on attending trade shows. It is where you will meet some of the most influential and smartest minds.

*Figure 32 - Lawrence and I at our first ASD event in
Las Vegas, Nevada, USA.*

ESTY PRODUCT RESEARCH

Etsy is an online buyer and seller community similar to eBay, except it focuses on hand-crafted or vintage goods. Most products sold fall into the category of arts, crafts, jewelry, paper goods, housewares, and artisan candies or baked goods. Vintage items must be at least 20 years old to qualify and can range from costumes, clothing, jewelry, photos, and housewares.

Etsy provides a marketplace specifically for crafters. These Etsy sellers typically work from home and have specialized skills. I like Etsy because it is full of creative products, many of which have not been sold on big platforms like Shopify or have had marketers that have tried to scale with paid ads.

A student once found a custom piece of jewelry that was selling organically on Etsy, but he could not find any signs of it being sold with Facebook ads. He took the product idea, made his own twist, and ran Facebook ads. To his delight, the product turned out to be a success for about a month until he ran out of audience size.

PRINT-ON-DEMAND PRODUCT RESEARCH (POD)

Another great way to perform product research (especially if you sell clothing) is to search Print-on-demand company websites like Teespring[24], Customcat[25], Gearbubble[26], Teelaunch[27], Pillow Profits[28], Viralstyle[29] etc.

Search for trends, holidays, best sellers, and new arrivals. Subscribe to their email lists for new product introductions. Take designs from other niches and apply them to yours. Have your designer also browse the sites. Join the POD company's Facebook groups, and subscribe to their newsletters for updates.

SPY TOOLS

Spy tools are software that allows you to crawl the Internet for the most viral products, giving lucrative information such as clicks, costs, sales, and much more.

Everything online is tracked today, from a visitor click to purchase, to how long people spend on your site. The level of granularity you can go to is mind-boggling. Through pixels, cookies, technology, and the use of API, the ability to essentially "spy" on what other brands, websites, and companies are doing is totally possible.

This first became apparent to me when I was searching one day on my Google Analytics dashboard to monitor where my traffic was coming from. I noticed that as expected, the biggest referrals were Facebook and Google, but then I noticed a weirdly named tool and I did some digging. The tool was a spy tool, and it is one of many sophisticated tools that allow marketers to find new and trending products that are doing well on the Internet.

Naturally, I was curious, so I signed up for a free trial. Within seconds, I was able to find trending products, what was working for my competitors, new product arrivals, and anything else that was performing well. I'll add the reference in the resources section.

If you are really stuck on product research strategies, you can use these spy tools to find out what is new and trending. Instead of spending hours testing and spending money on ads, you can use this spy tool option to find what is hot right now in the marketplace.

Personally, I prefer to use other sources, and of course my own intuition, I really want to learn more about my customer, and by doing the hard work, it will serve you in the long run. You must be prepared to get into the mind of the consumer and become one of them, to serve them at the highest level.

Also, there is also an option for you to find your competitor's ads on Facebook, visit their page, and see the ads they are running. The URL is https://www.facebook.com/ads/library.[30] I have no idea if this ad library function will be around forever. The ad library provides advertising transparency by offering a comprehensive, searchable collection of all ads currently running from across Facebook apps and services, including Instagram.

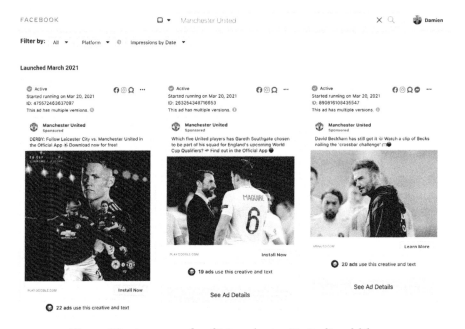

Figure 33 - An example of Manchester United's ad library.

YOUTUBE SEARCH

YouTube just keeps growing. "Over 2 billion logged-in users visit YouTube each month, and every day people watch over a billion hours of video and generate billions of views."[31] YouTube is the second biggest search platform in the world. Google, of course being the first.

Think about it, when was the last time you went on YouTube and searched for a product to find out more about it or compare the product to other competitors. Just last week, I was searching for a new monitor to use with my laptop, so I searched for YouTube videos that compared Samsung versus Dell's monitors. I watched a number of different reviews before choosing the monitor that got the best reviews and appealed to my needs and wants.

A lot of these YouTube product reviews are usually paid reviews, where the YouTube channel is getting paid an affiliate commission from the brand owner. For example, if I am a seller in the fitness space, my goal would be to search for fitness channels that are known for reviewing fitness related products. Once I start following these channels, I can see for myself what fitness items are trending and decide if and how I can model success.

The other benefit is you will be marketed to by other brands related to that niche who run YouTube ads on those particular channels. For example, marketers will target big fitness channels to run YouTube ads because they know their ideal audiences are subscribed to those channels. YouTube ads are awesome because you can run an ad directly to a YouTube video URL or channel.

The final tip is you can install the Chrome extension "keywords everywhere." Keywords Everywhere is a browser add-on for Chrome and Firefox that shows search volume, CPC, and competition on multiple websites. In summary, follow your competitor's channels, follow the big channels in your niche, and follow the review channels.

EBAY RESEARCH

eBay is an online shopping site that's best known for its auctions and consumer-to-consumer sales. eBay is one of the older platforms, but it can still be a place to find great products to sell.

My first introduction to selling online was with eBay. I sold football boots. eBay lets you put items you own up for auction to the highest bidder, which will attract many shoppers who are looking for used, unique, or hard-to-find items.

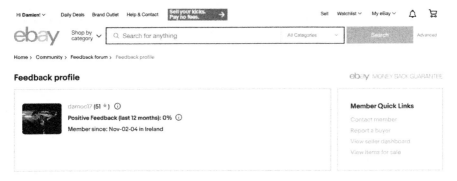

Figure 34 - My eBay account I set up in 2004.

Shopify and eBay have partnered to give you access to eBay's customer base of over 170 million buyers, and this new sales channel is ready to use. Watch out for sponsored posts because, most likely, if someone is running ads to a listing, it is selling quite well. eBay also gives you a top sellers category similar to Amazon.

WALMART PRODUCT RESEARCH

As of 2020, Walmart is the hidden gem of the e-commerce world. Known mostly for their giant number of retail stores and for being the largest retailer in the world, Walmart is now branching into e-commerce.

They are attempting to gain market share from Amazon. Currently, they have fifty thousand sellers compared to over two million on Amazon. Smart sellers know that if you can tap into the new world of Walmart.com, then you are one of the very few to jump into this new trend. Simply put, Walmart shoppers are now becoming more OK with shopping online.

Again, use the search feature to see what new products are showing up on Walmart's marketplace. P.S One great book to read is *Made in America* by Sam Walton. You can grab it on Audible also.[32]

WISH PRODUCT RESEARCH

Wish is an American online e-commerce platform that facilitates transactions between buyers and sellers. It is most known for its ridiculously cheap products, but its shipping times are really long.

If you buy something on Wish, you are likely buying directly from a manufacturer in China, despite the fact that Wish itself is a US-based company.

Wish usually has some of the most viral and new products on the market and can be a great place to source new product ideas, especially trending items.

CUSTOMER FEEDBACK & SURVEYS

You'll often hear the phrase that "customer is king." One fantastic way to conduct high-quality and rapid product research is by asking your customers!

Walk into any supermarket and I'm sure you'll see companies handing out free food samples or conducting market research on new products and services. This is a cheap and effective way to get really great customer feedback.

From an online perspective, you can survey your customers through email marketing in exchange for a gift voucher or discount code. Not only will it give customers an incentive to provide feedback, but your customers will acknowledge that you are involving them in the product creation and ultimate success of your brand.

Asking first-time buyers for feedback is a great way to gain insights into how you're seen by the outside world. Questions like "Why did you choose to shop at X?" "What other products would you like to see in our store?"

Having a live chat feature on your website is also a great way to get instant feedback as you'll often find the product that the shopper is looking for is not available.

In-person is also a great method to get face-to-face feedback. Imagine having one hundred dog owners in a room together—the idea generation would be incredible. You can also host local meetups and focus groups. If you do not have any customers, take to the high street and find your ideal customers and ask them a list of brief questions.

COMPETITOR ANALYSIS

One of my favorite quotes is by Jack Welch. He says, "Number 1: Cash is king. Number 2: Communicate. Number 3: Buy or bury the competition."

It is incredibly important to be aware of your competitors by identifying what they do well and what they don't do so well. When I decided to launch my dog store, the first thing I did was create a list of my competitors. I wanted to know what they sold, at what price, how fast they shipped, where they advertised, and what was their unique competitive advantage.

If you already know what niche or industry you want to sell in, you can go research the top players. On Facebook, you can click on a brand's page, click on the "info and ads" section and you'll see the current list of products that are being promoted with Facebook ads! You can also go to competitors' websites and search for new arrivals and best sellers. By modeling success, it cuts down on your advertising costs and helps you avoid mistakes if you are on a shoestring budget.

You should also subscribe to your competitor's newsletter, mailing lists, and who they follow on social media. By subscribing to their mailing list, you can see when new products launch and the various promotions that they run. Rather than blatantly copy, it is better and more ethical to model success, take inspiration, and put your own twist on the product and offer.

What to look at when analyzing the competition?

- Who is their target customer?
- Where is their main following established— Facebook, Instagram, YouTube, etc.?
- What market share do they currently own, and how long have they been in existence?

- What is their main differentiating factor or value-add for their business and products?
- What are they known for?
- What key features or benefits do they highlight in their products and websites?
- What is the price point compared to other competitors in the marketplace?
- How do they approach shipping, what tiers do they have, or do they offer free shipping?
- Where do they appear and rank in Google news search?
- Have they received venture funding?
- What is the customer experience like?
- How good is their abandonment cart flow?
- Have they a live chat feature on their site?
- What is the social media approach to content creation?
- What type of blog posts are they creating and how often?
- What type of marketing do they rely on; email, paid ads, radio, tv, etc.?
- What is their email marketing approach?
- How good are their customer reviews?

The above are just some of the questions that I ask myself when analyzing my competitors. The deeper you understand your competitors, the more you can avoid mistakes, cut out costs and ultimately deliver a better product to your customer. You can also look at the areas that your competitors are not doing a great job in and deliver a better customer experience.

Another great tool you can use is SEMrush.[33] It allows you to analyze competitors, find gaps, and inform your marketing strategy.

As you make moves in the market, you will gain attention from other competitors. If you have performed a SWOT analysis, you should be aware of your competitors and what differentiates them from you. It's important to understand what unique competitive advantage you possess and focus on those core competencies.

Naturally, as you grow and scale your business, more competitors will enter the market to try and grab a piece of your business. It happens very quickly in the e-commerce industry because everything is online, and people can find your products and reverse engineer the process. Maybe they saw an advertisement, or maybe one of their customers migrated over to your brand. Nonetheless, here are some tips for dealing with competitors. By the way, I love competition! It keeps my team and I on our toes and helps us realize we are in a great niche, and constantly pushes us to improve our products and services.

Here are some tips for dealing with competition:

Know your competitors: Keep an eye on your competitors, identify what new products they are launching, find their bestsellers, and note how they differ or how they are similar to you. You can use a tool called similar web to check their website traffic. You can also check their website for new arrivals (filter by date newest) and best sellers using the following links yourwebsitename.com/collections/all?sort_by=best-selling

Follow their social media and subscribe to their email lists: Model success by discovering how they run their social media and email marketing campaigns. Don't copy but get inspiration from each of your competitors. By subscribing, you also are in tune with what products they offer on promotion and what new products are being introduced.

Don't underestimate: The smallest competitors can soon become your biggest competitors. Just because a competitor does not appear to be a big threat doesn't mean that it won't change in three to six months. Companies grow fast online, and you never know what financial backing is behind each competitor.

Buy their products: Want to reverse engineer their sales process, packaging, post-purchase funnel, and after-sales service? Purchase their products and find out what they do well and what they do poorly.

We are stronger together than we are apart: Often, companies join forces for the benefit of all involved. Don't rule it out but do stick to a contract on what the terms and conditions are.

Become better: That's right, demand more from your team to do a better job not only in customer service but in how products are positioned and interpreted.

Innovation: By constantly innovating, you are adapting to change and bringing new products and ideas to the market.

Look after your team: Walmart famously refers to their employees as associates. Make sure to make your team feels part of the vision and reward them for staying ahead of the competition.

Beware of first-mover advantage and first-mover disadvantage: As with anything in life, there are pros and cons. Even though being first to market might be ideal, your competitors may follow with a better improvement or enhancement on your design or product.

Also, it may be the case that you launch unproven products to unsuspecting customers, and it does not work. The early bird gets the worm, but the second mouse gets the cheese. Constantly improve and tweak your product. Competitors should not be ignored. There are seven billion plus people on the planet, so there are plenty of customers to go around. Having said that, you have to study other competitors to learn how to deliver the best possible product. I encourage you right now to take a piece of paper and pen and list out every competitor in your niche. Find out what they do well and what they do poorly, and what they have that is open for disruption.

SOURCING AGENTS

Sourcing agents work on your behalf to find the best products for you to sell. They are usually closer to the factory floor and can often negotiate better products and faster shipping lines. My friend Nathan who owns **Sourcify**, and has also spoken at my masterminds, can help you find the right product for your business. He works with companies that are looking to scale.

There are many other domestic and international agents to assist you in finding your first or next product. For an introduction, you can message me directly through social media or go to the resources section.

DAILY LIFE

One simple example of a strategy you can do every day is when you're out in the street or with your friends, just be present to what is happening. What clothes are being worn, what style, what consumer products are popular, and what have the big brands positioned in their shop windows? Maybe you're watching TV, sport, or a movie, and some idea comes your way—write it down, document it, and come back to it when you are ready.

When I was selling dog merchandise, I used to go to the dog park and monitor what dog owners were wearing, the toys they would play with, and anything else that would give me a clue into what the market wants.

You have to be willing to obsess over your customer needs and wants. Just like an actor prepares for a movie, you must immerse yourself fully to do whatever it takes to understand your audience.

SUPPLIER RESEARCH
CHINESE SUPPLIERS

A lot of e-commerce entrepreneurs source their products and raw materials directly from China at much lower costs. After all, the majority of the world's products are manufactured there. China has become known as "the world's factory" because of its business ecosystem, low regulatory compliance, reduced taxes and duties, and competitive currency practices.

Two big websites to find Chinese suppliers are Alibaba, which is a B2B (business to business) platform, and AliExpress, which is a B2C (business to consumer) platform.

The basic difference is that Alibaba generally requires large orders and has a minimum order quantity, whereas AliExpress has no minimum order and is tailored to the smaller seller. I recommend if you are new to start off using AliExpress. I encourage you to always run a background check on the supplier you intend to work with first. You can use the filtering settings on the AliExpress site to find the best-rated suppliers and of course, find products that are currently trending with large order volume.

When choosing suppliers, I like to communicate with them individually and vet a couple of different options to see which one is best suitable for my business. You should not just choose the first supplier you see. Many of these Chinese suppliers will communicate with you via Skype, WhatsApp, or WeChat. You'll know pretty quickly how responsive they are, their skill level, and the level of experience they've got based on the communication and correspondence.

Eventually, once you start building a relationship, they will act as your own personal research counterpart. AliExpress has been the method of choice for e-commerce entrepreneurs for a few years now in finding winning products. Alibaba is usually the next step when you have found a winning product and you want to work more closely with the source of the product. Alibaba will always be more of a direct approach.

Category	Alibaba	Ali Express
- MOQ	- High MOQ	- Low MOQ
- Pricing	- Lower Pricing	- Higher Pricing
-Custom design & branding	- Unlimited design & branding offered	- Design & branding not offered
- Product Certification	-Products are generally compliant	- Some products may not be compliant
-Quality issues and risks	-You get what the supplier can offer	-You get what the supplier can offer
- Lead times	- Planning, due diligence, and production can take months	-Add to cart, pay, and wait a few weeks for delivery.
- Best suited for	- Experienced sellers and scaling	- Beginners and testing

  AliExpress

Figure 35 - Alibaba versus AliExpress comparison.

WORKING WITH US SUPPLIERS

Let's say you find a winning product that you are sourcing directly from China. Normally shipping from China is anywhere from 7-30 days, depending on your supplier and method of shipping. The supplier is shipping the product directly from China to your end customer, maybe via E-Packet from China to the United States.

Maybe you spent the past few weeks testing various products in your niche, and now you are starting to see consistent sales on one product. Again, there are many ways to test and source products, but I am using this particular example for simplicity purposes. Let's say the product is costing you $10, including the shipping. You are selling it for $30. That is a pretty nice profit margin of $20, and it allows you to spend up to $20 to acquire the customer through ads and other marketing methods.

However, there is a high chance that the AliExpress supplier is just another middleman between you and the factory. AliExpress stores are essentially bridging the gap between you and the factory floor. They provide a service of convenience in your testing phase. It is important to note that you are paying extra for this service. You could easily go and find that same product for maybe $6 or $7, including shipping, if you did a bit more research on other platforms like Alibaba.

However, there is a bigger and more pressing matter, and that is delivery times. You can probably ship your first fifty to one hundred orders from China and get away with long shipping times, but you need to plan for the next steps. People are eventually going to complain about long shipping times and therefore, you need a better and faster supply chain.

The next steps are as follows:
- Find a US supplier that has a warehouse and stock that can ship in 5-7 business days: or,
- Bulk order a shipment from China (Alibaba) to a fulfillment company in the United States.

The reason I say the USA is because it is a global seller's biggest market. This move to a faster and more streamlined shipping will allow you to start scaling with the confidence that your products will ship faster and with greater quality control. It will also increase the conversion rate on your store because people love fast shipping times, and it is often the main reason why people choose one brand over another. The other main benefit is that competitors are going to eventually enter the market and if there is one way you can destroy your competition, it is through faster delivery times and happier customers.

Many US suppliers and warehouses will also provide additional services like personalized and customized packaging. When you are selling at scale, you need to have a supremely run supply chain. I've seen a number of beginners get shut down by Shopify, PayPal, Facebook, Stripe and more, because of long shipping times. It is so easy nowadays for customers to win PayPal or Stripe disputes. If you need help with Chinese and US suppliers, please reach out.

SELL YOUR OWN PRODUCTS

Another way to approach the market is by not only being a retailer but taking control of the manufacturing too.

Just like the trend of Etsy, more and more people are turning their passion into legitimate businesses straight out of their garage or home. Go to Etsy.com and you will find everything from candle making to photography.

If you have a skill or a passion, you don't need a supplier; you can literally turn your passion into a business through Shopify and other platforms like Etsy.

One tip when selling your own products is to build your brand around the uniqueness of your product and how each order is carefully assembled and shipped with care.

Some people prefer shopping and supporting local businesses rather than big retailers. Be confident in your skills, trust the process, and leverage the power of online.

You can go to Etsy and perform a search to get an idea of some of the products being sold that may not be advertised and marketed on channels like Facebook and Instagram. In fact, most Etsy and homegrown sellers are not well versed in paid marketing strategies. By selling your own products, you can carve out a special niche for yourself and cut costs at every level of the supply chain.

PRODUCT RESEARCH & SUPPLIER CLOSING THOUGHTS

Summary: As you can see, I have listed quite a few different types of product research strategies. These are the exact strategies that my team and I use on a weekly basis. My students have also used these strategies to find their first or next winning products. Just because you have a product that is selling right now does not mean you shouldn't be looking for the next one. Eventually, products run their course and demand will drop. You don't want to be in a situation where you are not ready for the next season or in a position to not serve customers that demand a new product.

We went through a lot of product research because it is important. You may feel a little overwhelmed right now but don't. The goal is to slowly but surely, figure out which method works best for you and your products. You must be willing to spend at least a few hours per day researching the market to find what is working, especially if you are completely new. Without a great product, you will be unable to attract customers. Without customers, you don't have a business.

Every entrepreneur has failed at least once, so don't let a few failed product tests get you down! Remember, the more time you spend testing, the better you will become and the greater chance you have of finding a winning formula for success. And just for context, when I say testing, I mean creating simple tests to see how well a product does when you put it in front of your ideal customer. We will be discussing how to test later in this book through paid ads and organic strategies.

The goal of product research is not just finding winning products but to find suppliers you can trust. It is also a way for you to understand the different platforms and how they work. You are literally one viral product away from generating your first five or six figures in revenue.

Best of luck and start researching right now. As an example, go on AliExpress right now and type the word "dog" into the search bar and tell me what the first product is that you see. You can take a photo of it, tag me on social, and I'll give you my opinion on it as a viable product to launch!

Here is another bonus that I am scattering throughout this book. Watch me over the shoulder as I show you how to perform product research at a high level. Product research is required to find those "pockets of gold" that will help you discover which products are selling in the marketplace and what people are actually searching for. Visit EcommerceActivated.com/sell[34] to check it out now.

Action Steps:

- Create a tracker either through Google Sheets, Microsoft Word, Trello, or the Notes app on your phone. Record product ideas that you find in the marketplace and you wish to sell in your store.

- Block out time in your week to perform product research or have it as an ongoing thought in your mind. Ideas can come from anywhere, even out in the general public.
- Leverage social media and the Internet to perform keyword research on Facebook, Instagram, Google, Youtube, Etsy, Amazon, eBay, Pinterest, etc.
- Pay particular notice to trends, what are people wearing or buying, and what is something that is selling because of a season or holiday event.
- Go to the resources section of the book to avail yourself of the free documents to help you take action. I do recommend that you read this entire book first, though.

SECTION THREE

BUILDING YOUR STORE

PICK AN E-COMMERCE PLATFORM

Now that you have an idea of where to find winning products and trustworthy suppliers, and you know how to perform your product research, let's move to the building of your store. Before I begin, I must tell you that I am not the most tech-savvy.

Yes, I know I worked for Apple, but I am a farm boy at heart, and my real skills lie in marketing, problem-solving, building teams, and finding great products. So, when I searched for an e-commerce platform, I looked for a few key things: ease of use, simplicity, and scalability.

I looked at many options and the solution that made the most sense for me was Shopify, they are a Canadian multinational e-commerce company headquartered in Ottawa, Ontario. Shopify has been empowering independent business owners since it was founded in 2006. What I love about Shopify is that they built their platform for entrepreneurs like myself. My job as an entrepreneur is to work on my business and not in my business, and Shopify really does a lot of the heavy lifting of store creation and management.

To date, over 1,000,000 businesses in 175 countries around the world have made over $200 billion in sales using Shopify.[35] There are other platforms available like Wix, BigCommerce, WooCommerce, Volusion, LemonStand, 3dcart, BigCartel, Clickfunnels, Magento and many more. It really does depend on your needs and wants.

The beauty is that these e-commerce plug-and-play solutions allow you to literally set up your store in less than 48 hours without the need to be a coding or technical specialist. It is a lot easier than you think. Regardless of your technical skills, this will be one of the most rewarding parts of building your business as you see your store come to life. Embrace it and get that store going as soon as possible! Take massive decisive action every single time you feel a little bit of procrastination approaching.

ADMIN WALKTHROUGH

Every e-commerce platform has an administration section, where the store owner and its admins can see and control everything from customers to financials and settings. This is essentially the "back end" and private view of your store. You can manage all aspects of your store inside this view. You can also choose to add partners or agencies and give them partial access, so they can help you without accessing your personal data.

Over the course of your journey, you may hire developers or agencies to help you scale or optimize your store's performance. This is one of the services that my team and I provide. Often the slightest change can lead to the biggest improvement in your store's performance. Remember, you can grab my book resources to reference anything I discuss, from services to links to bonuses.

The following are some of the sections that your store admin might include but note that depending on your store platform, some of the features below may not exist:

- **Home:** A view of current activity on your store, including the day's sales and visitors and any notifications and alerts that need to be reviewed.

- **Orders:** A list of your total orders including the line item details.

- **Products:** The total view of all the products in your store. You can edit your product photos, sales copy, pricing, SKU's, and more inside this section. You can choose to hide certain products instead of deleting them from the customer-facing website.

- **Customers:** A total list of all your customers, including their purchasing history, their email, address, and more! This is one of my favorite views as it tells me who my top customers are.

- **Analytics:** I love to look at my analytics dashboard. Here I can quickly get an idea of how well my store is performing. Some of my favorite metrics to look at are my conversion rate, number of store visitors, and average order value. Custom reports can be built to specification, displaying the information you need and omitting any data that is not required from the report. An example might be pulling the number of orders for a particular product or calculating the amount of sales tax captured in a given month.

- **Marketing:** Your store may have a marketing section where you can choose different apps to help market your products and services.

- **Discounts:** You can create discount codes inside your store admin. They are very powerful when used correctly and are easy to set up and track. I use them when I am retargeting warm traffic that has already visited my checkout page. I may also use them in email promotions. The smallest discount can often persuade people who are close or almost ready to purchase. Along with the discount code, I might say something like: "Hurry, only 30 items remain, use code HURRY15 to get 15% off today." Discount codes are especially useful around special events and holidays. Most shoppers expect some type of store discount for example, on Black Friday and Cyber Monday.

- **Apps:** Apps help you increase the functionality and profitability of your store. Some of my favorite apps can be found in the book resources section. An example of a useful app is one that automatically compresses store images without ruining image quality. Large images or videos can slow the speed of your site, therefore increasing the chances of visitors leaving your store. Nobody wants to be on a site that takes forever to load its pages.

- **Theme Edit:** This section allows you to manage the store theme. Think of the theme like the visual layout and structure of your site. You may want to change the fonts or colors, or you may want to customize the menu items or add sections to the store layout. Remember I mentioned building a brand identity, well inside your theme is where you bring that brand to life.

- **Sales Channels:** There are new sales channels showing up every year. It is important to be omnipresent and have your brand represented across all of the various sales channels, new and old. Examples today include Pinterest, Facebook, Instagram, eBay, Walmart, Etsy, & Amazon.

- **Settings:** As the name suggests, this is where you manage all of your store and company settings. (Shipping, Domains, Preferences, General, Legal, Pages, Notifications, Gift Cards, Locations, Files, Store language, Billing, Capital, Checkout, Taxes, Plans & Permissions.)

As you can see, you can manage your entire store inside just one portal admin. Do not be overwhelmed; it's pretty easy to get used to once you set aside some time to explore. Again, I am not a technical wizard and I got used to it all within a week. My goal is to provide solutions for you that every person, regardless of their experience, skill set, or education can use. Go to my book notes EcommerceActivated.com/resources to see some of the additional references and tools I use.

THE IMPORTANCE OF YOUR STORE SETUP

There are generally three areas to look at when trying to understand why your store is not generating sales or performing how you want it to perform. They are 1) your website, 2) your store traffic, and 3) your product. Usually, it is the case that your website is not functioning correctly, or you are not targeting the right people, or people just simply are not interested in your product.

In this section, I will focus on the website itself. Before I begin to run any paid traffic or launch my store, I want to give myself the best chance of success. Today, people expect a certain level of quality and as more and more people buy online, these standards will only increase.

If your store is designed poorly, people will choose to buy elsewhere. There has to be some level of professionalism, quality, and branding. People often come to me saying they have visitors to their store but no sales, and they cannot understand why. The first thing I do is visit their site, and this is usually one of the issues that exist. The website is simply not up to standard.

Once you have your store designed, I recommend sharing it with a friend or family member and asking them if it looks professional and if they would buy from that store knowing it wasn't yours. Getting a second opinion is key to your journey as a new entrepreneur because everything you do is a learning curve and lesson. Store setup and optimization take time and experience. I will explain more in greater detail later.

There are also other issues that exist besides design. In my training, I have my students complete a thirty-point checklist before their store goes live. This gives them peace of mind before unveiling their store to the world.

Do not let perfection stand in your way, though. The minimum is to have a professional site that is easy to navigate. The world is moving fast, and I want to get your store up and running as soon as possible.

Areas to analyze when deciding if your website is set up correctly:

- Design.
- Navigation.
- Pages.
- Contact Info.
- Analytics.
- Tracking Codes.
- Pricing.
- Shipping.
- Storefront Password.
- Payment Gateways.
- App Setup.
- Domain Integration.
- Marketing Integration.
- Sales Integration.

NAMING YOUR STORE

Having a strong name can give you a huge competitive advantage in the marketplace over your competitors. Let's say you are selling the same dog bed as hundreds of other stores, but you own the domain name dogbeds.com. This is going to give you massive leverage and increase the chances that customers will buy from you over your competition.

Why? Because it has more authority and power, and it seems as if you are the original or go-too choice. Just look at how popular the buying of domain names has become today. People realize the importance of names for brand equity, trust, and instant customer recognition. In 2017, Walmart, one of the biggest retailers in the world, paid $9 million for the domain Shoes.com.[36]

Before you begin naming your store, you need to ask yourself the following questions:

- What products am I selling?
- What is the brand I am looking to build?
- What is the correlation between the store name and products?
- What is my mission statement?
- What does my store look like in two to three years' time?
- Is the domain name available to use?
- Am I choosing a name that may be trademarked?
- Would this name be powerful for SEO?
- Does this name translate inappropriately in other languages?
- Is the name available on social media?

Once you come up with a few ideas, you can go to the site leandomainsearch.com to help you choose the best name for your store.[37]

Tips For Naming Your Store

1. Start Brainstorming
2. Research The Current Market
3. Know Your Audience
4. Think Ahead
5. Ask For Help
6. Check Trademark
7. Make A Shortlist
8. Test Your Name
9. Get Feedback
10. Stick With Name If Happy

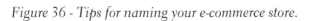

Figure 36 - Tips for naming your e-commerce store.

If a domain is taken and you really want it, it may be available for purchase. Perhaps someone had initially bought it with the intention of doing something with it but forgot. Also, people are known to domain squat, which means that they will buy domains in the hopes of selling for a profit. GoDaddy has a service where they negotiate the purchase of a domain for you. It may be worth checking it out.

If you are just starting off and have not yet decided on what to sell, you can go ahead and create a general store name. You can change it later as you decide what niche and products you want to focus on. Most people who are new to e-commerce go the route of creating a general store to test many different types of products. When they find a winning product or niche, they'll often rebrand that store into a niche-specific store and buy a suitable niche name.

DOMAIN MANAGEMENT

A domain is the URL or website address where your customers go to find your store online. As mentioned previously, I use Shopify as my e-commerce platform. Once you create your store, it will look something like this: yourstorename.myshopify.com.

Obviously, this doesn't look great from a customer's point of view, so you are better off purchasing a custom domain from a third-party provider. My domain registrar of choice is GoDaddy, and they have a simple integration with Shopify that will port over the new domain in minutes.

Your store will now show "yourstorename.com" instead of yourstorename.myshopify.com. I want everything to be brand congruent, from the name of the store to the domain name, to the email, to the social media. Remember, we want to build consistency, memorability, and quality in our brand messaging.

PROFESSIONAL E-MAIL

Creating the right business email allows you to be more professional, while also keeping brand congruency with the domain name. No one wants to visit a store and see that Gmail or Hotmail is listed as the store email. Trust me, I have seen stores that list Gmail as their contact details and it makes me cringe.

My students and I use Gsuite, which is a very simple, common, cheap, and easy alternative. It connects to the Gmail platform, with emails for your custom domain for a small fee per user per month.

This allows you to have emails like support@yourstorename.com or info@yourstorename.com instead of yourstorename@gmail.com.

Remember, as we are building and growing our brand, we are always thinking in terms of conversion rate optimization. Everything we do is a commitment to moving someone from being a complete stranger who knows nothing about our company to nurturing them, to eventually encouraging them to become a customer. If changing our email to a professional email is going to help, we do it.

MANAGING YOUR PRODUCT DATABASE

There are two ways you can add products to your store. You can manually add them or use apps to automate the publishing of products to your store. If you only have a few products, you can upload them into your store inside the product section of your admin view.

You will need to give your products a title and description. I also recommend taking high-quality photos and using keywords in your title and description to help you rank for SEO.

You will also need to add pricing. Usually, I like to have a before and after a price to show the value and percentage savings that my customers get.

I will also add the number of products available and of course, the SKU number. SKU is short for "stock keeping unit" and is used by retailers to identify and track their inventory or stock. The SKU is a unique code consisting of letters and numbers that identify characteristics about each product, such as manufacturer, brand, style, color, and size.

Shipping is also important, some of your products may have higher shipping rates because of size and weight, and those rates should be decided.

You can also upload products but choose to hide them from your storefront until you are ready to launch. There should be an active and draft setting where you can toggle on and off whether you want your products to be visible on your store or not.

You can also add variants if your product comes in multiple sizes and colors or other options.

Tagging products with keywords is another great way to identify and push various products into different categories and collections. An example might be a fitness store that has different categories and products, such as women, men, football, cycling, running, etc.

If you are someone who does not have any products and you are looking to drop-ship from other suppliers, they usually have an API that allows you to sync products from their database to your store. If you are sourcing from China and other locations, I recommend that you use apps like Oberlo, which is now owned by Shopify, to manage multiple products and suppliers.

I love the product section of my store admin, as here I can change pricing, colors, descriptions, tags, pictures, variants, and more. As a marketer, you will constantly find ways to improve your pages, descriptions, and pricing. The goal is to find the sweet spot for what your customer is willing to pay.

CREATING KEY PAGES IN YOUR STORE

There are a number of common and key pages that you will need to create in your e-commerce store. I've built and studied many successful stores, and the top websites have a common flow to how their stores are structured and designed. A key part of that design is the layout of the store pages.

Remember, the goal is to have a site that is optimized for conversions. We'd rather have a store that is built to generate sales, rather than having the most beautiful and artistic site in the world that is not set up for making sales. One of the ways to increase conversions is to give the person the right information, at the right time, in the most efficient manner. We want to move that person from someone who is just browsing to someone who feels trust, has the information and is now committed to making a purchase.

Figure 37 - A diagram showing how an e-commerce store may look and flow.

Before people make a purchase, they need to have trust in your brand, believe that they will get value from your product, and align with the company itself. As most people are browsing on mobile devices today, the layout is so important to move them along the sales funnel efficiently.

The following are some of the key pages on any e-commerce store:

- **Homepage:** The homepage is usually the first page to design when building your store. You can display promotions or special offers on the homepage header, like "30% off for Valentine's Day." The banner photo usually is a lifestyle image or a wide-angle shot of your best products. You can list your collections, include an email capture, have a featured product or video, list your mission statement and tag line. The homepage is a chance to showcase your brand and give a good first impression. Most store owners send their traffic directly to product pages, so often, homepages may not be viewed depending on the type of shopper. The homepage and product pages should have brand congruency.

- **Catalog/Category Page:** The number of products and collections you have will determine how many levels need to be in your catalog. The catalog is an easy way for people to drill down and find what they want. An example might be a store that sells all types of fitness products. Inside that category of fitness, there might be sub-categories like running, cycling, rowing, and so forth. This allows someone who found your site to quickly navigate to the department or section they want. Again, the goal is to enable a person to find what they want in the most efficient manner possible.

- **Product Page:** The majority of customer traffic is sent to product pages and it is here where people will spend most of their time. They'll check the product description, reviews, specifications, return policies, and shipping times. This is where they will decide whether to click the "Add to Cart" button and begin the checkout process. If your product page is designed poorly, or fails to give the right information, or just does not come across as trustworthy, then people will get frustrated and/or have second thoughts and will leave or what we call "bounce." It is usually very hard to get that person back to your store again, but it is possible through effective remarketing like customer testimonials, discounts, more company information, and perhaps a message from the founders. High-quality images, proper product descriptions, great pricing, scarcity, urgency, and trust are some of the most important factors of a high-performing product page. We will dive into product page secrets later when we talk about conversion rate optimization, but this is the most important page on your store.

- **Cart Page:** The cart page lists everything the shopper has added to their cart. You can also decide to list the estimated shipping costs, if any. There is also an opportunity to add a pre-purchase upsell at this stage. An example might be offering the shopper the chance to buy more of the same product in exchange for a price discount. This upsell, if taken, is incredibly valuable to the store owner as it raises the average order value of the customer. We will chat specifically about the average order value later. Again, adding more trust and urgency on the cart page is a great idea. Finally, you can add two options to continue; one is to move to the checkout, the other is to continue shopping.

- **Search Page:** The search function is usually located on the top of the navigation menu. This allows people to quickly search for products, keywords, or anything else that might prevent them from making a purchase. The search page can be designed to have an auto-suggest feature. As the person is typing the keyword search, it will show results similar in a way to a Google search. *Side note: I also recommend having the address auto-complete on the shipping and payment info page. This means that as soon as the customer begins to type their address, the form will automatically suggest the full name and address. This just means an easier and quicker checkout for customers. A faster checkout leads to higher conversions.* The search feature also allows you to look inside your shop analytics for the most commonly searched words on your store. This will give you an insight into what else your customers are searching for. Perhaps there is a product they want but that you do not stock.

- **About Us Page:** The about us page describes your brand, story, how you got started, and what you stand for. The About Us page is a great opportunity for you to outline the company's mission statement, culture, and values as a business. You can also decide to embed a video from the founders. It is a well-known fact that people buy from those that they know, like, and trust. Speak about why you launched your brand, how passionate you are, and how happy you are to serve your customers. Don't be afraid to jump on camera. Be proud of your brand.

- **Track Your Order Page:** One of the conversion tricks I discovered was adding a tracking page to my main menu. This gives customers the ability to enter the tracking number to get the latest delivery status of their shipment. When shoppers see this page, it builds more trust. This page also helps reduce the number of customer support tickets by quickly allowing them to get the latest delivery status by entering their tracking number.

- **Checkout Page:** This is the beginning of the checkout flow. This page is where people begin to enter their personal details. Some stores allow people to checkout as a guest or give them the ability to create an account, so their preferences are saved for faster checkout next time. The email address and shipping address are usually submitted here. Look at your checkout page and ask yourself is there anything which is confusing or distracting. If for one second, people feel doubt or uncertainty, they will shop elsewhere.

- **Shipping Page**: This page is a summary of the shipping price or to acknowledge free shipping.

- **Payment Page**: This page is where people enter their billing address if different from their shipping address. They will also add their payment details here. Some of the common payment methods are Credit Card, PayPal, Apple Pay, Google Pay, Amazon Pay, Shop Pay, Bitcoin, Stripe, Shopify Payments, Square, and cash on delivery. You also have the ability for customers to enter a discount code on the final purchase price. This discount code is often a code used by visitors who were about to leave your store without buying. As soon as someone attempts to leave your store without buying, you can trigger a discount code to encourage them to complete their purchase. If for example, people see a shipping cost, it may annoy them, and they'll end up exiting. But, if you show them a discount code offer, it may give them an incentive to continue.

- **Review Page**: The review page is where the shopper reviews the details they have entered before submitting the order button.

- **Confirmation Page**: This is where the purchase has been made. A summary of the customer order is displayed along with a thank you message. You can also add post-purchase upsells, which I will talk about later.

- **Terms of Service:** A terms of service agreement is a set of regulations that users must agree to follow in order to use a service. This is usually positioned in smaller text at the footer of your site.

- **Privacy Policy Page:** This page informs your store visitors about the private data you collect and manage on your store. This is usually positioned in smaller text at the footer of your site.

- **Returns Page:** This page outlines in detail your return policy. This is important so that in the case of a chargeback or dispute that you are covered. People will also look for this page to understand what claims they have and if they decide they want to return an item.

- **Contact Us Page:** A page that people can contact you via email, phone, or social media.

- **FAQ Page:** Give your customers as much information as possible in the most efficient manner by creating a FAQ page. A great way to build a FAQ page is to have your customer service team highlight the most common questions and update as you see fit. Often if you do not have a FAQ set up, you'll find customers searching your site for an array of topics. What this means is that shoppers do not have all the answers they need and are looking for site information to solve their questions. This is why I recommend creating a FAQ page.

- **Happy Customers Page:** As you grow your company and receive customer testimonials, a good idea is to build a page showcasing your happy customers. This is another one of my conversion tricks. Just like word of mouth, testimonials with product images are a great way to push people who are "on the fence" to go ahead and complete their purchase.

CHOOSING A STORE THEME

As mentioned earlier, a theme is a template that determines the way your online store looks and feels. Different themes have different styles and layouts and offer a different experience for your customers. Platforms like Shopify give you a selection of over one hundred free and paid themes.

Many beginner stores are run on free themes like "Debut," "Supply," and "Brooklyn." These free themes are perfect, to begin with. As you gain more experience and you want to increase the capabilities of your store, you can move easily to some of the more advanced themes like "Turbo" and "Retina." I'll add my personal favorite in the resources section.

Don't let the decision of a theme slow you down from setting up your store! Themes have their function, but ultimately there is a lot more to the success of a product or brand, than the theme. The beauty of platforms like Shopify is that you do not need to be a coding genius or expert in website design, as I mentioned in my introduction. It is literally a drag and drop style website build. I have built over fifty stores for clients, students, and of course for my personal brands, and I am not technical whatsoever.

One last tip is to choose a theme that is mobile responsive. The theme may look good on a desktop, but how does it look when you view it on your cell phone. That is the real acid test. Remember, 70 percent of your traffic will be from mobile devices. You can reach out to me for advice on the highest performing theme today.

Figure 38 - A website optimized for desktop, iPad, laptop, and mobile view.

THE SHIPPING DEBATE

Shipping is an interesting topic in the world of e-commerce. Amazon changed the game with free two-day delivery, and now more retailers—both physical and online—are playing catch up. The reality is that customers want their products delivered faster, with real-time tracking, with high quality, and competitive shipping costs.

If you are new to e-commerce, there was a period of time where lots of e-commerce drop-shipping stores were shipping products to customers from China with long delivery times, often anywhere between three to four weeks. The service was terrible, and companies like PayPal and Stripe started to crack down on those stores placing large holds and reserves on their accounts.

Simply put, chargebacks and disputes were rampant because many drop-shippers had no idea how to run a business, not to mention a complex supply chain. At first, customers that were first-time online buyers didn't know any better and were happy with the service. As e-commerce became more popular and consumers became smarter, the idea of shipping your product in three to four weeks was no longer a smart idea. Coupled with Amazon's grip in the marketplace with Amazon prime, e-commerce owners had to rethink their strategy.

Now, e-commerce owners are moving to faster shipping lines, shipping and sourcing agents, or simply fulfilling in-house to compete. You have a couple of options when it comes to pricing:

- Charge for shipping but deliver an exceptional service. In fact, make that service one of your competitive advantages.
- Do not charge for shipping and add the costs into the product price.
- Offer free shipping over a certain order quantity. (E.g., Free Shipping over $75 storewide)
- Cut costs in your operations and eat the cost of shipping.

For me personally, I like to have free shipping in the domestic home country. I want to acquire the customer at minimum break-even. I know that if I satisfy the customer, they will buy from me again, therefore raising the lifetime value of my customer. The majority of your money is made on the back end of your business.

There is a shipping setting in your store admin that allows you to set both domestic and international shipping rates. You can also work with local shipping companies to get the best rates for your products and services. An example of how your shipping settings may look inside your store is as follows:

Domestic:
> USA Shipping & Handling $4.99
> Free USA Shipping & Handling Over $75

International:
> International Shipping & Handling $9.99
> FREE International Shipping & Handling Over $75

I recommend you study your competitors and see what shipping model they use and the prices they charge. Another tip is for you to buy your competitor's products. This will allow you to model the areas that they are successful in and focus on being better in the areas where they lack in. An example might be discovering that they send thank you notes with a coupon in their delivery packages. It also allows you to go through their purchase funnel and record the various upsells and offers they show as you purchase their products.

CONFIGURE YOUR TAX SETTINGS

I am not a tax expert, so I recommend you consult with your local tax expert, as every individual may have a different use case or specific circumstance. You can also check out a company called Taxjar.

In your store admin, there should be a section where you can select your tax settings. Once you identify the tax specifics, the setup of taxes inside your store is very straightforward.

Again, this is an area that is worth getting professional advice if you cannot "google search" the information in your home country. In the earlier chapters, I mentioned that you should focus on working on your strengths and outsourcing the areas that you are less proficient in. Tax is a weakness for me, so therefore I let the professionals handle it when it comes to tax season.

EXTENT INTENT

When we sell, we want to make use of every single opportunity there is to either make a sale or capture an asset like an email address so we can remarket later.

An exit-intent or popup is a message that displays to users as they are about to leave your website. I am sure you have seen it before. You're browsing a website and you decide to leave the store, and as soon as you do, a message pops up and asks for your email or encourages you to remain on the site.

Figure 39 - An example of how an extent intent might look like.

The popup might display something the following:

- "Don't leave; sign up to our newsletter and get 15 percent off."
- "Purchase today using code 20NOW and get 20 percent off."
- "Did you know our products are organic, purchase today and get FREE shipping."
- "Subscribe to our newsletter for future promotions."

When thinking about conversion rate optimization and getting the most out of your traffic, an exit popup is a great way to start. Remember, there are many reasons why people will decide to leave your site. They include:

- Product price is too high.
- Shipping costs are too high.
- Lack of trust.
- Lack of product information.
- Uncertainty on delivery times.
- Slow site speed.
- Disorganized or complex site navigation.

If you find that you are attracting a lot of visitors to your site, but no one is buying, you can at least attempt to offer them a discount to cater to price objections or bring them into your email list and nurture them through more emails and offers, which will hopefully build additional trust. I use an exit-intent that comes with the email marketing tool Klaviyo. You can also use other apps on the market that can personalize your message for each type of shopper.

Finally, capturing emails is so important. You want to build a strong backend of emails so you can offset the cost of customer acquisition through paid ads. Go and install your exit-intent today.

"Among our key learnings, exit popups outperformed popups displayed on landing pages by +5 percent. If you're collecting 10,000 emails/month (congrats if that's the case), that would represent 500 additional emails/month and 6,000 emails/year." – Klaviyo[38]

SET UP YOUR PAYMENTS AND PAYOUTS

Payment gateways and processors allow merchants like us to accept credit card payments from our online customers. Shopify Payments, Stripe, and PayPal are a few of the most common ways e-commerce entrepreneurs take payments on their stores. You can also use Apple Pay, Google Pay, and Amazon Pay. There is also a new payment method called "SHOP" by Shopify.

I am sure there will be more options coming along but be sure to give your customer a choice. I know some customers who only purchase with PayPal, so they have the backing of PayPal and can easily raise disputes if a product doesn't deliver or the experience is not up to standard.

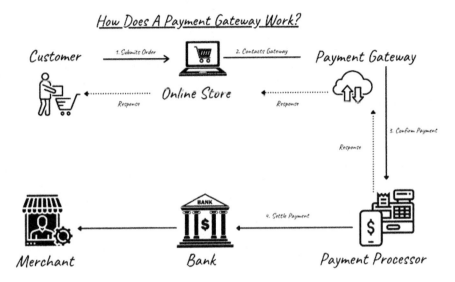

Figure 40 - A diagram illustrating how a payment gateway works.

KEY APPS

Apps are plugins to help grow your business and improve your marketing, sales, and social media strategies. There are many other uses but those are the most common for e-commerce stores.

You can find apps for all different platforms like Shopify, WordPress, Clickfunnels, and the list goes on. If for example, you use Shopify, they have their app store where you can find the best-rated apps by business function, either paid or free.

The first point I will make is that having too many apps on your site can be a bad thing, as it may slow the speed of your website. I recommend only using an app if it is performing a certain duty;

otherwise, remove it. When choosing apps, be strategic about what you need.

You will want some type of app that connects your supplier's inventory to your store. Examples might be the Oberlo app that syncs product information from your supplier to your store, or for print-on-demand products, I recommend Printful.

The next is an email capture app—something that can capture subscribers' emails and plug them into an email marketing software like Klaviyo. You'll also want an app that helps market your products via SMS. I recommend SMS bump.

Recart is another useful app that helps with increasing your store's revenue by engaging customers on the platform they actively use!

You might also want an app that compresses your images. Your site is made up of a lot of product imagery and general photography, which if large, can have an effect on the site speed.

There are also apps that help with shipping notifications that allow customers to track their orders. An example is Aftership.

If you love fast communication, you can install live chat, which can help you communicate with your visitors instantly and make the shopping experience more personal.

You should also add all the social media apps like Facebook, Instagram, Pinterest, along with the marketplace apps like Etsy, eBay etc.

I could list a host of apps, but I am reluctant to as, by the time you read this, better apps might have released.

For a list of my current favorite apps, which often change, visit my book resources or my groups for advice.

REGISTERING YOUR BUSINESS

Incorporation describes the process of creating a new business structure where that business becomes a recognized entity or person under the law. Since I am not an expert in the legal field, I recommend you reach out to a professional who can help find the best solution for you in your country and jurisdiction.

You will want to treat your new e-commerce venture like a real business and there are many benefits to incorporating your business like the protection of personal assets, easy transfer of ownership, separate credit rating, paying of fewer taxes, and increased durability.

When I saw success in my first business, I set up an LLC (limited liability company) in the state of Arizona in the United States, where I was living at the time.

PREPARING YOUR STORE FOR LAUNCH

Typically, my launch strategy will consist of the following five steps. This is a high-level checklist that you can use to ensure your site is created and launched correctly.

Phase 1: Pre-Launch Checklist: In phase 1, we are looking to secure the store name! You can use GoDaddy to check if your store name is available. I recommend going with a ".com" extension. If ".com" is not available, ".co" or another variation may be accepted as a last resort.

If you are undecided on a store name, visit leandomainsearch.com to find names best suited to your products and brand. Be sure to search the web to ensure there are no other brands that use the same name. If other brands are using the name, I would find some alternative options. You can use USPTO[39] to check if the name is already trademarked; if so, I would avoid and choose another name. Also, go to your state government website and look to see if there is any other company in your state operating with the name you want to use.

You will also want to go on social media and do a search for your name to see if it is available. If the name is not available for every channel, just adjust slightly to something like "**official**storename." Try this free tool to save you time on checking each channel. (https://www.namecheckr.com/)[40] Finally, be careful choosing a name, if for example, you name your store "Joessocks," then you are essentially stuck to just selling socks.

Phase 2: Site Launch Checklist. The next step is launching the site itself. Most platforms will have a 14-day free trial. Once you choose a platform, you can select a theme. Paid themes work great, but you can also use a free theme perfectly fine. Choose one that aligns with your product range, brand, and style. Test until you find the right fit. If you want my personal paid theme that I use for the highest conversions, you can reach out to me. The full list of Shopify themes can be found on their website.

Choose only the essential apps to get started, as mentioned earlier. Remember, too many unused apps will slow your site speed. Check the ratings of the app before choosing and see what other sellers have left as feedback. A full list of apps can be found on their website.

The next step is connecting your custom domain. By default, your store uses the Shopify extension. E.g.,

DogBeds.MyShopify.Com needs to go to dogbeds.com. You can use GoDaddy or Namecheap to purchase your domain. You are also going to want to set up shipping, both domestic and international.

Phase 3: Image/Graphics Checklist: Create a logo using a site like Fiverr or run contests on Freelancer to get a number of different options. You can also use a local designer or a free tool like Canva to create your logo. Canva is a simple user-friendly tool for all your design needs. Check how your logo looks on black and white backgrounds. Learn how to make simple graphics for your site. The dimensions of your graphics will be shown inside the Shopify admin. For example, the optimum image size for your slider on the Brooklyn theme is 1200px wide.

You can use Shopify image resizer[41] to reduce the size of the images. Ensure you have nice and clean site photography, especially product images. Remember, the quality of your site photography will say a huge amount about the professionalism of your company.

Add your collection images. Add Slideshow images. Add an "About Us" image. Use Remove.bg[42] to help remove unwanted backgrounds.

The favicon is the icon URL image that shows on the address bar. It is typically 100x100 pixels. Again, this is useful as it adds to the brand feel.

Often an introductory video can help with product descriptions, brand messages, and information about your company.

Phase 4: Integration Checklist: The next phase is your integration checklist where you need to ensure all of your tracking and connectivity is set up correctly.

Google Analytics: Installing Google analytics will allow you to learn more about your site visitors. Time of visit, pages visited, and time spent on each of your webpages. Google Analytics will also provide:

- Referring site details (such as the URL a user came through to arrive at your site).
- Type of web browser.
- Type of operating system (OS).
- Network location and IP address.
- Demographics.

Install the FREE tool here.
https://analytics.Google.com/analytics/web/

Facebook Pixel Tracking: The Facebook pixel is a piece of JavaScript that sits on your website and reports visitor/customer traffic information back to your ad account. Go to http://business.facebook.com/. The pixel records and fires on each activity like add to cart, initiate checkout, and purchase.

Social Media Linking: Link and integrate your social media channels into your store. Test the links to ensure they work.

Email Integration: Shopify and other platforms are designed to integrate with the email providers. The most common (up until recently) was MailChimp, but that partnership ended with Shopify and you need a workaround. There are other cheaper versions, but I use Klaviyo. The expense will pay for itself with the high level of customization, reporting, segmentation, and campaign automation. I am also a registered approved partner with Klaviyo.

Don't forget to set up payment details: You can use PayPal and Shopify Payments. Check your country for the best options.

PHASE 5: Go Live Checklist Ensure the password is removed and the site is live. Perform a subscriber registration test. Perform a site speed test at gtmetrix.com.[43] Perform a test purchase and you're set to launch the business of your dreams.

GO LIVE

Before you launch your store to the public, you are going to want to test it in as much detail as possible. I recommend having a work colleague, friend, or family member go through the different sections of your store and highlight any issues or areas of confusion. You can also have them record missing features or broken links. This is commonly known as usability testing.

It might be a good idea to test the site on different devices and brand names too, such as Apple iPhone, iPad, and desktop browsers, Nokia, Android, Chrome, etc.

You should also place a test order to ensure that purchases can be made in the store and that everything looks the way you want during the checkout and confirmation process.

Launching your store is an exciting time. You've spent hours of research and planning, and you are ready to showcase your product to the world.

I recommend having a countdown to the launch date. Build excitement, create social media buzz, invite family and friends, and run some prizes for the first few buyers on your store.

On e-commerce platforms, there is a password that you need to remove before you release the store to the public. You can find it in the preferences section.

Finally, it should be a moment of celebration and happiness for you, so do enjoy it. You've launched an online business to the world! Let's gooooo!

BUILDING YOUR STORE CLOSING THOUGHTS

Summary: In this section, we covered a wide variety of topics related to the building of your store. Your store is where shoppers will make the decision whether to buy from you or not. They'll either make a purchase, abandon their cart, or they may even bounce without even checking out your product page.

Remember, there are usually three areas where things may go wrong in the beginning of your e-commerce journey. It may be a poor product that no one wants, an incorrect marketing strategy where you are targeting the wrong audience, or finally, a poorly designed website with insufficient branding, trust, and security built in.

Your website is the one area that you can improve on pretty quickly and take control of by accurately tracking the changes and improvements versus the sales performance.

Ask yourself as you go through the site does it feel right, is it easy to navigate, is it fast, how does it look on mobile, and have all the information necessary to make a purchase decision.

One simple change can lead to a huge shift in performance. Finally, Rome wasn't built in a day and you must have a happy medium between taking action and improving on that action.

If you have any issues with the building of your store, feel free to reach out.

Action Steps:

- Think about what you want your store to look like, the name, the color scheme, the branding, and mission statement. Check if your name is available.
- Design the store with the mobile shopper in mind. As a result, think about how small a mobile screen is compared to a desktop screen. People will most likely be browsing your store on their phones.
- Ensure you set up the key pages on your store. Most people want to know, like, and trust you before they buy from you. Build trust, reviews, and a great "About Us" page.
- Add various payment options to your store. Most people want a choice when buying. PayPal is a common method that people prefer to buy through because of their trust and protection to the consumer.
- Take action and play around with the administration section of your store. The more you familiarize yourself with the backend, the quicker those sales will come in.
- Leverage platforms like Shopify to help you build awesome looking sites.
- You can go to the resources sections to grab assets to help you launch your store.

SECTION FOUR

SALES AND MARKETING

STRIKE WHILE THE IRON IS HOT

We are now entering quadrant three of my ESF framework. Our goal here is to take the products that we researched and the store that we designed and find a winning combination that we can scale by marketing the right products to the right people and optimizing the entire store and funnel for success.

In this chapter, we're going to talk about why it's important to strike while the iron is hot. We will talk about all of the different marketing strategies that you can use to scale your efforts to increase sales and your customer base.

Scaling is expanding by acquiring more sales faster than the rate at which you take on costs. Or in essence, your company is able to grow its operations either through more sales or work in a capable and cost-effective manner. In other words: make use of an opportunity immediately. The opportunity is that you have a product with the potential to scale to big numbers.

E-Commerce Success Framework

Quadrant 1 - Start	Quadrant 3 - Scale
• Learning	• Optimization
• Mindset & Focus	• Capital
• Planning	• People
Quadrant 2 - Sell	Quadrant 4 - Systemize
• Testing	• Systems
• Sales	• Processes
• Data	• Technology

Figure 41 - My E-Commerce Success Framework.

I remember when I was young and worked on my dad's farm, we had a saying, "make hay while the sun shines." Everyone in the family—there were seven of us—would help to ensure we made the best quality hay by bringing it into our farm sheds as soon as possible to keep it dry and safe from the imminent wet weather. Living in Ireland, you were never guaranteed long periods of sunshine.

Your specific opportunity is that you found a pocket of gold, a product fit for the market and it is currently showing signs of being a winning product. A product that if scaled correctly, can easily make five to six figures in sales per month.

As a result, instead of resting on your laurels, it's important that you take immediate action and double down on this newfound product success. Now, don't get me wrong. Enjoy the moment of getting your first few sales and first real achievement in making money online, but now comes the serious business. I said before; it usually takes one in every seven or eight products to find that winning scalable product—that pocket of gold.

For most people, the experience is amazing, especially if it is your first online business. I remember when I got my first sale, I was over the moon. I couldn't believe it. I had to double-check to see if, for real, I had a paying customer. The same applies when it comes to my students and clients. The first sale is always a special moment.

Usually, I get messages from clients like: "Oh my god, I just woke up to my first sale." "Is this real, I cannot believe I made money while I was sleeping." "What do I do next? I'm in panic mode." And that's the truth of it, that's how it usually works, and it comes when you least expect it. That's the power of actually building an online business, it's a 365-day, 24-7 cash flow business and you never know when your sales are going to arrive.

Here is where people too often make a big mistake: they make a few sales and they don't have a strategy or a plan. All of a sudden, things start to get out of control, whether its competition entering the marketplace, not having enough orders, slow response time to enquiries, a lack of communication with suppliers, a lack of real understanding of where the product is coming from, and a lack of confidence in your marketing strategies.

If you're not ready to double down, if you're not ready to take massive action, someone else will enter the marketplace and seize control. So, the first thing is realizing the opportunity you have when it comes first mover advantage.

This means you've probably got a product that is unique in the marketplace. It means you may have total control over your competitors by delivering a unique product to your target audience—a product they may not have seen before.

By being first, you can establish your product as the industry standard. You are able to find customers first and make a strong impression, which can lead to brand recognition and brand loyalty. You may be able to control resources, such as premium contracts with key suppliers or hiring talented employees who see the vision.

The drawback to being first is that you will have competitors enter the market after you, with a possibly better and more improved product if you do not constantly innovate and listen to your customers. The capital you invested is larger since you are doing a lot of product research and testing. Essentially, later entrants can reverse-engineer new products and make them better or cheaper.

Later entrants can identify areas of improvement left by the first mover and take advantage of them.

So, what I'm saying here is that you have to realize that as you start making sales, more and more competition is going to enter the marketplace. So, what do you need to do? Essentially, work faster to get so far ahead that it will be difficult for those who try and copy you to compete.

There is no doubt that hungry sellers are going to start seeing your ads, people are going to be using social media and spy tools to go and find your products, and all of a sudden, the product that you're selling has a lot of competitors.

Focus is key. It's time to get very clear on what you need to do in order to move fast. You need to start by fulfilling existing orders and asking these important questions:

- Are products getting fulfilled?
- Are there product quality checks?
- Who is sending tracking numbers?
- What are the estimated delivery times?
- How fast can you get customer reviews so you can use them to increase conversion rate and as user-generated content for marketing purposes?

It's important to get clear on the numbers and projections. Daily communication with your suppliers is key. You have about 48 hours before customers will start looking for confirmation of their orders, often sooner.

Other key tasks are monitoring your ads, monitoring customer emails, including whether you're sending out the appropriate communication and auto-notifications. Make sure that you are posting on social media and have a team handling any tasks that require a ticket to be created.

You are going to want additional help. Hire the right people to take the pressure off of you. Things move faster, orders come in and now, all of a sudden, you're not in test mode anymore; this is a real-life business, you got to double down and strike while you have the advantage. As you start to scale both vertically and horizontally, you need a really awesome marketing strategy.

Some key questions to ask as you develop your marketing strategy:

- How are you testing different audiences?
- Are you being omnipresent across social media?
- What are the daily metrics and KPIs?
- What demographics give you the best ROI?

You also need to start building audiences. Luckily, with advertising platforms, we have the ability to track everything. This is extremely important because you can double down on targeting the customers who are most interested in your product and can deliver the best return on investment (ROI). Naturally, you start to double down on what works and turn off what does not. With custom and lookalike audiences, we can expand beyond into new territories. I will talk specifically about advertising later.

It is important to start writing down a list of to-do items in order to help you focus on the things that matter and the things that don't. Start with the most important first and work your way down. The area of focus in the initial sales is where my clients need the most help. You need to be running on all cylinders. As I said before, you have a window of a few weeks to really push before the competition starts to figure out what you are selling. Above all, don't panic; embrace the moment. You have achieved what many haven't.

THE YEARLY MARKETING CALENDAR

As many of you may know, I love to plan and organize my week for optimum performance. I truly believe that if you don't value your time, someone else will take that time from you.

Setting clear weekly goals will make you reluctant to give your time away and allow you to fulfill your true potential.

The same applies to the yearly e-commerce calendar. Before I begin my marketing efforts, I map out the entire year. I want to get clear on the efforts needed so I can base my life, my team, and my efforts around these yearly dates.

E-Commerce is incredible and gives us unlimited reach and scale, but only if we leverage it correctly. For example, you need to properly prepare for the months of November and December, which in some cases can generate up to 70 percent of your total yearly revenue because of the holiday and gifting season.

One of the ways I plan my year is by using a tool called Trello. I can integrate Trello with my team calendar and ensure that we properly prepare for each holiday event. Below are some, not all, of the ideas you can use to plan your year. Burnout is real, so chose the days in the year that you can plan to take time off for yourself and your family.

January: New Year's resolutions are always a big focus for people at the beginning of the New Year. A great product to sell in

January is anything related to fitness and health, especially after the holiday season. January can be a great month to begin the preparation for a big Valentine's promotion in February. Another great idea is to use clearance sales to get rid of any excess inventory from the previous year.

February: Valentine's Day is a huge event across the globe. Shoppers are looking for special gifts for their loved ones! People will do anything for their loved ones, so don't be afraid to push some big promotions and offers in the month of February.

March: St Patrick's Day is another big event. As an Irishman born and bred, I can tell you, especially in the states, that Americans celebrate it almost as crazy as the Irish do. This is an opportunity for more sales with an Irish twist.

April: Spring season is here; shoppers are looking forward to holidays and travel, and Easter is a big event. April is also a time to plan for family-related gifts in May and June.

May: Two big dates are Mother's Day and Memorial Day. One of the reasons I love to sell jewelry is that it can be sold year-round to any member of the family. It also has a low cost of shipping and is a high perceived value product.

June: Summer is here. People are outdoors, looking for products to enjoy the good weather with and use on vacation. This is a great time of year to sell bikes, camping equipment, fitness, and sports-related products. Father's Day also happens in June. This is a great opportunity to market father related items like DIY products, men's fashion, and jewelry.

July: Independence Day falls in America in July. There is a broad range of American-themed apparel and gifts that can be sold.

July is typically a slow month for e-commerce sales, but it might be an opportunity to do a mid-year review, improve your site, get clear on the second half of the year, and focus on hiring for a much busier winter.

August: August is back to school month. Laptops, school clothes, and books are heavily discounted. August is another great month to start preparing for quarter four (October, November, December).

September: A relatively slow month before the madness of quarter four. Those that prepare the best will reap the biggest reward. September is also a good month to start selling winter-related products.

October: The beginning of Q4 is October, followed by November and December. These three months are massive in the world of e-commerce. This quarter represents a shopping bonanza, where stores can generate multiple millions of dollars in revenue if planned correctly. The big shopping opportunity in October is Halloween. It keeps growing year over year. In 2020, 148 million Americans celebrated Halloween and spent $8 *billion* dollars.[44]

November: The biggest month of the year arguably for e-commerce sellers. Black Friday and Cyber Monday are huge shopping days as consumers look for bargains and holiday gifts. Over the last couple of years, Black Friday has turned into Black Week, where instead of just one day, there is a week of promotions. In 2020, consumers spent $9 billion on the web the day after Thanksgiving, up 21.6 percent year over year, according to data from Adobe Analytics.[45] The month of November also includes Veteran's Day and Thanksgiving.

December: The goal in December is to finish the year strong. Continue with Christmas promotions, but remember your cut-off delivery dates, so customers are aware of when the drop-dead delivery dates end. The last situation you want to arise is a bunch of unhappy customers because they never received their gifts in time for Christmas. One way to avoid this disappointment is by clearly outlining the delivery dates on your homepage and product pages. December is also a great month to plan for January and the New Year.

Most e-commerce entrepreneurs usually work right through the entire quarter four. Each year, I gather with a bunch of other marketers to work and brainstorm so that the sum of our combined efforts exceeds individual performance.

Note: As you go through the year, make it a habit to be in the activity of acquiring subscribers regardless of if someone has bought from you or not. Over time the goal is to eventually turn a subscriber into a customer.

BECOMING OMNIPRESENT ON SOCIAL MEDIA

Attention is the new currency. Let me ask you a few questions:

- How far are you in distance from a delicious pizza at Domino's?
- When was the last time you saw an ad on tv for Domino's?
- When was the last time you received coupons in the mail for Domino's?

Dominos and other large companies have the resources, power, and money to literally be everywhere at once. The reality is that there is no such thing as too much marketing. Dominos knows exactly how to keep their product in the minds of its customers at all times.

These types of companies know that by being everywhere, eventually, you will associate their brand name with the product they are selling. Subconsciously, they want you to think of Domino's when you think or crave pizza.

The benefits of being everywhere are as follows:

- **First to Mind:** When you think soda, you think Coca Cola! When you think cell phone, you think iPhone (Apple). When you think luxury car, you think BMW.

- **Brand Recognition:** By being everywhere, acceptance of your brand and products are more easily adopted.

- **Reduce Price Sensitivity:** The more people resonate with your brand, the more they will be less resistant to paying a premium price. The authority and presence that you build with being everywhere subconsciously attract consumers into paying a premium.

- **Authority Positioning:** Eventually, by being everywhere, people will link your brand to a specific industry that can be very powerful. When this happens, people will refer or recommend you naturally.

- **Higher Conversion Rates:** People don't often buy on the first visit; by constantly showing up, you improve the chances that the visitor or follower will eventually buy.

- **Remain Competitive:** By being omnipresent, your marketing strategy never goes stale, and you never take your eye off the competition.

- **Natural Expansion:** You may not know it, but by diversifying into new sales channels and social media outlets, you are reaching another subset of your total audience. e.g., You may sell dog products but not every one of your potential customers has a Facebook account.

Now, I know what you are thinking. Damien, there is no way I have the budget and resources to be everywhere like the big brands. Well, it may be a little easier than you think. In today's world, we have unlimited reach through free social media channels. Just recently, we have seen a mass movement of new social media stars and platforms emerge.

Just recently, TikTok provided the biggest opportunity to gain first-mover advantage in the world of super-competitive Instagram and Facebook domination. Addison Rae leads a new list of the top-earning TikTok stars, generating income of about $5 million for the 12-month period ending in June 2020, according to a report from Forbes.[46] She saw a gap in the market and jumped on the trend. She knows that attention is the new currency, and it can be easily monetized.

She wasn't a Coca-Cola or an Apple brand, just someone that knew how to get attention. TikTok represented a new and untapped market with more demand than supply.

On Sept. 5, 2020, Vlad TV reported that Warner Music Group purchased IMGN Media for $85 million. The company creates Instagram, Snapchat, and TikTok pages and post memes and videos that are likely to go viral. The owner of the Black-themed Instagram page "Daquan" has reportedly sold the brand for $85 million.[47]

For starters, this shows you the power of social media and how giant companies are willing to pay for traffic and followers. That's right; this company has no actual physical product; its product is its follower base. I think the reason for this acquisition is it has to do with data watching and better understanding the habits, actions, and predictions of teenage audiences.

I will chat further about how similar Instagram "meme" and content pages can make a fortune by promoting other people's products, and in most cases, they are e-commerce products.

With this introduction, I hope it inspires you to start creating content for your brand, understanding that each piece of content you publish is another stepping-stone to building something of value.

In this section, I will be talking about all the different possibilities you have to leverage the power of social media inside your sales and marketing strategies. Think of social media as the gasoline to your car. Without gas, you won't be able to drive. Social media is a mixture of organic and paid content.

Our goal is to create enough organic content and build up an audience of followers so that we can slowly turn that audience into buyers through paid ads.

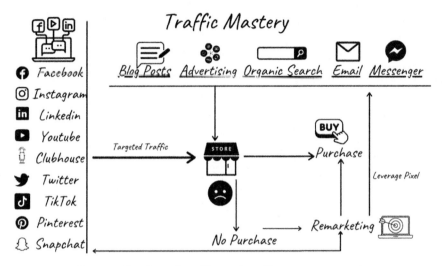

Figure 42 - Social media and traffic mastery overview.

You can see that as long as you keep feeding the machine, which is your website, the process of generating sales will keep occurring. Whether someone buys or not, they go back into a loop of remarketing.

This is why you'll often wonder why a product that you just visited or a video that you watched will appear on your timeline, offering you a chance to continue watching further and/or make a purchase.

The following is a strategy to leverage social media as a way to become omnipresent across the Internet.

Step 1: Create social media accounts across all of the current social media platforms. e.g., Facebook, Instagram, Twitter, TikTok, YouTube, etc.

Step 2: Create a monthly calendar for posting valuable and fun content across all channels.

Step 3: Take one day a week to record video and capture images. This is called batch work and it allows you to become efficient in your workload.

Step 4: Use a social media management tool like Hootsuite to automatically schedule content throughout the week.

Step 5: Engage and interact with your followers.

Step 6: Leverage hashtags and keywords to attract more people to your brand.

Step 7: Add your store link to the bio of your social media accounts.

Step 8: Become better, follow your competitors, and model success.

I encourage you to begin sooner rather than later, or at least just secure your social media handles (@names). Finally, model some of your competitor's social media pages and discover how to have a mix of value-based and sales content. No one wants to follow a social media page that constantly sells. Discover what content your audiences enjoy engaging with and optimize it towards those insights.

WRITE COMPELLING COPY

Sales copy is a text that persuades people to want and buy a product or service. When you browse a restaurant menu, it's written in a way that sounds delicious and appealing. When you scroll through a holiday catalog, you feel like you are already on the beach sipping cocktails. Copy entices us and engages us by using words to sell.

The art of storytelling and writing sales copy is something that comes with practice, experience, and knowledge of your niche. I had never written a book before, so it is something that I had to study and learn to overcome the limiting belief that I'm not good enough to write a book. The one thing I did have was knowledge of my customer, which is you because I was once in your position, and therefore I am able to tailor the content in a way that I know will deliver value.

With your brand, everyone loves a good story and if you can convey it in your messaging, it's going to lead to success a lot quicker. Let's first talk about the story behind your brand.

As mentioned earlier, when you create your store, it's important to put time and effort into the "About Us" section, which is also known as "Our Story." This page only needs to include 200 to 300 words about the company and maybe a photo of the CEO and founder. A good story will gravitate people to your brand. Remember, most people do not know who you are, and they don't trust you, so you have to give them a reason to shop with you.

If, for example, you own a dog brand, tell them about your passion for dogs, why you created the store, and how you are different. Tell them about your employees, your mission, your contribution to society, and your focus on customer satisfaction.

I discovered that dog owners don't just want to hand over their money to some faceless corporation, they want to purchase from someone that they know, like, and trust, and the more authentic and real you are in your story, the better. Do you have office dogs? Add pictures of them, too.

Now let's talk about sales copy. Sales copy is what a retailer or brand uses to persuade a potential customer to take an action. The two areas of copy you will want to work on are in the advertisement you create (via Facebook ads or another traffic source) and the page where your advertisements link to (product page or homepage).

The following are some tips for writing great sales copy:
- Know your audience, the way they speak, and what they want.
- Tell an interesting statistic, story, or something which makes them want to read more.
- Avoid wordy sentences. No one has the time to read long paragraphs.
- Focus on the benefits that come from the product.
- Use action words.
- Add scarcity if you have a limited number of units available.
- Integrate keywords and emotional triggers in the copy.
- Use bullet points for ease of reading.
- Highlight why you are better than your competitors.
- Show results and/or photos of the product in use.

I was never that good at writing in school, but it's something I am getting better at because I know the impact words can have on the success of any business. If that sounds like you, all I can say is that once you start writing about things you love, you'll soon find that you are much better than you think.

FACEBOOK MARKETING

Let's move now to one of the most powerful ways to scale your business, and that is with online advertising like Facebook.

Have you ever seen the giant billboards on buildings or alongside highways in the US? This was once upon a time one of the most popular ways to advertise. While they still exist, more and more companies have moved to digital methods of advertising. The main reason is because attention has moved online. People are on their phones and laptops for two to three hours per day. The real benefit is that digital marketing like Facebook is quantifiable. What I mean is that the results can be easily measured and tracked, and you can target your ideal customer. A billboard on a highway is hard to quantify the performance.

Thanks to social media and the way we interact in today's world, platforms are able to gather endless amounts of data on their users. Facebook, Google, YouTube, and other social media channels have hundreds of different data points on each one of us, all feeding into their data centers.

Firstly, based on the social media profiles that we create, Facebook can gather our age, gender, location, and much more. They also know what we like based on our likes and shares, and they can track as we scroll through our social media newsfeed. They also know which videos and images that we comment, like, and share. It can tell our favorite brands and sports teams and the list goes on. As a result, social media algorithms and artificial intelligence are able to construct who we are and what products and services we are most likely to engage with and buy. It's like a giant data center of consumer information.

It is no wonder that Facebook CEO and founder Mark Zuckerberg is always under scrutiny by the Federal Trade Commission. The world is still coming to terms with tracking and consumer data. If you want to get a good look into how social media companies work, I suggest you watch the movie "The Social Dilemma" on Netflix by Jeff Orlowski.[48] I already knew a lot of what was in the movie based on my years of experience, but this really does accurately portray how we humans have become addicted to social media.

With all this information at their disposal, it gives Facebook, and other social media companies, massive opportunities to capitalize on it. Here's an official statement from Mark Zuckerberg on how Facebook helps advertisers. There is a lot more to it than this, but this is a general overview of what Zuckerberg had to say:

"What we allow is for advertisers to tell us who they want to reach, and then we do the placement. So, if an advertiser comes to us and says, 'All right, I am a ski shop and I want to sell skis to women,' then we might have some sense because people shared skiing-related content or said they were interested in that, they shared whether they're a woman, and then we can show the ads to

the right people without that data ever changing hands and going to the advertiser."

So, you may ask how you can get started with Facebook ads and how you can use them to scale your business. This is not an exact blueprint but it's a basis for beginners. Let me break it down into steps. It might be easier to explain through video, so for more details; you should visit my free bonus at EcommerceActivated.com/scale.[49]

Step 1: Create an account with Facebook. You can go to business.facebook.com.

Step 2: Install the pixel on your website. This is a very simple and easy process as Facebook integrates with most e-commerce platforms like Shopify. The pixel is a piece of JavaScript that reports and tracks what happens on your site and sends the data back to your ad account, such as who visited your website, who added a product to the cart, or who purchased, etc.

Step 3: Decide which type of campaign you want to run. Facebook has many different types of campaigns depending on what you are looking for, like conversion ads and brand awareness.

Step 4: For e-commerce specially, we run conversion ads. A conversion ad is when someone takes a desired action on your site. For example, we can tell Facebook to find us people who are interested in dogs, who are male, over 35, live in the US, and match the characteristics of people who shop online.

Step 5: Start with small budget ads and divide up targeting into adsets.

Step 6: I like to divide my budget into different audiences because I want to know which audience converts the best to my product offering. An example might be as follows: One Campaign selling Dog Shoes with four adsets targeting four different groups, those groups might be "Dog Products," "Dog Breeds," "Dog Associations," and "Dog Owners." Each audience gets the same budget.

Step 7: Let the ads run for forty-eight hours and analyze the data. This is where the magic happens.

Step 8: Cut the losing adsets and focus on the winning adsets.

Step 9: Start to increase the budget on the winning adsets and see how it reacts with the change. Ideally, you want to see the same pattern of positive ROI.

Step 10: Find more interest groups that you can add in and repeat the process. Testing helps you find the pockets of people that react the best.

Step 11: As this process of testing is happening, the pixel is feeding the ad account, and data you are acquiring is allowing Facebook to optimize for your ideal audience. The more data points Facebook has on your ideal customer, the easier and cheaper it will be to find your next customers.

Step 12: With a Facebook ad strategy, there is no one right way. You have to test. What works best for you may not work for someone else. It is all about your products, your site, and your ad account and how they perform.

Step 13: Look at your columns to read the data. Here are the following columns that I use when analyzing my results.

Delivery, Frequency, Reach, CPM (Cost per thousand), CPC (Cost per click), CTR (Click Thru Rate), View Content (FB Pixel), Add to Cart (FB pixel), Purchase (FB Pixel), Cost Per Purchase,

Purchase Conversion Value, Return on Ad Spend (ROAS), Amount Spent Today, Total Amount Spent.

Step 14: As soon as you have built up your audiences. You can create a lookalike audience. These audiences typically give you the cheapest acquisition costs.

For other platforms, the process is pretty much the same: You rely on data and metrics, and you raise your budget in accordance with your results.

This is just the tip of the iceberg; I could not cover all of the strategies in just one chapter. As mentioned in other chapters, think of Facebook ads like a machine. The more information you feed it, the smarter it becomes. The smarter it becomes, the better results it can bring to you as an advertiser.

If you are unsure of the best way to target your customers using Facebook, then I highly recommend a free tool called Facebook Audience insights. It can be found inside your Ad Manager.[50]

Audience Insights shows you data about your ideal audience so that you can compare and contrast different targeting options, plan your campaigns, and create relevant advertisements.

It can be used to learn more about your target audience or if you are seeking additional interest groups to target. Two key metrics you should look at are "relevance" and "affinity."

Facebook defines "relevance" as: The pages that are most likely to be relevant to your audience based on affinity, page size, and the number of people in your audience who already like that page.

They define "affinity" as: How likely your audience is to like a given page compared to everyone on Facebook.

Imagine if you wanted to find out more about the dog niche, what pages dog lovers visited, the brands they associated with, and the average age of that niche. Well, audience insights give you a number of different data points that can be broken down by the following:

- Age and gender.
- Relationship status.
- Education level.
- Job role.
- Top categories.
- Page likes.
- Top cities.
- Top countries.
- Top languages.
- Frequency of activities.
- Device users.

Imagine the boost this gives you if you do not know where to start. Without this tool, I wouldn't have been able to scale into different audiences and markets and skip the majority of testing because Facebook already had the data behind my ideal buyers. The beauty with Facebook is that you can also target Instagram users through the Facebook advertising platform since they bought Instagram in 2012.[51]

Figure 43 - Another example of a sock company leveraging Facebook and Instagram ads.

INFLUENCER MARKETING

In this section, we're going to talk about Influencer Marketing. I define Influencer Marketing as a form of social media marketing where people, or organizations, who may possess an expert level of knowledge, or influence in a particular field, promote someone else's products or services to their own followers in exchange for some type of compensation.

An example might be a fitness model on Instagram who is a fitness coach, gym instructor, or health expert, and they agree to promote a supplement product to their followers in exchange for compensation or some other agreement.

There's no doubt that having a strong social media presence matters as I mentioned with the emerging TikTok "stars." One way of getting your products out to the masses is by finding influencers who already have a powerful and loyal following and use them as a traffic source.

These influencers are regarded as experts in their particular niche and have built up a strong and loyal following for a reason. They could be models, celebrities, or just people with a unique style or possess brand-aligning characteristics.

How do you go about finding the right influencers to work with?

- The first question is, what product are you looking to sell?
- What are the characteristics of this product?
- Who is your ideal audience?
- Where do they live?
- Where do they hang out?
- What kind of styles and personality traits do they possess?

Once I have answered those questions, I want to define the goal of the marketing campaign. How much am I looking to generate in sales, or is the goal purely to improve brand awareness or to grow a social media channel and email list? Once you define your goal, it's important to choose the social media platform.

Is it Instagram, Facebook, Twitter, Pinterest, Snapchat, TikTok, or YouTube?

Once I answer those questions, I like to go through a list of different influencers.

I usually list them out on a Google doc and rank them based on their follower size, engagement, product to market fit, and price.

A simple way to determine price is by emailing or direct messaging that person on their social media channel. Usually, there will be a contact email associated with their profile also.

In order to find Influencers, I would first search on Instagram, or I might go on Facebook, or I might start looking for related hashtags.

For example, if I am searching for someone in the fashion niche that is an influencer in leggings, I might search "leggings" or "gym leggings" on Instagram. The main goal is to find a fit between the product you sell and the influencer's content and audience. Without the right fit, their followers will not buy.

6 Things I look For In An Influencer

- Posts Relevant Content
- Large Passionate Following
- Omnipresent Across Social Media
- High Engagement Rate
- Experience Promoting Brands
- Not Working With Too Many Companies At Once
- The Right Fit For My Brand

Figure 44 - Things to look for in a great influencer.

Once you narrow your list down to say your ideal top three, you can begin to negotiate and test what works on a small scale. I like to start small and test out my campaigns before scaling. I'd much rather learn early that my $50 campaign was a failure rather than agreeing to a $500 or $1,000 monthly campaign. One benefit of Influencer marketing is that you are diversifying your traffic. It means you may be reaching other people that your competitors are not.

I'll usually negotiate a price with the Influencer for an introductory campaign. This type of campaign is usually a 24-hour only post. It could be a story post or a swipe up story. If the results are good, then I will renegotiate and create consistent promotions with the Influencer that produced positive results. If the results are bad, at least I started with a small budget and I can eliminate that Influencer from my list.

Eventually, through trial and error, you will find the right Influencer that gives you positive ROI, brand exposure, and a great strategic partnership. One important thing to note is just because an Influencer has a large following does not mean that their audience is highly engaged or is going to want to buy your products.

There are tools and websites to help you find how to put value on Instagram promotions and how best to find the right influencers for your niche.

Finally, treat this type of marketing differently as you are working directly one to one with the individual and not some big corporation. Be very specific with that person, perhaps even writing out a simple agreement, so you are both clear on the agreed-upon deliverables and compensation.

GOOGLE ADS

Google ads[52] have been around for quite some time and are still a fantastic way for you to attract your ideal audience. The main difference between Google ads and Facebook ads is that Google is *search intent.* What this means is that people are searching for products to buy or at least looking for information. An example might be a search term like "Best Dog Organic Shampoo" for dogs. People are in a buying behavior and if you can match your ads to specific keywords, you are on to a winner.

Most people who buy on Facebook buy based on *interruption marketing.* Facebook ads are about interrupting a person's scroll and showing them an offer that they did not know they need. This is the main difference between these two social media giants.

Google is intent-based advertising, and Facebook is interruption-based advertising.

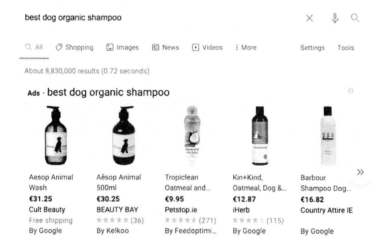

Figure 45 - Google search results based on "best dog organic shampoo."

YOUTUBE ADS

YouTube instream ads play before the intended video that the user is about to watch. As I talk about these different platforms, it's simply too much for me to give you the entire strategy in one book, so I'm sharing the golden tips and a high-level overview on each. The beauty of e-commerce is that you can market in many ways, so I'd rather give you high-level overviews in each one rather than a deep dive on just one single platform.

For YouTube ads, I use "instream ads." In-stream ads are sometimes skippable and sometimes not. If your ad is longer than thirty seconds, you are charged when someone hits the thirty-second mark. If your ad is shorter than thirty seconds, you are charged if someone watches the entire ad. And, obviously, if someone skips your ad, you're not charged.

What is beautiful about YouTube ads (which is owned by Google) is that you are advertising on a giant video platform that is search-based intent, as I mentioned earlier. What this means is people go on YouTube to find information. For example, "How to Groom Your Dog." Dog grooming is a giant niche, so naturally, there will be YouTube channels dedicated solely to dog grooming or dog-related products.

What you can do is put your video ad in front of these YouTube channels and specific videos, so as someone is about to watch a video, your ad shows up before it plays.

Key Youtube Ad Metrics To Look At

CPV (Cost per view): A bidding method for video campaigns where you pay for a view. A view is counted when a viewer watches 30 seconds of your video ad.

CTR (Click Thru Rate): CTR is the number of clicks that your ad receives divided by the number of times your ad is shown; clicks ÷ impressions = CTR.

ROAS (Return on Ad Spend): Return on an ad spend tells you for every dollar you spent, how much are you returning in revenue. Return on Ad Spend = Revenue / Ad Spend x 100.

Watch Time: Watch time measures the total amount of time people watched your video ads, shown in seconds.

Earned actions: Earned actions can include clicks but also new channel subscribers or engagement. This metric can also indicate relevance.

Conversion rate: How many people are clicking from the ad to the landing page and then converting into buyers? For example, if you had 50 sales from 1,000 interactions, your conversion rate would be 5 percent.

Figure 46 - Some of the useful Youtube (Google Ad) metrics to look for.

Youtube ads are run through Google ads. You can sign up for a free account at https://ads.google.com/.

SNAPCHAT ADS

Snapchat is another popular mobile app that allows the sharing of photos, text, and video, but the main difference is that the messages disappear from the recipient's phone after a few seconds.

Snapchat Ads work for all advertisers, from global brands to small and medium businesses. There are about 249 million daily active users on the platform. You can use the Snap Pixel and the goal-based bidding to optimize your ad campaigns. The audience is typically that of a younger demographic.

As you have seen, nearly all big social media channels have their own ad platform. What works for others may not work for you, so it is best to test.

Also, remember there is a saying, "if you don't pay for product, you are the product." Essentially these social media companies would not be able to deliver value and generate revenue if their users, which is us, were not posting and engaging in content. As a result, the ads you create should represent the content that is familiar with the users of the platform. Gain insights from Snapchat's Ads Manager, a self-service platform, where you can easily test, analyze and optimize campaigns.

TIKTOK ADS

TikTok has about 1 billion monthly active users. That is quite astonishing for a platform that's only a few years old. TikTok gained huge popularity for its viral videos and proved a great alternative for content creators who were late to the game on Instagram.

Simply put, TikTok had more demand for content than supply and so people became viral stars overnight. It is still a little early to know if TikTok will continue to be a social media giant and not just a one-hit wonder.

Recently, I got an invite to check out their advertising platform. I will begin running ads in 2021 on TikTok and I advise you to check it out too. Being omnipresent allows you to find the best advertising ROI for your particular niche. In the case of TikTok, the average age of their users is a lot younger than, say Facebook and Twitter. According to Reuters: "60 percent of US TikTok users are aged between 16-24, according to a November 2019 release."[53]

If you sell products to the teenage and younger demographic, then TikTok could be the route for you. There are rumors that

TikTok will integrate the buying and selling of consumer products into the app in mid-2021. To get started, you can visit: https://www.tiktok.com/business/.[54]

TWITTER ADS

Twitter is a 'microblogging' system that allows you to send and receive short posts called tweets. Twitter was one of the first social media platforms that I ever joined. I must admit though, I never really got into it until recently. Part of the reason for my newfound love of Twitter is because it really does have stimulating conversation and a lot of great knowledge that can be consumed in short-form content.

Twitter users like me are seeking more intellectual pursuits, news, and informative content. This is the type of user you'll be targeting, compared to a Facebook user, where people are looking for entertainment, photos, and family/community content. Twitter is probably one of the less popular places that e-commerce entrepreneurs advertise on and I think they are missing out. I believe Twitter ads are open for disruption. The fewer advertisers you compete with, the cheaper the acquisition costs will be, leading to greater growth and profits. According to Twitter, its users are 2.7x more likely to purchase a product after seeing it on the platform. If you can partner with influencers, then that purchase intent increases to 5.2x![55]

Twitter gives you a list of objectives to choose from:

- **Awareness:** To get as many people as possible to see your message.

- **Followers:** To build your audience and grow your number of followers.

- **Promoted video views:** To get more people to see your video or GIF.

- **Website clicks or conversions:** To get people to visit your website and trigger lead generation or sales.

- **Tweet engagement:** To get people to share, respond to, or like your Tweet App installs or re-engagements: to get people to install or open your app.

Twitter also allows for conversion tracking that enables you to measure your return on ad spend by tracking the actions people take after viewing or engaging with your ads. This again is why I love digital marketing because we can track every dollar we put in and calculate how much we get in return.

RETARGETING YOUR AUDIENCE

You'll hear a lot of marketers talk about "low-hanging fruit." It can be defined as something or someone that can be won, obtained, or persuaded with little effort. Retargeting is the low-hanging fruit of online shoppers that you'll be able to capture and turn into sales easily via paid ads.

Retargeting is where you target people that have already viewed your website, product, or offer and try and convince them to return back to the product or page that they were viewing. Distraction is one of the many reasons that people do not buy on the first attempt.

Retargeting works by leveraging the pixel code. The pixel is a piece of JavaScript that is installed on your website and reports what is happening on your site to your ad account. Usually, each social media platform has its own pixel. The pixel is able to determine who visited certain pages and who is most likely to convert. By having the pixel data, you can create custom audiences that essentially bucket people into categories based on specific actions they have taken on your site. For example, you'll be able to build audiences that have people who added a product to the cart but did not buy.

Some of the best retargeting audiences are as follows:
- All website visitors, excluding buyers.
- Visitors to specific website pages.
- Visitors who viewed a product page but did not buy.
- Visitors who added to cart but did not buy.
- Visitors who initiated checkout but did not buy.
- Visitors who added their payment info but did not buy.
- Visitors who watched 50 percent of a video.
- Visitors who watched 75 percent of a video.
- Visitors who watched 95 percent of a video.
- Visitors who engaged with your social media pages.
- Your email lists. (You can load emails into a custom audience)
- Your Instagram Page followers. Etc.

The big return on your digital marketing is in your retargeting, so set it up immediately. You can capture retargeting sales at a fraction of the cost of cold traffic because those visitors have already seen what you are offering and have expressed interest. Do not neglect retargeting, as it will always give you the best return on ad spending when it comes to paid ads. Please note retargeting can be performed on any social media platform that has a pixel and you have it installed on your website.

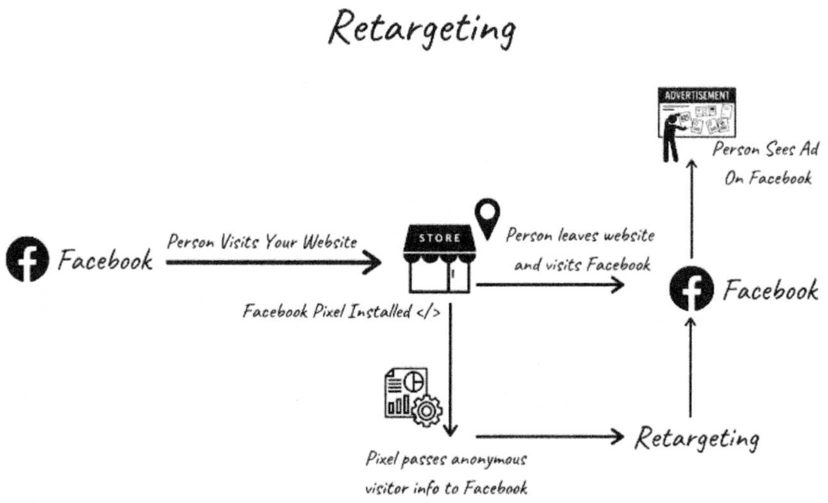

Retargeting

Figure 47 - Retargeting explained.

THE NEXT BIG PLATFORM

When I mention the words "The Next Big Platform," what I am referring to is any new social media platform that you can jump on where your ideal customer may hang out.

Social media gives you the opportunity to post relevant content that your potential customers will resonate with. It is the first step to giving value to future customers. For example, a video showing puppies to dog lovers with a call to action to visit your website.

If I asked you right now to post a video on TikTok and Instagram, I am 99 percent confident that the video you post on TikTok will get more reach and engagement. Why is this the case? Well, it comes down to supply and demand economics.

Instagram has been around since 2010, but TikTok was just fully released in 2020. TikTok has less of a supply of content, so if you start posting there, the chances of you going viral will be far greater. Instagram is now a lot more competitive and requires you to be different to stand out from the millions of content creators and users.

My best advice is to study all available platforms and see which ones work best for you and your business. Just because a social media platform is new and you may not be familiar with it does not mean you should not try out its effectiveness. You must be willing to do what others are not.

Finally, let's say you are one of ten people selling the same product. Nine of your competitors are all focused solely on Facebook and Instagram. You, however, are on both of these platforms but recently just joined TikTok. Essentially you have an advantage when it comes to targeting users on TikTok. The first-mover advantage is your friend! Jump on trends and keep innovating and expanding your business. Keep an eye on the next big platform so you can be one of the first people to jump in as an early adopter. A classic example as I write this book is Clubhouse. By the time you're reading this, it'll be something else.

ORGANIC DIRECT MESSAGE SELLING

Organic selling is a method of sales where you communicate with your followers and fan base, usually through direct messages on social media.

Before I begin, I want to say that this is not a scalable method as such, but it is a way for you to leverage your following if you have one and turn your followers into customers. As you know, social media allows us to build large followings through pages and groups.

Usually, when one of your social media pages or groups reaches a certain level of followers, it begins to grow much faster on its own. On YouTube, most people spend six to nine months uploading content before any of their videos take off. When one video goes viral, the channel itself begins to grow dramatically. Essentially you have triggered the YouTube algorithm, and it will begin to show more people your content because it is seen as something of value to a particular niche.

The same applies to groups and pages; eventually, after a lot of hard work, your page grows naturally by people tagging their friends and sharing your content because it is meaningful and engaging.

So, let's get down to the actual direct messaging process. What happens over time is your follower base will start messaging you through the direct message (DM) feature. In my case, when I was growing my social media dog pages, I was getting a least 20 to 30 messages a day from dog lovers. These messages would range from thank you messages to messages about products they could not find on the site. It became a great way for us to conduct product research.

Not only is this a chance for you to satisfy your follower's needs by communicating with them, but you can also recommend products to them based on your interaction and what they want. One of the best ways to convert non-buyers to buyers is through a meaningful, one-to-one conversation.

The next time you get the opportunity, train your virtual assistants or admins to give value first inside a direct message and sell only after the value has been provided. You'll be surprised, most people just want to chat with a real person, and once they know you are real and not a bot, they will happily spend their money with you.

Again, this is a small technique that I have learned through the years. Ensure your direct messages accept messages from "all" people and not just the people you follow. There is a setting inside your social media profile. I highly recommend direct message selling if you are tight on an advertising budget and you want to grow an impressive social media following.

FREE JUST PAY SHIPPING

"Free Just Pay Shipping" is a marketing strategy that online entrepreneurs use to capture new emails and customers. By finding low-cost products and selling those products for free but charge for shipping, the hope is to acquire new customers at breakeven or less. The bigger goal is that those customers will eventually ascend up the value ladder and purchase more products at higher prices throughout their customer journey.

The other advantage is that you are building your pixel and ad account with buyer data, which gives the likes of Facebook more data to optimize for your ideal customer. If you are trying to break into a particular niche, this is a great strategy to acquire customers with a low-cost product but with a high perceived value attached.

I also have students that give away free digital products. Let's say you create an e-book that is full of content on dog-related tips and tricks. The e-book can be used to give away content for free, and inside the book can be suggestions of products to complement the value you have given.

Here is an example:

1. The e-commerce owner wants to branch into the dog market.
2. They build a giant email list so they can eventually promote products to their list for free.
3. The owner contacts a supplier and buys thousands of dog reflective collars for $2 each to promote to dog owners.
4. They sell the dog collar for $0 but as a $19.99 value on Facebook. The store owner offers it for free and the customer only pays for the shipping, which might be $8.99 (The Free Plus Shipping Offer).
5. The shipping cost is expected to hopefully cover the cost of the dog collar plus the cost of acquiring the customer.
6. As long as the business owner can gather thousands of emails at a low cost, he or she will then be able to remarket and sell via email for higher-priced products.
7. If the first-time customer experience is positive, then there is a likelihood that they will purchase again via other promotions and through email marketing,

8. As more customers are acquired, your social media grows, and your customers will also refer their friends and family to your website.

Figure 48 - An example of a "Free - Just Pay Shipping" product page.

THE POWER OF THE PIXEL

You've heard me reference the pixel a few times, so now might be a good opportunity to go into detail about what it is and how it functions. The pixel is a piece of code provided by advertising platforms. It allows you to create and install your own pixel onto your website so that you can accurately track what is going on.[56]

Have you ever wondered what people do when they visit your website, what pages they visit, and what actions they take? Well, the pixel is essentially a tracking mechanism that allows you to record that activity at a high level. Let's talk specifically about the Facebook pixel to keep things simple.

Imagine a snowflake tiny in size; it's not that powerful right? Gather some snow and now you have a snowball. Roll the snowball and it gets bigger and strong. Push the snowball off a hill and it begins to roll and gather speed and size on its own accord. This example is how I am going to attempt to describe the Facebook pixel. As you add more snow, it grows into something much more powerful than what it began with, which was a simple snowflake.

Probably not the best analogy but you hopefully you get the idea. Now imagine a new website that you have just created, and you added the Facebook pixel to track your traffic. There is no data at this point, as no one has visited. Now imagine you start selling dog products on your store and you start marketing—Facebook ads, blog creation, anything to do with sending traffic to your site. What happens next is the Facebook pixel starts to record activity as it receives useful insights about visitors to your website, like where traffic is coming from, the devices people use, and other demographic information. (This is your snowflake stage) As you send more traffic, it learns more about your ideal customer. It starts learning and tweaking its algorithmic machine. It also tracks what type of people are moving along your sales funnel, like adding a product to a cart or making a purchase. It's essentially learning faster and growing stronger the more you feed it with data. Just like the snowball as it rolls down the hill, the pixel too is getting stronger, smarter, and it's beginning to understand what you want. So, in essence, the more data you have, the stronger the pixel becomes, just like a snowball as it grows in size.

Eventually, your pixel and advertising account get so strong that it is able to predict the customer you are trying to attract. Imagine

Facebook's entire data center; they literally have billions of data points. So, if you are selling to a particular type of person, for example, a dog owner, as the pixel gets stronger, the easier it is for Facebook to deliver better results to your advertising account and ultimately your return on advertising spend.

So, in the beginning, treat the pixel just like something small; you'll need to feed it in order for it to grow and produce results. The best way is to feed it through targeted ads and other organic methods of traffic to your website.

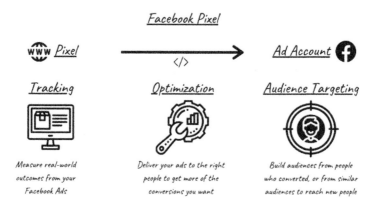

Figure 49 - The benefits of the Facebook pixel.

AFFILIATE MARKETING

Affiliate marketing is a promotional model where a third-party person gets paid a commission for any customer; they directly refer to a product and who makes a purchase.

Let's say a dog brand launches an affiliate program. Generally speaking, this is how it works:

- It offers to pay affiliates 20 percent for every sale they refer.

- The affiliates themselves promote the products via social media, word of mouth, friends and family, email, or paid traffic.
- Each affiliate is given a unique link to promote the company products, such as yourstore.com/affiliatename
- Through software, digital referrals can be measured, and compensation is paid out automatically on a specified date to the affiliate.
- Payment is usually made via PayPal or another common online payment system.

Refersion is the software that I use when implementing an affiliate marketing program on my online store. Refersion powers affiliate networks for over 19,000 merchants. What I love about the platform is it takes care of all of the technical aspects of managing my affiliates.

As mentioned before, I love simplicity, and if a software or another partner can take the responsibility off my shoulders of something complex, then I will delegate the responsibility.

A simple example of an affiliate is … me. I am a loyal customer of Shopify; I have used the e-commerce platform since 2016. I get paid a small commission for people I refer to the platform. I am happy to refer people because I believe it is the easiest model to get started on; my past experience with Shopify is a pleasant one, and my team and staff are well-versed in their features and applications.

Now, how do I know that affiliate marketing works in e-commerce? Well, going back to my dog store example, I discovered that my dog followers and customers were referring to people naturally. We had over 120,000 dog fans on our Facebook page. Our page followers tagged their friends and were commenting on our daily posts. These posts were a mixture of regular dog-related content and sales content.

I came up with the idea to incentivize people that were fans of my brand. I offered the chance for my followers to become affiliates. This led to more customers, and it started to drive some incredible new user acquisition and higher average order value. My fans/affiliates were now getting paid for their marketing efforts. It was a win-win for everyone.

Figure 50 - How affiliate marketing works.

WEB REMARKETING

Typically, you'll have on average, a three percent conversion rate on your store. That means for every 100 visitors to your store; three people will make a purchase. The good thing is we can remarket to those other ninety-seven people who visited but did not buy.

One company I have used in the past is Criteo. Criteo helps you re-engage shoppers throughout their path to purchase with tailored video and display ads delivered across the world's best publishers and designed for measurable performance. Criteo Dynamic Retargeting utilizes machine learning to serve up the most relevant ads in real-time.

You can add Criteo to your remarketing efforts along with your standard Google and Facebook retargeting. The reason you should try other forms of remarketing and capitalize is that you need to do what your competitors are not willing to do. Also, with Criteo, your ads will show up on other popular channels and news sites, and not just the social media platforms. Do not neglect retargeting; you need it running all of the time when you have traffic coming to your store. I promise you that retargeting will be the single biggest return on ad spend for your digital marketing efforts.

EMAIL & SMS MARKETING

You'll hear me talk about email marketing throughout this book and in my student training. Why? Because it is one of the key components to building a strong backend of essentially free money. With email marketing, you have the power to consistently send email promotions and newsletters to people who have opted in to your company's email list. As you can imagine, your companies email list can be a huge asset to your business and top-line revenue.

Over the past few years, SMS has also become a valuable asset to e-commerce companies and acts as a more direct type of interaction. SMS is incredible for abandonment cart recovery. Your

SMS promotions have much higher open and click-through rates. Someone is much more inclined to open a text message than an email buried in their inbox. I think we can all admit that we are subscribed to more emails than we need.

The beauty of email and SMS is that you've already done the hard work of acquiring someone's email or phone number, and now you get the opportunity to either: a) sell more products to the same customers; or b) nurture subscribers to buyers.

According to VentureBeat, email is the most effective advertising channel that generates $38 in ROI for every $1 spent.[57] Let's take a look at some of the simple lists and segments you can create to ensure you get the best delivery rates and return on your flows and campaigns.

Lists are static, meaning they grow as people subscribe or are manually added. Segments, on the other hand, are dynamic, meaning they grow as people meet segment conditions and shrink as people no longer meet them. Moreover, segments update in real-time.

Here are some of the most popular lists you can create:

Preview List: This is a small internal list that you can create as a test before sending emails to a mass audience. No one likes to open emails with broken links or typos. Usually, the list is made up of my team members. By sending your broadcast to a small test audience, it allows you to test the content, links, fonts, colors, and subject titles.

Unengaged (One Year): This segment won't populate until you have at least fifty-two weeks with your email provider, and the criteria is that your subscribers have had at least received ten emails but haven't opened or clicked on any of them. Usually, these subscribers are not really interested in your brand or product offering, and I often exclude them from my promotions, so I can receive higher open rates.

Unengaged (Three Months): Similar segment but shows the unengaged profiles for the past three months.

New Subscribers: These are profiles that have recently subscribed to your email list over the past fourteen days.

Engaged (Three Months): My favorite segment is the three-month engaged profiles. These people have opened or clicked an email in the past ninety days. I am confident that these users will give me my high open rates.

Newsletter: The newsletter is anyone who has subscribed either by opt-in on your website, via checkout process or any other email opt-in. I recommend excluding unengaged subscribers when sending a large email broadcast to hopefully get above ten percent open rate.

Here are some of the most popular segments you can create:

For me, my email provider of choice is Klaviyo. It is fully integrated via API to your e-commerce store. In doing so, you will be able to create segments that allow you to really dig deep into your most valuable customers.

Churn Risks: These are people who have purchased from your store at least once but have since lapsed in engagement and may eventually move to another brand that sells similar products. My tip is to re-engage those profiles with content that is specifically related to them. Also, try using upsells and cross-sells to sell similar products to the items that they have already purchased.

Potential Purchasers: These are people that have had engagement recently on campaigns, your site, or in general expressed interest in your products and brands. You can cleverly send them a little nudge by presenting an irresistible offer to make them a first-time buyer.

VIP Customers: These are our very important people. They have typically purchased over x amount or have purchased from you on a number of occasions. For me, VIP customers typically have spent more than one hundred dollars on my store or have made three or more purchases from me.

Win-Back Opportunities: These people have bought from us before, are still engaging with our emails, and may be ready to make another purchase. Typically, it has been over 180 days since their last purchase.

Repeat Buyers: These are customers who repeatedly buy your products. You can drill down even further if you want by segmenting your list by-product or collection. For a dog niche site, that could be Husky buyers, Dachshund buyers, or Bulldog buyers, etc.

I've attended private Klaviyo workshops in Miami, and I am a partner with them, promoting their products that my students and I use and love. If you'd like an introduction to their product, just let me know and I'll help you get set up. You can also visit the resources section of this book. The below is an example of one of the many simple configurations inside Klaviyo that you can set up to segment your buyers from your non-buyers.

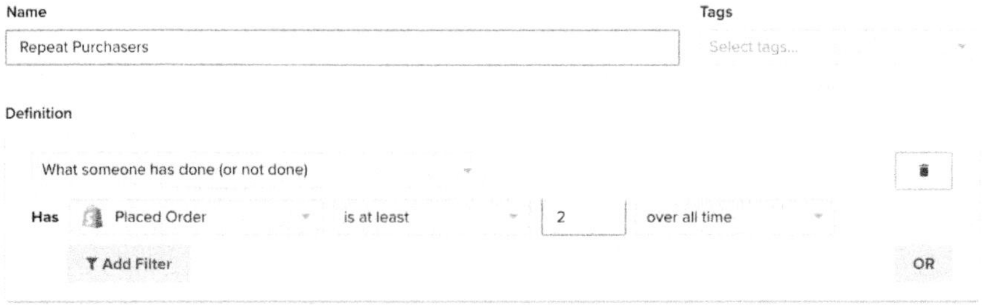

Figure 51 - The Klaviyo admin view of how-to setup a "repeat buyer" segment.

BLOG SETUP

Who loves free traffic? Ask any business owner what they would like more than anything; well, organic sales is likely high on their list. If your advertising account got shut down today by social media giants like Facebook, where would you source new traffic from, other than your social media pages or an email list?

I highly encourage you to start creating blogs. It does take time to create blog content and be consistent, but it is so important to the long-term success of your business. The immediate return may not be evident, but it will stand to you in the long run.

Ideas for blogs are endless and can be scheduled out automatically over the month. You can also invite guest bloggers to help you write if you find that your time can be more valuable elsewhere.

When I sold in the dog niche, I had a very passionate dog customer of mine who found a blog article I wrote and asked me if she could write about her life with dogs. Of course, I said yes and to make it a win-win for everyone and to encourage her to write great articles, I offered her free dog merchandise.

One or two posts a year will not cut it, though. Invest time, effort, and whatever money you can, and create a concrete blog posting schedule. Shopify has its own section inside your account that allows you to create blogs. Inside the blog articles, you can link to different products and collections inside your store. I like to structure blogs with "attention," "story," and "offer."

An example might be as follows:

Attention: The day my dog almost died.

Story: Traveling in the car without a safety belt.

Offer: I designed this safety belt for dogs.

Of course, there are many other ways to write blogs; this is just one example. The more content you create, the more Google will start to rank your store and move you up their rankings. If you have a site without a blog, start writing today, your existing customers will appreciate the fact that you are providing value and not necessarily pitching your products all of the time.

PRE-ORDER SALES

A favorite strategy that many people overlook is pre-order sales. I generally use this strategy for testing the marketplace. Pre-order just means offering a product for sale that has not yet been released.

Imagine you found success in a niche, and we'll use the dog niche example again. I want to share with you what worked for me. Let's say you have sold different types of dog-related products; you've accumulated a bunch of dog customers, email subscribers, and social media followers.

Your dog supplier reaches out to you and mentions that they have received news of a brand new and exclusive product that is about to hit their factory floor. The problem is that it is an unproven product, but it is unique and very similar to other products that sold well in the past. The other problem is that the product will not reach the factory until four weeks from now.

Some people may view this as a problem or may say, "let's wait until four weeks," but for me, I see it as an opportunity to be the first mover in my market. Pre-sales can be easily created through Shopify and other e-commerce platforms. So here is what I will do.

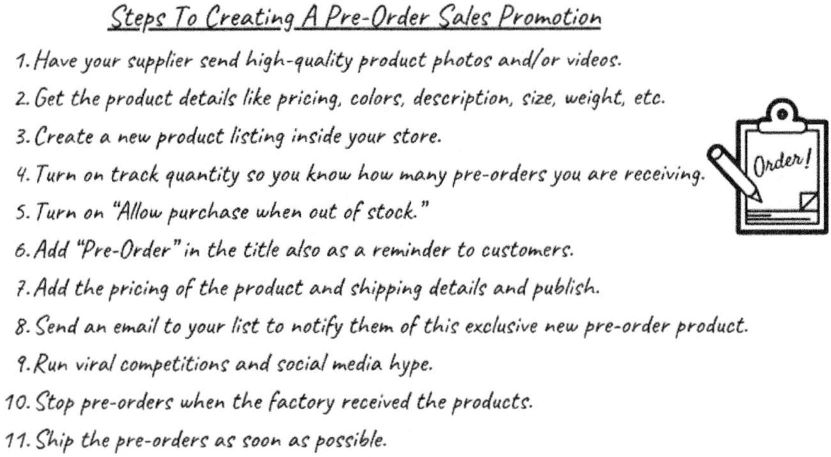

Steps To Creating A Pre-Order Sales Promotion

1. Have your supplier send high-quality product photos and/or videos.
2. Get the product details like pricing, colors, description, size, weight, etc.
3. Create a new product listing inside your store.
4. Turn on track quantity so you know how many pre-orders you are receiving.
5. Turn on "Allow purchase when out of stock."
6. Add "Pre-Order" in the title also as a reminder to customers.
7. Add the pricing of the product and shipping details and publish.
8. Send an email to your list to notify them of this exclusive new pre-order product.
9. Run viral competitions and social media hype.
10. Stop pre-orders when the factory received the products.
11. Ship the pre-orders as soon as possible.

Figure 52 - How to create a pre-order sales promotion.

There are also Shopify apps that do this for you in an easier and more advanced fashion, but this will get you started for free. Pro tip: if you are selling just pre-order items and nothing else, you can change the "Add to Cart" button to "Pre-Order" through the language settings of your code. In Shopify, you will find it here:

Dashboard > Online Store > Themes > Actions > Edit Languages and change your "Add to Cart" button to read "Pre-Order."

SEO STRATEGIES

Another core marketing strategy to generate free and quality traffic is SEO (Search Engine Optimization). Yes, it takes a little time, but it is rewarding in the long run. We have all been in the following situation: We create something we are proud of, but we are left disappointed when no one purchases or shows interest. How do we help customers find your new store?

The quickest way is through paid ads, but the other way is through content creation and SEO, as mentioned earlier. SEO helps your store rank higher in search engine traffic. Chances are, if someone finds your store through an organic search, they are in a buying mood.

The first way to improve SEO is by adding keywords to your site and landing pages. If for example, someone searches "Electric Bikes in Ireland," the chances are if you have the keywords "Electric" "Bikes," "Ireland" consistently added throughout your site with other relatable words, you are going to appear in the search engine results. If you sell Electric Bikes, you are going to want to try and add as many keywords as possible throughout your store's pages.

You can use a tool called "keywords everywhere" to show you what research terms are mostly correlated to what you are selling. You'll want to update your title and meta description of your store and then inside each product description.

Another tip is to name your file uploads with keywords and ensure links and images are also named with keywords. So, if you have photos of your products, make sure you name them with the keyword attached, such as ElectricBikeIrelandSku1234.jpg.

You'll also want to work on backlinking. This is where one website links to another website. An example might be if a cycling magazine wrote an article about bikes on their own website and inside the article is a link to your site where they can visit your page to purchase products. Backlinking is awesome because search engines like Google see it as votes of confidence. A great way to have other sites link to your site is by creating engaging and relevant content.

Another tip is to create a site map and verify your store with Google. SEO is a long-term game but rewarding. Remember, focus on constantly improving your store by adding keywords to every page, from products to blog posts. Google wants their customers to have a great experience, so the better your website is, the longer people will stay, and therefore the higher Google will rank your site.

Figure 53 - The many ways to optimize SEO.

SALES & MARKETING CLOSING THOUGHTS

Summary: I hope you enjoyed this section on sales and marketing. I gave you a number of different strategies that have worked for millions of different e-commerce entrepreneurs, including myself. If you have ever wondered how brands like Kylie Jenner, Fashion Nova, GymShark and more, have scaled so aggressively, it is because they have used many of the methods I've outlined in this book.

They've all spent millions of dollars on Facebook and Instagram ads for a giant return on ad spend. They all use Shopify to build stores that are optimized for conversions. They know the importance of building large followings on social media while leveraging influencers to promote their products. They each build giant email lists to sell on the back end to raise the lifetime value of their customers. These brands have literally grown in a few years to hundreds of millions of dollars in revenue.

Throughout this book, I want you to keep in mind my E-Commerce Success Framework (ESF): Start, Sell, Scale, and Systemize. You cannot start without taking action and choosing your e-commerce business model. You cannot sell without building your store and researching products to bring to market. You cannot scale without finding a great product and doubling down on what works. And finally, you cannot systemize the entire business until you have people, processes, and technology so that you can remove yourself gradually from the business.

I am excited for you because you are at the beginning of what is going to be a new era of commerce. The world is changing, and you have an opportunity to satisfy this new online consumer demand. One big tip for you is to choose one ad platform at the beginning. I started with Facebook and Instagram ads because I felt they were the easiest and most common. As I became more confident, I diversified into lesser-known platforms.

I think we are spoiled today. Advertising today is much easier than it was prior to social media and tracking codes. You can literally have an ad created and running on your store in five minutes. It's just like riding your first bike or going on your first date. At first, it is going to feel strange or overwhelming and you may fail a few times, but it is all part of being a successful entrepreneur.

The following video link breaks down the system that is digital marketing and how you can replicate it to either start or scale your business online. This is a fantastic overview of how big social networks operate and how they leverage data. Visit EcommerceActivated.com/scale.

Action Steps:

- Create your social media accounts if you have decided on a store name. You will want to secure the handles. E.g., @mystorename

- Setup your free advertising accounts. You can begin with the most popular ones and start off slow.

- Learn about what the pixel is and why it is so important in capturing data on your website.

- Create custom audiences if you are running traffic to your store currently. These audiences will help you categorize visitors based on the actions they performed, e.g., "visited page," "added product to cart," "purchased," etc.

- Learn how to write compelling copy or go to your favorite shopping websites and check out the product descriptions.

- Create an opt in on your website to build a list of subscribers. Create email marketing and SMS campaigns to turn your lists into free money-making campaigns.

- Start creating blog posts related to your products to help bring organic traffic to your store and help you start to rank and build authority.

- If you are overwhelmed at this point, or you are not in a position to take action, I understand. This is great but detailed information! Keep reading this book to completion.

SECTION FIVE

STORE OPTIMIZATION

PROGRESS IS BETTER THAN PERFECTION

"Look at my success. I didn't achieve it overnight. It has been the product of many years' struggle, and every year, my times have shown gradual improvement."– Mo Farah – Most successful British track athlete.[58]

One of the biggest tips I give people who are just starting off is to take imperfect action. There is no way you are going to find a home-run winning product on your first attempt. It takes a few tries, so embrace the challenges and failures along the way. Just like riding a bike for the first time, you'll only learn after you fall a few times and get back on the saddle.

Figuring out what works and what doesn't is something we all need to go through. Successful entrepreneurs will tell you that they'd prefer to quickly identify what doesn't work, so they focus on what does work because time is a finite resource.

When I first started my business, I knew I wasn't going to have everything perfect, and you won't either! One issue that often holds people back is that they try and execute based on perfection. They want the perfect script, or the perfect video, or the perfect lighting. No one cares in the beginning of your business because you have not yet reached a large enough audience.

The entrepreneurs who succeed are the ones who take immediate action with a first iteration. That task might be launching your first advertisement, or creating your first store, or hiring your first assistant. These successful action takers are not afraid to make mistakes, and they realize that progress is better than perfection.

Only after you have taken action can you then begin to optimize and improve on your first iteration.

In this section, I will offer clear strategies to improve your overall website and business so that it brings more sales, customers and converts your traffic at a higher percentage. This section focuses on improvements to your offer, your website, your customer experience, all of which are needed to make your business a success. Optimization is never-ending: Coca-Cola, Nike, and BMW never stop launching new products, testing new marketing and sales strategies, and neither should you.

You must learn to love and embrace change and improvement. Just like a bodybuilder, they dedicate their entire life to building the perfect body and becoming the best version of themselves. They will do anything to build the perfect body: drink little to no alcohol, get lots of sleep, eat healthy foods, and adhere to a strict gym routine. Just like a bodybuilder looks in the mirror trying to find weaknesses in their physique, the same applies to you in your business. You must be willing to embrace change and fall in love with the process of making things work more efficiently. "A rolling stone gathers no moss!" - Publilius Syrus

When people reach out for help, the first thing they will say is, "My ads are not working; can you look at them?" Usually, I won't even look at their ads until I can rule out the other possible causes for their "ads not working." The issue can be as easily identifiable as a poorly optimized website or a sub-par product that no one wants. An e-commerce site's performance can be evaluated in five to ten minutes to determine if the site has issues.

Here are some real-life examples, along with actionable plans, on how to gradually improve your site's optimization over time. Remember, the slightest improvement in conversion rate, especially when you are running thousands of dollars of ad spend, can lead to a significant increase in profits.

Again, do not feel overwhelmed; I'm here to tell you that you don't need to be a coding expert and you don't need any type of degree. You need to be someone who wants to take on new opportunities, seek growth and challenge, and set a goal of becoming a better, more well-rounded entrepreneur, which, in turn, brings success through trial and error.

CONVERSION RATE OPTIMIZATION

Conversion Rate Optimization (CRO) is defined as a system for increasing the percentage of visitors to a website that converts into customers or more generally, takes any desired action on a webpage.

Have you ever had difficulty making a purchase online? If so, there's a strong chance that the website was not optimized correctly and, as a result, the owners of that store are leaving a lot of money on the table.

Like many of the strategies I outline, CRO is an ongoing process. For me, any additional percentage increase is a guaranteed path to more sales and profit. Naturally, as a result, it makes sense to focus on constantly improving that conversion rate number.

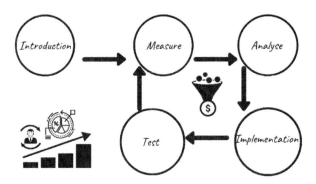

Figure 54 - The CRO process.

According to Monetate, the average conversion rate is about three percent globally.[59]

The following are a few of my favorite strategies on how we improve our conversion rate. With each strategy I outline, imagine yourself as a shopper and let your subconscious guide you as you navigate the website and enter the purchase funnel. You can also experiment by opening up your favorite store and navigate your way around the site.

Conversion Rate Improvement Strategies:

Improve Product Pages: Your product page is likely your most visited page as it is typically where you are driving most of your paid traffic. If a customer sees my advertisement for a dog product, then I am going to send them directly to the dog product page. If I sent them to the homepage, then they have to go looking for the actual product they originally saw and clicked on. Remember: A confused buyer is a non-buyer.

On my product pages, I have high-quality images of all my products and a very clear and easy-to-read product description. You must explain the benefits of the product. An example is fitness products. People buy for the potential or implied transformation the product will bring and not the actual product specifications. In addition, I usually offer an incentive for shoppers to "buy now" with a free shipping promotion marked as "today only." It's important to always include scarcity and urgency in your sales copy.

You can also make your product pages better with SEO-friendly product titles. This will allow your products to show up across various search engines higher in the page rank.

Another important trick is to list whether a product is on sale or if it comes with free shipping. The lack of free shipping is one of the biggest factors to poor conversion rates. Simply put, online shoppers do not like paying for shipping, so it may be a good idea to build shipping into your product's price.

Use product ratings or product reviews to build trust and make people feel like you are a brand that can be trusted. Finally, make sure the product page is compatible for mobile view. Customers will also want to know what recourse is available to them, so be sure to include policies, refund, and terms of service links on the product footer page.

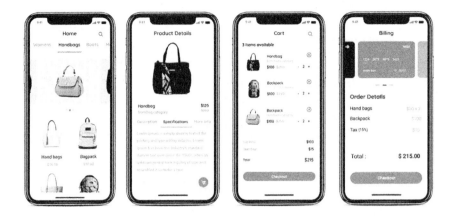

Figure 55 - The entire mobile product page view split in four for demonstration purposes.

Optimize your Pricing: You need to find the sweet spot for your product's pricing. It takes split testing and surveying your customers to see what they are willing to pay. What I have done in the past is create two identical product pages with the same product and same content; I simply listed one product at $39.99 and the other at $49.99.

I discovered that my conversion rate dropped significantly at $49.99. Even though I was gaining $10 extra, my conversion rate was much lower, which meant my overall profit was down. Another example: I had a student who sold a baseball cap in the Texas market for $19.99 for three straight months. I asked him if he ever tested the product at $22.99 and he said that he hadn't. The following week he raised the price and conversion rate remained the same. So, he spent three months selling a product he could have been selling for $3 more if only he had split-tested the pricing. Again, every scenario is different so perform your own price testing.

Having a Clear Call to Action: You have to treat every potential customer like they have never bought anything online before. Having clear buttons and descriptions will move customers along the sales funnel more quickly. On the product page, I use the text "Add to Cart" on my button as opposed to "Buy It Now." I feel "Add to Cart" is less of a commitment and helps to nudge people along the funnel.

Figure 56 - An image of the "Add to Cart" button on a product page view.

Also, if you have a special offer on your site, make sure it stands out. It could be a storewide twenty percent discount promotion or a "buy one get one free" deal. I like to include those offers on the store banner or header bar. Try playing with different colors to discover which colors pop the most.

Figure 57 - An example of a "buy one get one free" deal.

Reduce the number of options: Have you ever been to a restaurant with a giant menu? The waiter or waitress passes by and asks, "Are you ready to order?" Usually, you are still deciding, right? There is so much food on the menu that you try and take as much time as you can to ensure you make the right choice, even if you are hungry and cannot wait for your food to come. It is just the way we are as humans; we want to make the best choices for our money, and we want an exchange of value regardless. By reducing the number of options in your store, you can actually improve decision-making and therefore, your conversion rate. If you look at some of the most popular burger restaurants on the West Coast, their menu is very simple. The idea is that less is more, and you focus on quality and efficiency over complexity. If you have too many options, it may overwhelm the customer and they may decide to abandon what they came to buy.

Personalization: As you probably can tell, I love meeting and exceeding customer needs and wants. They are the true CEO of your business. One trend I have followed this year is personalization. Just look at some of the billion-dollar companies today that are moving to focus on customer personalization. By allowing people to personalize their products, you automatically add value and deliver a product that is perceived as having more value.

DOUBLE-DOUBLE®

CHEESEBURGER

HAMBURGER

FRENCH FRIES

BEVERAGES

SHAKES

NOT SO SECRET MENU

Some of the products I currently sell allow my customers to personalize their gifts. This gives me a huge competitive advantage in the marketplace because no one else is doing it right now in my niche. Giving a piece of jewelry to someone is a wonderful and common gift. Now imagine engraving a customized message inside the gift and having it delivered right to the person's door. This increases the perceived value, grows my brand, and raises my conversion rate because I am adding value and offering a unique product. Everyone wants to be the first to own something new.

Every day I receive emails from happy customers who are delighted with the final product. What you'll notice, because of this unique product, is that more and more people will ask my customers, "Where did you buy it?"

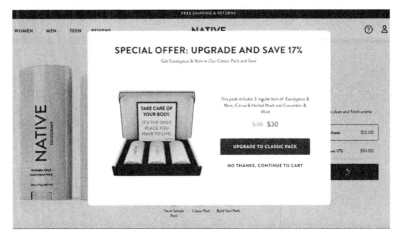

Figure 58 – An example of pre purchase upsell.

The other art of personalization can be done through your email marketing. By segmenting your audience, you can personalize particular products to people who have demonstrated a likeness or style to that item. This leads to higher open rates and happier customers. This can be done through Klaviyo, my preferred email service provider.

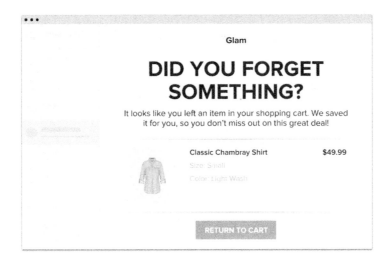

Figure 58 - Personalized emails lead to higher open rates and builds trust.

Optimize for mobile traffic: You will also want to optimize your product page and entire website for mobile traffic. The majority of your traffic (more than 65 percent) uses their cell phone to browse. Just because your site looks amazing on a laptop or desktop does not mean it will look good on mobile. Have your friends or family members give you feedback on the mobile shopping experience.

Navigation: Another important optimization strategy for scaling is to ensure that your site has all the information necessary for customers to make a purchase decision and an optimized layout and navigation flow. Here are some of the menu items I will have on either my header or footer menu bars: Home, Catalog (e.g., All Products), Sub Catalog (E.g., Shoes, Shirts, Jeans, etc.), About Us, Contact Us, Track Your Order, Privacy Policy, Return Policy, Terms of Service, Blog, FAQ, Store Locator, Reviews, and Social Media links.

The question you must ask: When you look at your site, how easily can people find what they are looking for? People have very short attention spans and will leave your website if they cannot find what they want.

Imagine if you could use the suggestions provided and fine-tune your store to really focus on building trust and delivering a great customer experience? Here are some scenarios:

Scenario One: Store Conversion Rate at 2%.
You are selling a $50 product.
Ads: $10,000
Visitors: 20,000 people.

CR: 2 percent

Buyers: 400 buyers

Revenue: $20,000.

ROAS: 2x.

Product Cost: $10 per unit.

Cost of Goods Sold (COGS): $4,000

Gross Profit: $20,000 - $10,000 - $4000 = $6,000

Scenario 2: Store Conversion Rate at 4%.

You are selling the same $50 product.

Ads: $10,000

Visitors: 20,000 people.

CR: 4 percent

Buyers: 800 buyers

Revenue: $40,000.

ROAS: 4x.

Product Cost: $10 per unit.

Cost of Goods Sold (COGS): $8,000

Gross Profit: $40,000 - $10,000 - $8000 = $23,000

As you can see, the profit margins skyrocket when the conversion rate increases, all other things being equal. Don't get me wrong, this takes time, but it is possible. So, if you are running a lot of paid traffic right now, do not neglect your website. Focus on constant improvements to raise the conversion rate and turn visitors into buyers.

Payment Options: One thing I have learned is that you need multiple payment options on your site. After all, we want to get paid, and we want our customers to feel safe. Check your country to find the best merchant processing companies to work with. Shopify Payments and PayPal are two of the most common ways e-commerce entrepreneurs take payments. You can also use Apple Pay, Google Pay, and Amazon Pay. There is also a new payment method called "SHOP" by Shopify. More will be developed, but the main point is to give the customer choice.

I know friends of mine who only purchase through PayPal so they have the backing of PayPal and can raise disputes easily if a product doesn't arrive or the product quality is substandard. Cryptocurrency payments are also on the horizon and expect them to be requested soon.

Keep A Visible Cart: Another important trick is to show the customer their cart. If it is hidden, they won't know where to click, and you may lose them as an abandoned cart. Usually, on the top right corner is the best and most common place to position this cart icon. If someone adds a product to their cart, the number of items will display over the cart icon.

Exit Intent: Not everyone who lands on your website makes a purchase. One of the reasons is that they may feel the product is too expensive. Often people can be pushed over the line to make a purchase by using an exit-intent popup. It is a little incentive for people to purchase now. It might be something like "Leaving already? Grab 15 percent by completing your purchase now."

Trust Factor: Trust is a huge factor in the success of your store. Just like the actions we take in our day-to-day lives, the same applies to making decisions in the world of e-commerce. You shop at your local Nike store because you trust the brand. You drive in your Ford car because you trust it will get you from A to Z, and you drink the coffee from your local shop because you've done so for years.

Don't expect people to purchase from you if you cannot portray a sense of reassurance and trust. Building trust could be something as simple as either a thirty-day money-back guarantee or on-site customer reviews.

SITE SPEED ANALYSIS

The average attention span of humans today is nine seconds, which means if you've gotten this far in the book … congratulations! As you can imagine, no one likes a slow website. Site page speed measures the time it takes the content on a page to load.

More and more marketers are coming to terms with the fact that you literally have a few seconds to grab someone's attention. Since most people are visiting your site for the first time, it is important to give them a pleasant shopping experience.

As I mentioned earlier in this book, one of the biggest factors to a slow website are images and videos of a larger size.

To perform a site speed test, visit gtmetrix.com. This site is free, and it allows you to check how your site performs, reveal why it's slow, and discover optimization opportunities.

One of the discoveries I made when I first started to scale was that I had a bunch of uncompressed images on my store. I found this out by going to the GTMetrix website and entering my store URL. Normally this would not be that bad, but I had over 230 products in my store and that quickly adds up in terms of file size.

By using an app to decompress, I was able to reduce the site speed from nine to four seconds. A recent survey from Shopify reveals that if a site is generating $100,000 per day, a one-second improvement generates another $7,000 daily, while the opposite is true.[60] It can be easy to neglect your site speed when the money is coming in. This is why I've made a point to mention that you must become obsessed with the data to find every possible way to improve. One little tweak or improvement can put you ahead of your competition.

BROWSE ABANDONMENT

Just because someone came to your site, browsed your product and left, doesn't mean that they are not interested in buying from you.

Life gets in the way sometimes; people's batteries die, they might be dealing with a work issue, or they may be putting their phone down to have dinner. Persevere, follow up, and close that sale. A browse abandonment email or SMS is an automated message you can trigger from your provider to anyone who visits a product page or product category and does not add to the cart or make a purchase.

According to Klaviyo, "In Q1 (2019) alone, browse abandonment emails made our customers $17,627,349.83."[61]

By now, you probably know that I love automation. By using a simple email provider, you can set it up once and forget about it; the software is that intelligent! A simple API integration will integrate most e-commerce platforms with your email provider. I usually send two automated emails: one within two hours of the person visiting the store and one after twenty-four hours.

Some of my favorite subject lines for sending visitors browse abandonment emails are as follows:

- We caught you looking.
- Did you forget something?
- We kept this for you!

Hi Damien,

We know life is busy. It looks like you are just one step away from completing your purchase!

Complete your order within the next 15 minutes to get 15%off!

Figure 59 - An example of an abandonment cart email.

Don't leave money on the table, especially when automation allows you to "set it and forget it." The beauty of automated emails and texts is that they can be customized to add discount codes and even a link that takes the shopper right back to the product.

CART ABANDONMENT

"Damien, your dinner is ready" - My mom shouted from the kitchen!

I was in my late teenage years about to purchase a very expensive stereo system. It was something I had wanted for a very long time. It was my first big purchase, and I was at the checkout page of some random foreign website, but I was so ready to buy.

Was this call from my mother a sign?

Should I abandon my plans of purchasing?

Will I regret it?

Will I find a better deal?

Is this the best brand?

Several "what if" scenarios ran through my mind: I felt confused like maybe I should think about it a little more, so off I went downstairs to the kitchen for dinner. Like turning down the radio volume when you are driving and you are lost looking for directions, it was one of those subconscious responses: We just do it! I just had a feeling that I needed to wait. This was my first real experience of cart abandonment and it happens to people all the time in different circumstances.

While shoppers in brick-and-mortar stores rarely abandon their carts, abandonment of virtual shopping carts is quite common. As a result, it is very important to maintain a close eye on your store's abandoned cart rate. The average cart abandonment rate in 2020 was 88 percent.

Figure 60 - Reason's people abandon their shopping cart.

Customers scrutinize every aspect of your site, looking for reasons not to buy. This is more likely to happen if more than one store is selling the same product. Just go on Amazon and you'll find many different sellers selling the same product. What did Amazon do? They created what is known as "Amazon's Choice" to help customers make better decisions and ensure customer satisfaction. Amazon's Choice is a listing that shows that many buyers have purchased and are satisfied with that product, as told by its customer reviews. If you do plan on selling on Amazon, you must realize it is very competitive and as a result, you have to be different and stand out.

The slightest improvement in your cart abandonment rate can lead to a huge increase in revenue. Let's take a simple example: In a given day, Company A has twenty sales, but the number of shopping carts initiated is eighty. What a difference! The cart abandonment rate would be obtained by dividing twenty by eighty; after multiplying the result by one hundred, we would have twenty-five percent, which means that lost sales (abandoned carts) are seventy-five percent. As you are scaling, you may be uninterested in looking at your abandonment rate. I get it. Seeing your sales fly-in at unbelievable rates can be distracting, but if you make slight improvements and optimize your sales funnel over time, it can lead to an even greater return on investment. I will speak primarily to the main three culprits which stop people from buying.

Trust: As mentioned before, you have to make people feel like they can trust you and whatever you are selling. People buy products to solve a problem or emotional needs and wants. If you have a site designed and developed in a sub-par manner, your conversions will be equally sub-par. Give people as much information as they need, show your happy customers, ask them for feedback, and give them an attractive offer to bring them in as first-time buyers. Add trust badges, include a page that shows customers who have used your products, and create a meaningful message that resonates with your customers.

Unexpected Charges: Most people have a set budget in mind when shopping. They may see your product page and commit to buying your product for the listed price. As they go through the checkout process, you hit them with a $5.99 shipping cost. Now, this may seem small, but for some, it can be a deal-breaker. One way to offset this "surprise" is to offer more value in some way, like express delivery or mention shipping before the checkout process begins so they are not surprised. One tip: If people abandon their cart, create a pop-up that offers them "free shipping" or "15 percent off" if they purchase now. As with anything, you'll need to test what works best for you.

Poor Shopping Experience: How good are you at delivering a positive shopping experience? Is your site easy to navigate? How fast does the page load? Is it easy for customers to find the products they want? Is it easy to view products on a mobile device? The more you optimize with the customer in mind, the higher your conversion rates and sales will be.

Refer back to the earlier section devoted to setting up your store and discover how you can design and develop better landing pages and websites. The main purpose of this section, while short, is to give you an insight into something that not a lot of people focus on, which is cart abandonment.

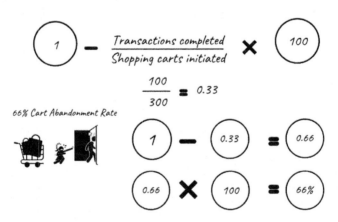

Figure 61 - The cart abandonment rate formula.

GOOGLE ANALYTICS

Who loves numbers? I must admit I used to hate numbers as a kid, but now they are at the core to every decision I make. Google

Analytics is one of the most popular analytics software available, and it happens to be totally free. Essentially, it allows you to analyze in greater detail the traffic on your site.

I am all about delivering great results, and the more I can understand data, the better I can tailor marketing and sales strategies towards what works. It was not always like this. I was pretty bad at math in school and was regularly called to the front of the class. "Damien, come up to the blackboard and solve this equation," my primary school teacher used to say. Math was just one of those things I did not like or understand, but I knew the teacher was just trying to help me, even at the expense of a little embarrassment.

When I reached corporate America, I worked as an analyst and everything was about reconciliation. Numbers had to match to the cent, and often it would mean hours of Excel troubleshooting. Despite these companies making millions, everything had to match at an executive and summary level before management would approve it. As a result, I became older and wiser, and I started to study numbers and how to look at data through charts, graphs, and tables. I treated my bank accounts, expenditures, gym stats, and so forth as information to help me become a better person and optimize my life. Luckily for us e-commerce entrepreneurs, companies like Shopify and Facebook have fantastic reporting and analytics dashboards.

In my first few months as an e-commerce entrepreneur, I was doing quite well, I was at about $70,000 in sales and I was pretty much wearing many hats all at once. It wasn't until the end of the month that I looked at my Google Analytics account and saw something interesting. Out of the total revenue, I noticed the main buying trend. Even though I was targeting a wide demographic of the United States, it was mainly men and women older than forty-five years of age who were interested in my products.

The next month I decided to focus solely on that specific forty-five plus audience. The result was my profit margins went up, my conversion rate increased, and my ability to focus on who my ideal customer was became much easier. I had learned the importance of studying data, this time as an entrepreneur.

Benefits of Google Analytics:

- Once installed it essentially tracks everything on your site through a piece of code.
- A buyer will want the lifetime stats of your store if you choose to sell.
- Google Analytics is completely free.
- Data visualization.
- Custom reporting.
- Real-time data.
- Monitors your website channels.
- Monitors your website pages.
- Discover how people find your store.
- The ability to fine-tune your store.
- Easy-to-use documentation.
- A comparison to Facebook Analytics.
- UTM parameters.
- Integration with Ad words.

Now that you know about Google Analytics, if you have not already, install it whether you have traffic coming to your store or not. The next step, once you get traffic, is to study what is going on inside your store and how you can get a more detailed look at the type of user or customer who is reacting favorably to your product and brand. Once the stats reveal who is actually converting, you can tailor your advertising, branding, messaging toward that niche subset audience.

FACEBOOK ANALYTICS

Facebook Analytics is built on the insights from Facebook's two billion users and is focused on the customer journey and the details about who engages with your brand. It plays a similar role to Google Analytics but on a more granular level. Many companies are using Facebook Analytics to test new opportunities and strategies in customer acquisition. Most of the time, what we think is an accurate reflection of our business is usually not the case. The more we can understand our customers, the better we can solve their problems and deliver better products.

What does Facebook Analytics Provide?
- Engagement Metrics
- People Metrics
- Location Metrics
- Monetization Metrics
- Growth Metrics

It also allows users to create their own custom dashboards to look at the data that is meaningful to them.

Figure 62 - The backend view of Facebook Analytics.

HEATMAPS

A heatmap is an aggregated visual record of all of the activity on your website, including clicking, scrolling, and tapping on mobile. Heatmaps provide powerful visuals because they tell you what part of your site is attracting customers and what areas they ignore.

Let's say you discover through heatmaps that your customers are ignoring an important piece of information on your site. This would be a signal for you to reposition or improve the way you show this particular piece of information. If this information is beneficial to the sale of your product, it will generate more sales once it's repositioned.

I had a recent student who was having trouble with her conversion rate. She was getting a lot of customers who were abandoning their cart. She was getting high "Add to Carts" but not enough purchases based on industry-standard metrics. For context, here is how the sales funnel looks like for most e-commerce stores once someone decides they want to purchase:

1. View Content (Start)
2. Add to Cart
3. Initiate Checkout
4. Add Payment Information
5. Purchase (Finish)

Once we started to dig into the metrics and installed some heatmaps, we found that her store was set up only to begin the checkout process once someone had created an account. That was the problem: asking people to make a commitment and create an account before they made a purchase. People avoid doing anything that takes up their time. The customer wants to buy, so eliminate distractions and hurdles that may impact the number one goal—an easy and straightforward purchase process. When my student removed the account creation, her conversion rates increased.

Start thinking of all the other pieces of data and knowledge you can acquire through heatmaps. Hotjar is a useful tool that you can integrate with your store. It allows you to get a real-time picture of where customers are clicking, and the drop-off rates at the particular stages of the sales funnel.

Key information heatmaps provide:

Find top exit pages: If they leave the product page as an example, perhaps the product is priced too high, or there is not enough trust built!

Finding elements on important pages: Discover which elements on the page are clicked on and which are ignored. An example is the "Continue Shopping" button on the cart page. Instead of sending people back to your site to purchase more, you may want to have them continue down the sales funnel instead. If so, make the "Continue Shopping" button less obvious and highlight the "Proceed to Checkout."

Key page interactions: You can see how people navigate on key pages; for example, on the final page of the sales funnel, shoppers might be clicking on the privacy policy and terms of service. If they are, make them less obvious, or ensure that they provide all the key information, so the customer has peace of mind.

Eliminate bugs: Heatmaps will allow you to identify errors or issues on your site; for example, you may be missing shipping rates for a particular country. If shipping rates are not set up, customers cannot make a purchase.

Post-purchase surveys: Once a purchase is made, you can survey the customer with key questions related to the store. Their feedback can be used to improve the optimization of the store.

CHARITY DONATIONS

A new trend is emerging where e-commerce companies donate a portion of their profits to local or national charities. Educated consumers have plenty of options these days to spend money with companies that align with their values, and one way to separate yourself from the competition is by showing how purchases, in turn, support a cause. Increasingly, consumers believe it is not just a company's obligation to make money but to give back. Think Ben & Jerry's or Patagonia.

By adding a simple message on your product page, just underneath the "Add to Cart" button, it lets shoppers know that a portion of profits will be donated. It essentially gives the customer an extra incentive to support your business while also putting you in a favorable position as a brand that cares. It's important to align the recipient of the donation with the brand. For example, donate to dog shelters if you own a dog brand.

According to Cone Cause Study: Eighty-five percent of consumers have a more positive image of a product or company when it supports a charity they care about. Eighty-three percent of Americans wish more of the products and services they use would support charities. Eighty percent of Americans are likely to switch brands (equal in quality and price) to the one that supports a charity.[62]

Not only are you making a contribution to others, but you'll also have higher conversion rates, not to mention happier customers and your contributions are tax-deductible.

CUSTOMERS REVIEWS & FEEDBACK

In 2016, I was one of the first sellers to introduce product photo reviews for print-on-demand. This is where a customer sends a photo review of the product they bought from you in exchange for a future discount. You can also create regular text reviews, but at the time, I was selling sneakers and wanted to showcase the shoes. What better way than to allow my customers to send in authentic and powerful photos of the products they just received. Photo reviews are much more powerful when they are in photo form.

I use an app called Loox that automatically sends an email to my customers with a link to review the product once they receive it. This email would only be sent after I knew the customer had received their order. This gave me a lot of powerful content for future marketing.

Why did I do it? Several reasons:

- I was able to see my customers' satisfaction or dissatisfaction both in terms of delivery, timeliness, and product quality.
- It allowed me to demonstrate to my customers that I cared.
- It provided me with photo images that I could automatically add to my store or send bad reviews to my supplier if there were quality issues.
- It increased my conversion rate because customers will buy from you if they know, like, and trust you. By placing other customers' reviews and photos on my website, it gave people who were on the fence a little nudge to follow through with the purchase.
- It allowed me to use my customer photos as marketing collateral by running ads or using the material for email marketing purposes.

If done right, your customers can become your best marketing tools.

"A customer talking about their experience with you is worth ten times that which you write or say about yourself" – David J Greer

PRICING PSYCHOLOGY

When you first launch a product, you obviously need to set a price. After all, we are in the business of making money. How do you know what to charge? Well, that comes from testing different price points, looking at your competition, your audience, and finding that sweet spot at which your customer is willing to purchase.

I must admit, I am a little obsessed with price, and you could classify me as a bargain or value shopper. I'm always looking to get the best bang for my buck. On the other hand, I know friends of mine who do not care about price; they just focus on the benefits and neglect the cost to their pocket. Other friends are short on time and never take into account alternative options. They will literally run to the store and grab the first item they see from the shelf, regardless of the price. The truth of the matter is that every buyer is different.

High Price High Value? If you look at Apple, a company I worked with for years, they focused on selling a small number of products at a premium price to tech-obsessed and loyal customers. Apple found a market willing to pay a premium for a great product, great customer service, and a luxury brand appeal.

Personally, I am a big "Apple fanboy," and I suspect I have spent over $10,000 with Apple on various products. So, if you want to learn anything from Apple, it is that you can indeed brand yourself as a high-priced product, high-value type of product or service. Some customers associate higher-priced items with better quality

251

and are therefore willing to pay extra. That is something to keep in mind when you are trying to price yourself in the marketplace.

Ending in 9? Another tip on pricing psychology is that studies have shown that instead of pricing your products in whole numbers, it's better to price one cent below. An example is, selling a t-shirt for $19.99 instead of $20. The reason is that shoppers tend to read from left to right. If we go back to the Apple example, Apple won't list a laptop at $2,000 but rather $1,999 as it appears more valuable and cheaper to the human eye. I've tested pricing on my own stores, and I can tell you that the highest converting price always ended in a number of 9's.

Adding More Product options? Are you able to add more options for the same product? *National Geographic* ran an experiment on popcorn and the results were pretty interesting.[63] First, they set up a popcorn stall at the movies, selling a small popcorn for $3 and a large popcorn for $7. As suspected, most people went with the $3 option. They then added a medium option for $6.50. This is known as the decoy option. To their surprise, sales increased on the large option of $7. Why? Because the large was only 50 cents more than the medium popcorn. Customers explained that the large option looked like a much more valuable offer compared to the medium. Even though they were spending more, it was the association of more value that made them choose the large option over anything else.

You need to find the sweet spot for your product's pricing. It takes split testing and surveying your customers to see what they are willing to pay. As mentioned earlier, what I have done in the past is create two identical product pages with the same product and same content and ran the same traffic to both offers and compared the results. Because of the Internet and social media, today's shopper has a lot more data, information, and options compared to previous generations. They can literally do a five-minute search and compare your store price with that of your competitors. At the end of the day, you must test.

Figure 63 - The decoy effect showing the $6.50 price point as the decoy.

AVERAGE ORDER VALUE & LIFETIME VALUE

Two key metrics in the world of e-commerce are Average Order Value (AOV) and Lifetime Value (LTV).

Average Order Value: AOV can be calculated by simply dividing the total revenue by the total number of orders. For example, let's say that in the month of August, your e-commerce store sales were $31,000 and you had a total of 1,000 orders. $31,000 divided by 1,000 = $31, so the August monthly AOV was $31.

Naturally, when scaling and growing your company, you want to raise the AOV over time. Why? For every incremental dollar it allows you to spend more money on the front end to acquire more customers.

With paid ads, you are competing with other sellers for the same customer. Imagine if you could now raise that $31 AOV to $40 AOV by adding upsells to your post-purchase funnel. This allows you to spend more money in acquiring a customer and outperforming your competitors in the auction and bidding. Facebook ads work on an auction basis. The winner of the auction (the advertiser) is the ad with the highest total value from the "bid," "estimated action rates," and "ad quality."

How do you raise AOV? Here are some of the strategies available and messaging you can use to increase that dollar value per customer:

- **Cross-selling:** "Here's a one-time offer to add a pair of dog socks with those dog sneakers."

- **Upselling:** "Would you like this leather option for only $10 more for the watch in your cart?"

- **Volume discount:** "This bracelet costs $20, but you'll save 30 percent if you buy two or more."

- **Free shipping:** "Free shipping for all orders over $65."

- **Coupons on next visit:** "Spend $100 and get $20 off your next purchase on any product!"

- **Return policy for expensive goods:** "If you're not satisfied, send them back."

The customer is everything to the success of your business! If your customers decided to leave in the morning, you would not survive. It is far cheaper to retain and nurture existing customers than find new ones. Therefore, it is important to satisfy and retain your customers the moment they make a purchase from you. That begins from the "Thank You" page after they make a purchase.

Lifetime Value: Another important metric in the world of e-commerce is Lifetime Value (LTV). This is the total worth to a business of a customer during the entire relationship.

Imagine if you acquired a customer in January, and at the end of the year, they bought three t-shirts worth $20 each, then the LTV of that customer so far is $60. LTV goes hand in hand with CAC (customer acquisition costs). How much does it cost to acquire a customer? Here's a worked example of the customer lifetime value calculation using the simple formula above.

Customer Mary's revenue per year = $100
Customer relationship duration = 5 years
Cost of acquisition = $25
Cost to serve = $25 per year ($125 over 5 years)
So, the math looks something like this:
$100 x 5 = $500
$500 – $125 = $375
CLV for Mary = $375

Obviously, the more you can raise the lifetime value of the customer, the more attractive your profit and loss (P+L) will be, the more competitive you'll become in advertising, and of course the more attractive you'll be to investors and lending institutions.

You can raise the LTV by being strong on social media, building really great relationships, working on email segmentation, and surveying your customers for new product ideas.

When I had my dog store, the dog buyers were so passionate that they would purchase two to three products per year. That's why the dog market is such a popular but competitive market to be in. So, the bottom line is to work on your AOV and LTV for the maximum benefit.

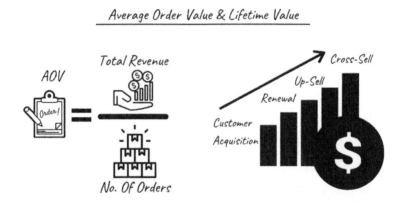

Figure 64 - Average order value formula and a graph of lifetime value.

SALES FUNNELS

Sales funnels are another way to sell physical products online. An example of a software that allows you to make simple and easy sales funnels is Clickfunnels. I use Clickfunnels for my book funnels and other digital products. You can grab a free trial in the resources section. Clickfunnels comes with ready-made funnels for any type of product that you are selling, from digital to physical products.

Sales funnels are a great idea when you have a product that is selling really well, and you want to test if you can improve the conversion rate, average order value, and in general, just get more revenue from the same traffic.

Funnel companies like Clickfunnels say that most people are "focused on selling a product, rather than creating an irresistible offer."

With a funnel, you are focusing on taking your potential buyers through a very tailored and specifically designed series of pages.

A funnel is different from a Shopify store in that a funnel is focused on selling one core product offering, whereas a Shopify store has potentially hundreds of products.

The funnel has the goal of awareness, interest, desire, and action.

As a result, the conversion rate on funnels is a lot higher. Not only that, but you can also add a number of different upsells and down-sells to raise the average order value of each customer.

Let me show you a comparison between a Shopify store and a Clickfunnels sales funnel.

Regular E-Commerce Platform Flow:
1. Visit's store
2. Visit's product
3. Adds product to cart
4. Starts checkout

5. Offers Upsell

6. Makes Purchase

Sales Funnel Flow:

1. Sales landing page

2. Order page

3. Upsell 1

4. Upsell 2

5. Downsell 1

6. Downsell 2

7. Order Confirmation

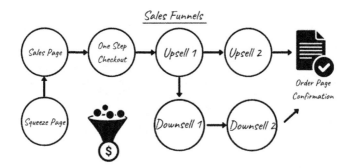

Figure 65 - The flow of how a sales funnel usually looks like.

CUSTOMER LOYALTY PROGRAM

"The purpose of a business is to create a customer who creates customers." – Shiv Singh, senior vice president of global brand and marketing transformation, Visa.

My mother Mary, is an extremely hard-working mother, rearing five children, and of course, supporting my dad, Gerard in his business endeavors.

One of the biggest expenses I can remember as a child was putting food on the table, and as you can imagine groceries bills added up over time. One thing I remember is my mother's commitment to "value" shopping. Essentially, she would try to make the Irish pound (before we as a country went to the Euro) go as far as possible.

Our grocery shopping was mainly done through supermarkets like "Dunne's Store" and "Super Valu" that sold a wide variety of products at low prices. I remember my mom kept a bunch of coupons, vouchers, and points in her handbag. She would accumulate them over time and when she had enough points, she could cash them in for something at the store.

Every time we would go shopping, I would pack the bags at the checkout and the cashier would say, "Mrs. Coughlan, would you like to use your points today." My mother replied, "no, thank you, I am saving up for the month-end special." I guess that was my first introduction to customer loyalty programs and I could see how valuable my mother's business meant to the supermarket.

Not only was my mother shopping at a reputable store with quality and fresh products, but she was also being rewarded for her loyalty and consistent shopping. Today, things are no different, but those loyalty programs are now available online and in digital form. Instead of a piece of paper like the old days, shoppers are now given laminated key ring cards and barcodes that they can conveniently scan at checkout.

Successful supermarkets understand the power of customer retention. They realize the power of a shopper's lifetime value. You probably have seen a consistent theme throughout this book, which is my reference to the customer. I constantly refer to customer satisfaction and doing whatever you can to retain that customer over time.

I can tell you right now, these large supermarkets with millions of fresh products stored in refrigeration do not want a drop in daily consumer spending habits.

So how do you create a loyalty program online and how can you set one up for your e-commerce business?

Before I begin, here are five reasons why you should create a loyalty program:

Customer experience: When people realize they can get more than just the product they are buying, they have a positive experience. They feel as if they are being valued as a customer and are being encouraged to gather loyalty points to enjoy free products. Customers don't just want to purchase products. They want to be part of your brand story. They want to connect with other like-minded individuals and feel part of the community. An example might be dog lovers who get to be part of a dog community by enrolling in a loyalty program. Anyone who purchased a product from my store was automatically subscribed to a special weekly newsletter involving other dog owners in which those dog owners shared stories, tips, and tricks on their relationship and life with their dogs.

Customer referrals: Most referral programs today have a program where you can gain additional points for sharing a referral link with others. If you have already gained a positive experience, and you know you have friends who would benefit from the products you buy, it is a no-brainer to share your link and get rewarded in the process. It is a win-win for the existing customer, the new customer, and the company.

Social proof: How many times have you searched online before making a purchase? If you did, chances are you saw a social media post where people shared their experiences. I think we as humans look for validation before making a purchase. I constantly search hashtags on Facebook and Instagram for products I am about to buy. One of the features of a referral program is the ability to reward people for sharing content on their social media pages. This could be a post-purchase review in the form of a product image or product testimonial video.

Build a long-term brand: If customers are happy, they buy from you repeatedly and act as a referrer. Ultimately, they contribute to your goal of building a long-term brand in a major way. Think long-term; think of how valuable your business becomes when it goes from just a regular shop website to a brand name.

Tracking: Loyalty programs allow you to track exactly how well a campaign is performing. If you know me, I love data, and I love to focus on the parts of my business that produce consistent ROI. If, for example, you test a loyalty program for your business, you can accurately see how well it is performing, who your top customers are, and the overall value that each campaign brings to your top line. I've used many different types of referral apps to help me manage and grow my loyalty programs. One really good app is Referral Candy.

LIVE CHAT

Live chat is a great feature to add to your store when you begin to scale your traffic. You can often have from fifty to two hundred people checking out on your store at once (which is visible inside your live store dashboard).

Let's face it, when you shop online, you lose the personal one-to-one interaction you get when shopping at your local traditional brick and mortar store. Live chat allows online shoppers to click on a little button to access your support team in a live setting and ask questions regarding your products or services. Remember, people have very short attention spans and are impatient in nature. If they cannot find the right information on your site, or they don't get a sense of security or trust, they will leave and shop elsewhere.

Most first-time shoppers will not be familiar with your brand, so having a live chat feature gives the shopper peace of mind and can be used to address concerns they may have before making a purchase. Some of the live messages I have received included questions about product material, where the company was located, what the refund policy was, or if the product was available in another color. Even though this information may exist on different pages of your site, not every shopper is going to spend time looking for it.

Most of the time, the same questions arise, so you can create a little button that links the shopper to a FAQ page before the customer has an option to chat with a live representative from your team. Having a live chat feature is also another way for you to recommend additional products and raise the AOV.

During quarter four, I may have anywhere from 100 to 200-plus shoppers on my store browsing at any given time. One exercise I perform is called "Chase the Sun," which is around-the-clock live chat support. Because we sell every hour of every day, I have 24 hour site coverage during the peak holiday seasons and break the coverage into three, eight-hour shifts. My team is based in the Philippines, Ireland, and the United States. I learned this strategy during my corporate days at Apple during major product launches.

As you can see throughout this book, I leverage technology wherever it makes sense. In this case, it is much more efficient to have customers send a live chat request instead of sending an email to "support." Adding a live chat feature will also improve and optimize your site and boost the overall customer experience. You'd be amazed at how a live chat feature will improve sales, customer satisfaction, while also getting you valuable information on how your customers think and act.

CUSTOMER SUPPORT

When you scale, you need to have an efficient and prompt support staff. When I first gained success selling in the dog niche, I really didn't know what I was doing. I had found a winning product and it was doing really well, but I was like an apprentice on a construction site, learning on the job, one day at a time.

I guess I had one advantage in that my business was online, and no one could see me sweating profusely in front of my computer screen on a daily basis, as I got hit with task after task. I remember the day as if it was yesterday. The first query came through to my support email and the subject line was "Where is my order?"

If you ask any e-commerce entrepreneur, they will tell you they've gotten this type of email on many occasions. As humans, we want our products, and we want them now. Even though we list the shipping times, people always want it faster.

The second email arrived. And then the third. Soon there were more than 50 emails in the space of three days, ranging with questions from size issues to shipping and from discount codes not working to credit card issues.

It really did start to get out of control and no matter how hard I tried to clean the inbox, the next morning, there would be more. It was then I met a gentleman from Florida named Nathan, who was a specialist in online hiring. We held a meeting, and it was clear that he was experienced in the recruitment side for online businesses.

The first thing I did was to hire a virtual assistant. I was a little afraid of letting go but I knew I had to hire, both to relieve some of the stress and to ensure my customers were happy. My new hire was responsible for answering customer support emails, answering live chat, and responding to social media messages.

A day later, customer support was under control and it was a huge breath of fresh air for me. That got me thinking about the next task I could outsource that did not need my personal touch. The lesson I quickly learned is that you need a team to help you scale. You may feel like you are superman or superwoman but trust me, that gets old quick. Find the tasks that you can get off your plate and outsource them to the right people at the right cost.

Some of my mentors have told me that one of the biggest mistakes they made in their early careers was not going all in faster. They described how success came a lot later in life when they dropped their ego. What took five years to build their first successful business could have been done in two years if they had asked for help, advice, and support. Most people have huge egos and are very prideful. As a result, they do not seek advice or feedback for fear of being judged. So, don't be afraid to seek help; go out there and find the knowledge and support you need to succeed faster.

UPSELLS & CROSS SELLS

The next strategy to help you scale is upselling. Just look at the following stats from Sumo: "Upselling increases revenue by 10-30 percent on average. Upsells are 68 percent more affordable than acquiring a new customer." - Sumo[64]

Again, the goal when scaling is to look at ways to tweak the elements of your business to generate more revenue or find ways through systems, processes, people, or technology to grow your business without losing efficiency.

Have you ever been to McDonalds and the cashier asks if you'd like to upgrade your medium fries to large fries for $1? If you are like me, you are a sucker for taking any upsell! At six-foot-four-inches tall and 230 pounds, I love my food, just not McDonalds—yuck! However, McDonalds is upselling at its finest.

Essentially, McDonald's is trying to get you to spend more money for a larger sale. The larger the sale, the bigger the profit, and the more profit, the more it allows McDonald's to grow its business. Most upsells are very enticing and are marketed in a way to convince the customer is getting a better deal.

Look at your current line of products, and check if there are more expensive options available for you to add, so you can have a number of different price points to raise the average order value. You might have products that vary in size or metal finish, or you may be able to provide a premium shipping service.

The other option for optimizing maximum revenue per customer is cross-selling. A cross-sell means you offer similar products that complement the product the person is buying. A simple example is if someone is buying a pair of running shoes, you can present to them a pair of running socks that will complement their order. That is why you'll often see socks at the checkout counter of a physical Nike or Footlocker shoe store. Let's face it, if you are going to buy a pair of Nike shoes for $120, a pair of socks for $10 isn't much of a major purchase decision. Besides, who doesn't like new socks in new shoes right?

There are a couple of ways to offer these upsells and cross-sells in your online store.

1) **Pre-Purchase Upsell:** This is an upsell you can have on your product page. You can give the option for the shopper to combine products together or choose a more expensive offer. A pre-purchase upsell is offered before the customer begins the checkout process.

2) In-Cart Upsell: The next option is an in-cart upsell offer. Here, the customer has added the first product to their cart, so you can now either embed the upsell offer or have a pop-up that gives the customer the option to choose a more premium offer or a combination of more products. This for me is a little bit intrusive and through my tests I have found that it hurts conversions. Remember if you are sending people specific offers, and they are ready to buy, I recommend not showing additional products, as I do believe it's best to acquire the sale first before showing the next offer.

3) Post-Purchase Upsell: The benefit of a post-purchase upsell is that the customer has already made the purchase of the first product. Now, you have an opportunity to offer them a one-time offer on the "Thank You" page. This is my favorite type of upsell as my goal is to get the sale without interruption and confusion. Once I have the first sale, I can then easily present the offer through a one-time discount. In the case of the shoes example, as soon as someone buys the shoes, I can present socks at an irresistible price.

4) Email Post-Purchase Upsell: Another option is to send customers a "Thank You" email based on the product they just purchased and present them with an irresistible one-time email offer. The confirmation and thank you emails have high open rates. The majority of people check these types of emails because they include important information like receipts, confirmation numbers, and other shipping details related to what they just bought.

Upsells and cross-sells require a lot of testing. Keep an eye on the conversion rate of your store to see the impact it has on your sales.

Figure 66 - An example of a post-purchase offer.

Two key goals of any store owner:

1. Convert more visitors into paying customers (Conversion Rate).
2. Increase customer spend per conversion (AOV).

You can use many different apps to plug into your store to help with upsells and cross-sells.

Zipify OCU has a great one-click upsell that integrates with most e-commerce platforms and you can literally connect it to any of your products in minutes. There is no coding involved; the app simply connects to the products in your store. Find products that complement each other for the best conversion on the uptake.

Figure 67 - One click product upsell example (shoes & socks).

STORE OPTIMIZATION CLOSING THOUGHTS

Summary: Optimization is an ongoing process that is crucial to the growth and success of you and your business. I love talking about optimizing one's life and business because I am fascinated by human potential and the unique and special superpowers each one of us possesses.

As someone who is constantly looking to improve my own life, whether it is measuring calories, sleep time, or how my students react to my training, I too want to want to adjust, test, and improve my value in the marketplace. There is no such thing as perfection, but that doesn't mean we should settle for average. As humans, we should never stop trying to improve who we are, so you shouldn't neglect improving the performance of the system that brings revenue to your business, which is your store.

Storeowners who fail to continually look for micro improvements are those who eventually get squeezed out of the marketplace. A successful storeowner constantly tests different tools, strategies, and experiments with ways to drive more traffic, convert that traffic at a higher level, and increase the conversion rate and revenue in the process.

By making slight changes and adjustments to our stores, we can improve the performance, success and ultimately change the lives of our customers. To effectively make micro improvements, I suggest testing one improvement at a time. If you make multiple changes to a system, it is much harder to measure the impact of those changes. Instead, focus on improving one aspect of your store, move to the next improvement, and so on while keeping an eye on the analytics that your store reports on a daily, weekly, monthly, and yearly timeframe. These small changes will have a cumulative effect and, hopefully, will dramatically increase your profits. Life is easier when you tackle it in small bite sizes.

Action Steps:

- Use the strategies mentioned in this section to look at ways of optimizing your store for success and keep asking: How can your website and business be improved?
- Install Google Analytics on your store. You can set up an account for free.
- Live chat is a great way to answer customer queries; add it to your store if you are getting a lot of questions. It will also help shoppers convert quicker to customers.
- Survey your customers and/or your friends to find out what they like and dislike about your store?
- How does your store perform in terms of industry standards?
- What are your key performance indicators? (KPI's)

- If you are struggling to find the reason why people are not buying, install heatmaps on your store to try and pinpoint the problem. You can also use tools like Lucky Orange, which is an all-in-one conversion optimization suite.
- Identify and research other competitors and top brands to see what they are doing in their store to improve conversion rate.
- Don't leave money on the table; if there is a chance to sell more to the same customer, do so. Average Order Value (AOV) and Lifetime Value (LTV) are key to the long-term success of your business.

SECTION SIX

BUILDING YOUR EMPIRE

A WELL-OILED MACHINE

"Automation is good, so long as you know exactly where to put the machine." - Eliyahu Goldratt.

The idiom "well-oiled machine" means something or someone that functions very well or efficiently.

My dad worked extremely hard all his life, and it showed based on what he accomplished as a farmer. He owned one of the best farms in the country of Ireland. He was featured in countless news articles and was often asked for advice from other farmers. When peers in your industry reach out to you personally, it is often a sign that you are seen as the subject matter expert. Even myself, I have close connections with other e-commerce experts who I can call upon and vice versa. You must be willing to build strong connections no matter what industry you operate in.

As my younger brother began working on the farm, he added a next-level of thinking. He had farming degrees, computer skills, along with possessing our family's hard work gene. This next-level thinking brought technology and processes into an already successful business. My brother had a goal to systemize the farm and relieve some of the workload from my father. You see, it can be fun running a business in the early stages, but eventually, you will get to a stage where you need to take a step back and work *on* your business and not *in* your business. My father loved to work, but it was time to work smarter, not harder.

As my father got older and reached retirement, my brother decided to transform the beef farm into a dairy farm. Beef farming could be unpredictable and dairy farming brought more predictability and structure to the farm's operations. Every single day cows produced milk and there was a system to milk those cows. The routine was optimized for speed and efficiency: Every day, the cows were milked, fed, and watered. Every month, there was a paycheck from the milk factory. Every morning and night, the workers turned on the milking machines to milk the cows.

Because of this routine and predictability, my brother was able to turn the entire farm into a "well-oiled machine." And, because most things didn't change, my brother and father were able to work on the strategic side of the business and hire others to work on the tactical side. Tactics are the specific actions or steps you undertake to accomplish your strategy. This delegation and automation of work through people, processes, and technology allowed my brother and father to become advisors and managers, rather than the people doing the majority of hard and predictable work.

I share this story to give context that any business is made up of structures and systems that can be identified, organized, and executed for optimum performance. The same applies to your e-commerce business. While you'll need to learn how to build a successful company, once you identify the strategies and tactics, the goal should be to systemize and outsource the majority of the daily work. In this section, which is quadrant four of my ESF framework, you will learn how to implement a plan to document, systemize, and automate the day-to-day operations of your business. If you have gone through the process of launching your business, finding a winning product, and scaling a winning product, you know there are opportunities to make the process better. Now is your chance to focus on areas that need improvement. This new and improved process is what will be used for the next product you launch and scale, only this time, you won't be the operator doing a thousand things but rather the high-level advisor or coach. The goal is to build a well-oiled machine that eventually works for you.

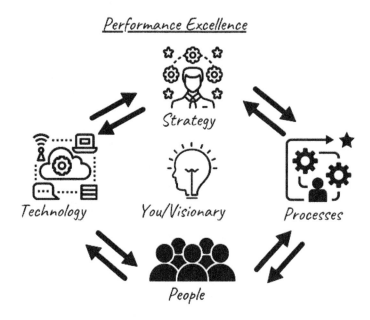

Figure 68 - A well-oiled machine has everything working together in harmony.

REPEAT THE CYCLE

If you remember quadrant two of the ESF framework, the main goal was to find a winning product to sell. This process required extensive research to discover what was working in the marketplace, what trends exist, and ultimately what customers wanted.

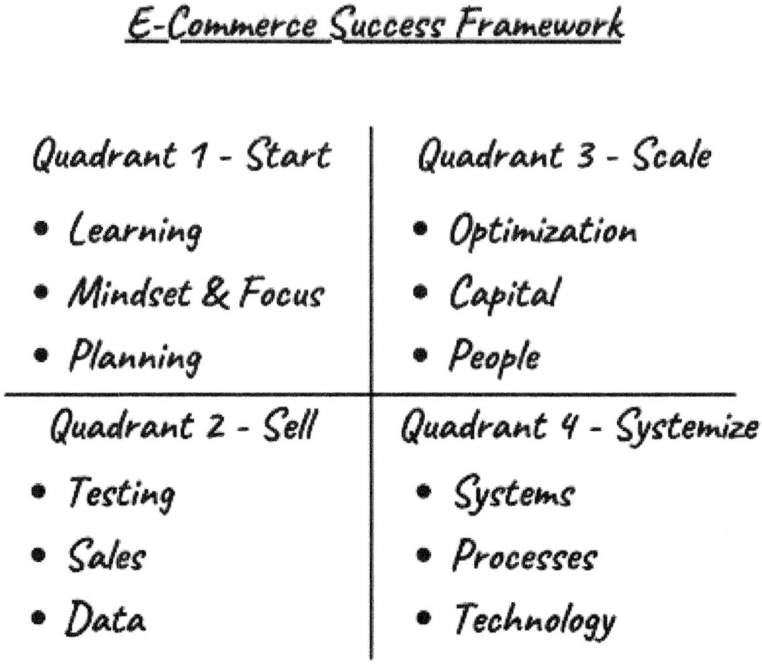

E-Commerce Success Framework

Quadrant 1 - Start	Quadrant 3 - Scale
• Learning	• Optimization
• Mindset & Focus	• Capital
• Planning	• People
Quadrant 2 - Sell	Quadrant 4 - Systemize
• Testing	• Systems
• Sales	• Processes
• Data	• Technology

Figure 69 - E-Commerce Success Framework.

This process can be tedious and time-consuming and is not what everybody likes doing. Some people can get lucky early and find a winning product within a week, while others may take a little more time to crack the code. Either way, be patient with the process and maintain the necessary long-term view that is critical to the foundation of a solid brand.

Once you find that first home-run product, repeating the process is much easier because you have a greater understanding of your customers, what they want, and don't want.

In this section, we are going to take this new level of success and learn how to repeat the process. Just like a factory has an assembly line, our business works in the same way of feeding new and improved products to our customers. Just look at Apple; they began with the Mac, then the iPod, then the iPhone and so forth. If someone loved their iPod, they will most likely have bought the iPhone as it was the next relatable product.

If you have already found winning products to sell and this is your first time achieving success, be sure to document it: How did the process look like? What changes would you make? What is the blueprint you would like your employees to follow?

Have you ever noticed how some things seem impossible in the beginning and then once you accomplish them, they don't seem as big as you initially perceived? All of a sudden, more and more people within your team seem to follow your lead with ease. They replicate your skills of finding products and almost become better at it than you.

"It always seems impossible until it is done. A winner is a dreamer who never gives up" - Nelson Mandella.

In the case of e-commerce, the goal is to test different products until you find that one winning product.

As you scale any product, you should be on the lookout for the next one. So in the case of the dog sneakers, my next mission was to find a similar product. And you guessed it; it was more shoes! Since we knew high-top sneakers worked, we started to source low-top sneakers. After low-top sneakers, we sourced socks.

Now, why would I choose similar products? Well, because it allows me to take advantage of my existing customers, my email list, a strong and mature pixel, and my ad account data.

I found my pocket of gold and was building a brand around the dog niche. So now, my store sold dog sneakers (high-top and low-top versions), dog socks, and dog boots. As soon as I saw that it worked, I moved to dog leggings and dog bags.

Expanding Product Range For Maximum ROI

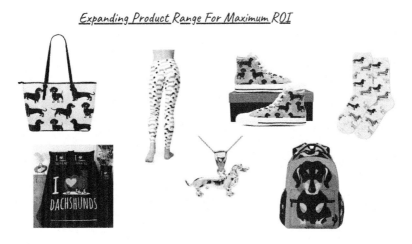

Figure 70 - Leveraging existing customers and offering relatable products.

Here are some of the key strategies I used to repeat the cycle of company and customer success.

Start With the End in Mind: As always, you have to have a strong answer to the question: Why? Set clear and actionable steps with an end goal in mind. If you just want to build a store to make money, it might not be a good enough reason to keep going when times are tough. But, on the other hand, if you truly love what you do and the impact you are trying to make, nothing will stop you from reaching your final destination.

To help you answer the "why?" question, answer the following: How many sales do you want to make? How many customers do you want to have? What is the retention rate? How big of an email list do you want? What companies would you like to partner with? What celebrities would you like to onboard? How many customers do you want to become affiliates?

There are many different things you can decide upfront. These are important goals to have and give you a clear picture of where you want to head, just like a basketball player in college perfecting their craft with the ultimate goal of playing in the NBA in two years or less.

Mission Statement: A mission statement can be defined as a formal summary of the aims and values of a company, organization, or individual. Remember, most people who shop on your site have never heard of you. One way to gather trust is to create a strong and powerful mission statement. For a purchase to occur, people must not only want the product but feel a level of trust and resonate with the brand. A strong mission statement summarizes the values of a company in five seconds or less. Another reason for a mission statement is to help guide the employees of your company to an end goal and provide a sense of identity. A well-written mission statement has the power to communicate the company's purpose to its customers, competitors, employees, vendors, and other stakeholders.

One of my favorite mission statements is from Disney. "To entertain, inform and inspire people around the globe through the power of unparalleled storytelling, reflecting the iconic brands, creative minds, and innovative technologies that make ours the world's premier entertainment company."

The moment you start venturing away from your core values as a company, the harder it is to maintain a level of consistency from your employees to your customers. That's why a lot of celebrities have to be careful in the public eye about what they say and how they represent their brands. Most celebrities will hire public relations managers who are experts in dealing with social media and the press.

If you have not yet created a mission statement, the following questions should be answered before formulating your own unique mission statement.

"What do we do?"

"How do we do it?"

"Whom do we help?"

"What value do we bring?"

Customer Journey: The customer lifecycle and journey are critically important, as I have discussed throughout the book. You may have found your first customers, but what was that experience like for them and what was the actual process in acquiring those customers? Once you answer those questions, keep going. Where did you source each customer from? What worked and what didn't? What was the feedback like on your product reviews? Where did the cheapest acquisition costs come from? What marketing worked and what didn't? What are the areas for improvement? What documents and SOP's need to be created to increase the satisfaction levels?

Let's take an example: I acquired my first customer after three weeks of testing. Let's call this customer Mary and walk through the phases of just how Mary's relationship, and the relationship of all customers, to our business will increase over time as we deliver more value and ensure a great customer experience.

Phase 1 - Mary is worth $60. Mary found my husky sneakers through a Facebook ad. I was targeting women 45+ who were interested in Huskies and the keyword "converse," but also those who were part of dog associations and federations. Mary spent $60 with the company. (This type of layered audience ad can be done through what I call "flex targeting" with Facebook ads.)

Phase 2 - Mary is worth $100. After Mary's purchase, she subscribed to our email list. Based on our segmentation (placing our subscribers into relevant groups) she is part of a number of campaigns and flows (involving huskies) through email marketing, as well as being an active follower on social media. By building more trust and indoctrinating Mary into our brand and mission statement, Mary decides to take up an exclusive offer to buy a second product, which was our new range of husky hoodies. Based on the initial purchase information we had about Mary, we were able to send her an automated birthday email with a twenty-five percent discount coupon. This is a perfect way to combine sales with a personal connection. We weren't selling Mary; we were acknowledging her on her special day while including an offer that resonated with her tastes and preferences. The hoodie was also a perfect purchase for her as we entered the winter season. The hoodie brought in $40. (Note, we did not have to pay to acquire the customer, as Mary is already an existing customer)

Phase 3 - Mary is worth $150. Black Friday comes around in November. We have been promoting our offers for the past few weeks on social media. Mary follows us on Instagram. On Black

Friday, we did a sitewide forty percent off all products. We added code "40BLACKFRIDAY" to a social media post and published it across our channels. Mary used the code when placing the order on our site. Mary purchased a blanket from our store at forty percent off. That brought in $50. Mary has now spent $150 over her lifetime with us.

Phase 4 - Mary is worth $150+: We created a loyalty program where existing customers could sign up as ambassadors and refer people to our program. Mary signed up as an affiliate and we gave her a unique link that she could use to promote to her friends. Mary has a blog and regularly posts about her dogs. Someone came across Mary's blog and decided to make a purchase through her link. As soon as the purchase came in, we were able to attribute the purchase to Mary through her unique link, and she got paid. While Mary did not make the purchase, she did refer the purchase. This is a little more complicated as her value technically remains the same, but she is now referring other customers through her own marketing. Those additional customers now also have lifetime value associated with their profiles.

As you can see from Mary's example, there is power when you nurture people who know nothing about your brand to become valued customers and who later become some of your biggest marketers by referring more people to your products.

If you are unclear of what your customer journey is, I encourage you to create one or map it out and worry about the details later. Remember, two of the most important metrics in e-commerce are AOV (Average order value) and LTV (Lifetime Value).

People: The next area that needs consideration, attention, and optimization is people. How valuable to your business are the people who work with you: What roles do they play and what value add and ROI are they producing for your company? What role do they play in the success of your business, or is it perhaps time to find a new role, or define a more valuable contribution to the team?

Or maybe after reflection on past performance, they are not a good fit and need to be let go? Either way, human capital is crucial to your business and you need to invest in finding the right people to help you. Most entrepreneurs who do not like hiring complain that they do not have enough time, but in order for you to truly succeed, you will need to find and hire the best people possible. Never hire for the sake of it. Hire for the right reasons. Find the areas of your business that will produce a ROI and find the best possible person to run that department.

An example might be after sales service. If you know that it's far cheaper to retain existing customers than to find new ones, then focus on ensuring your current customers are extremely satisfied with your service.

Hire people that fit your brand, have a passion for helping others through customer service, and knows exactly what it takes to move people along the value ladder.

Eventually, through hiring and firing, the leaders and employees that fit your company and brand will emerge. Without people, it is very hard to scale to new heights and maintain momentum.

You will also need to review your own performance. If after the scaling phase you realize that you worked way too much and were too focused on low-level tasks, then refine your process and pay attention to only the activities you as the CEO need to worry about.

Processes: How do you make something run smoother? You create a process. A process can be defined as a series of actions or steps taken in order to achieve a particular end. Human beings are far more effective and efficient when they are familiar with a process. Let's say you want to automate the process of product research. An example might be, what were the steps you took to find your first winning product?

It might look something like this:

Step1: Set aside five hours per week to perform product research.

Step2: Break product research into sixty minutes per day.

Step3: Identify what products are selling on social media.

Step4: Identify what is trending on Google trends.

Step5: Ask customers for new suggestions and improvements.

Step6: Search for best selling products through ad spy software tools.

Step7: What important holidays are approaching and what will trend in the future.

Step8: Create a Google sheet or Excel file capturing every product you discover.

Step9: Find the suppliers and competitors who sell those products.

Step10: Create your unique selling angle and decide if and when the product should be released to the marketplace.

Now, as you can see above, this is a series of defined steps. If you had just onboarded a new team member, this would be a perfect way to illustrate at a summary level how successful product research should be managed. You can pair these steps with a simple video showing how to perform the product research in more detail. This is going to incentivize and give confidence to the person assigned the duty of fulfilling product research.

Humans are awesome but really do need standard operating procedures and processes to be successful in the workplace. The other problem is if that person gets sick, promoted, or leaves the company, how do you train the next person? I will discuss hiring later in a chapter on finding and retaining the best employees.

I remember when I was scaling during my first year and I had one person on customer service. That person called in sick one day and I had no backup. I had no time to recruit and no contingency plan, so I had to literally go 24 hours without replies to my support tickets. Luckily, my employee was back the following day. When she came back, I knew I needed her to document her weekly processes so the next time it happened, I was covered. That process of documentation was implemented into all departments of the business thereafter.

Technology: How do you work smarter, not harder? One of the ways is with technology. Technology allows you to run leaner, with greater efficiency, output, and control. Technology can produce hundreds of data points, which allows us to make smarter and more accurate decisions. One piece of technology that I have spoken about before is Slack. Slack allows you to combine departmental conversations and communication into specific and unique channels. This allows all marketing communication and team members to centralize their work in one place, without the need to disrupt or notify other team members that may not need to know about the inner workings of other departments.

Slack is essentially a single place for internal messaging and sharing files. In the case of my customer Mary, imagine if my marketing team on a daily basis were able to communicate and share real time information in one channel regarding our best marketing strategies. Instead of one person knowing that information, the entire department was now being subtly educated on what is working and what is not working through quick, real-time conversations. Each department has a unique set of goals and objectives and using Slack helps managers maintain and streamline those targets.

Reporting: Another important practice is reporting. This is where you get insights into spending, growth, profitability, and much more. They say if you don't know your numbers, you don't know your business. Most business owners run their business with their eyes closed—like swinging a baseball bat with your eyes shut, hoping you'll hit a home run.

I don't blame them because data and numbers can often seem like the less sexy side of being an entrepreneur. But, knowing your numbers is crucial to identifying the costs associated with acquiring customers. A pop quiz: Who is the one true CEO of your company? If you said "the customer," you are correct.

Since this section of the book focuses on repeating the cycle, the main goal here is acquiring more customers through a series of processes and systems but done so profitably. Acquiring customers at break-even or less is every marketer's dream. If you do not know how much it costs to acquire your customer, then you will go out of business pretty quickly.

With reporting through advertising dashboards, spreadsheets, and e-commerce platforms, we can quickly put together daily, weekly, monthly, and yearly reports. These figures allow us to extrapolate data to determine costs and future sales targets.

An example of reporting might be the daily reporting of return on ad spend (ROAS). ROAS is a column that can be found inside your Facebook ads manager. The formula as defined by Facebook is as follows: "The total return on ad spend (ROAS) from purchases."

Amount Spent 98.48

Purchase Conversion Value $161.30

ROAS 1.64

By calculating the minimum ROAS for your business, you know the minimum ROAS you can go to before losing money. In simple terms, how much can I afford to pay to acquire a customer?

How to determine your minimum ROAS?

Cost of goods sold (COGS) $3.26

Shipping $7.36

Total COGS $10.62

Sale Price $19.99

Gross Profit $9.37

Break Even ROAS 2.13

As the example above shows, for every dollar you put into ads, you need to make $2.13 to cover ad spend & COGS. I recommend identifying every report that you need and how best to automate it so that it can be produced daily to you and/or during an ad hoc request.

Repeating the cycle is taking what works and building momentum. I hope this chapter showed you some interesting strategies and also to let you know that this process never ends! You must constantly work to improve your people, processes, systems, and technology.

Summary:

- Build momentum off what worked and repeat the steps you took when you saw initial success.
- Know why you started, create a powerful mission statement to help guide your customers, employees, vendors, and stakeholders.
- Understanding the customer journey is key to success.
- You need to document what worked well and what did not work so well.
- Create systems and processes that human beings can follow for efficiency purposes.
- The process of documentation and improvement never ends.
- As you repeat the cycle, every iteration will lead to greater optimization.
- If you lack resources, hire more people to help you. They don't have to be full-time; they can be part-time workers or contractors.
- Technology is your friend; use it to your advantage.

- Never stop testing new products. You never know when one product just stops selling or it loses its appeal or competition enters the market and sales decline.
- Knowing your numbers is one of the most important parts of being a business owner.

How to Create an Action Step:
- Identify a successful time in your business. It could be making your first 10 sales.
- List the steps involved in achieving that target.
- What are key areas involved and could it be automated?
- Who were the key employees involved?
- What was your role and can it be outsourced?
- What were the numbers and profitability of that achievement?
- What are the areas that can be improved on?
- What areas can be eliminated?

HIRING

As a kid, my parents used to tell me stories and old tales as a way to illustrate something complex. So for the next few chapters, I'll talk about how I managed to systemize my e-commerce business and hopefully, the insights will give you some direction on where to begin.

If you have not yet reached quadrant four in your business where you can systemize and outsource, do not worry! This book is meant to be read cover to cover, so think of it as a guide for what lies ahead.

Hiring is an essential component to ensuring your systems run. Regardless of technology or processes, humans are essential. Just like the farming example I shared earlier, humans are needed to turn the machines on, feed the right amounts of minerals, proteins and vitamins, herd the cows from the fields to the farm, and ensure no animal is sick or unhealthy.

When I first thought about hiring, I took inventory of every single one of my tasks. I listed out every single responsibility and rated it from one to ten in order of priority, one being the highest priority to the success of the business. Hiring is an expensive and time-consuming process but you have to hire.

Here are some tips for hiring the right candidate:
- Identify the ideal candidates for the position.
- Create great job descriptions that clearly define the job role.
- Use the power of digital trends & social media.
- Fit the personality to the job.
- Create mini case studies and see which candidate produces the best results.
- Monitor your reviews; your candidates will also vet you.
- Pay more for the right candidate.
- Your hire's success will depend on onboarding and training.
- Get better at your interviews.

When I was selling dog merchandise, it came to a point where I was overwhelmed with customer emails. I knew I needed to outsource customer support. Even though it is a lower-level task and something anyone can do, I wanted to hire the right person for the job. I ensured that I found someone who loved dogs, saw the value behind our product, and could communicate in a way that reassured dog lovers and gave them confidence in our brand.

You may have to go through a number of bad hires to find the right hire. Do not be afraid to fire fast. Put your bias aside and avoid keeping the wrong employees as there is nothing worse than prolonging a firing because it does affect the rest of your team. If you need help hiring, I will list some resources in the resources section of this book.

HOLDING ON TO KEY PLAYERS

I want to talk about the importance of hiring and retaining the best employees. I've hired both good and bad employees and trust me; it can be expensive and time-consuming to replace key players. Quadrant four, which is the systemization section of my ESF framework, won't work unless you have confidence in your employees to manage the day-to-day operations of your business.

Top caliber employees have a tendency to move to the companies that treat them the best. An example is Silicon Valley, the home to many startups and technology companies. Companies compete here for the best talent, especially when it comes to graduates from some of the top universities.

Many of the smaller startups just can't compete with the likes of Facebook and Google because of the incredible focus they put on employee happiness. At Google, employees get free food, free rides to and from work, free massage credits, and employee development is at the core of their company values.

Now I know Google is Google, and they have many advantages, but success leaves clues. Obviously, we can't compete with Google, but we can learn from how they approach employee retention. I will discuss that shortly.

What makes a great sports team? It's not just one individual player, but it's a combination of everyone on that team; each player pushing with their unique strengths and working towards the common goal of winning the game.

Sure, Cristiano Ronaldo is a fantastic player and scores a ridiculous amount of goals, but he is supported in winning by ten other players with specific roles and a manager leading and orchestrating their efforts on and off the field.

You see, there is no "I" in TEAM. This was one of the major shifts I had to make entering entrepreneurship. I initially wanted to do everything myself and could not let go of responsibility. I quickly realized that this was no way to run a business and began hiring the right people to help me grow and scale.

Let's first chat about retention and why people quit? So how many people quit their jobs? Let's use the United States as an example. More than three million people quit their jobs every month; this is quite a staggering statistic. Why are people quitting their jobs and what can we do about it?[65]

Just like I've always preached about looking after your customers and ensuring they buy from you again, the same applies to your employees. It's far cheaper to retain great employees than to find and train new ones. The cost of rehiring, training, and adding new employees to your business costs a lot more than just their salary. Also, during times of a strong economy, people have more choices and options. If there are more jobs, people will be more willing to search for other job opportunities that match their needs and want.

If a person is earning $25,000 per year with you, there may be a similar opportunity out there to earn the same amount, but where they are treated better and have the opportunity to work on things that they are truly passionate about.

These are the types of scenarios that exist every single day. Another reason why people leave is because of their boss. Poor boss performance makes employees four times more likely to quit.

Finally, with the world moving at such a fast pace, uncertain times, and a global pandemic, managerial styles need to change. What worked in the past no longer works today. A lot of the traditional ways of doing business are no longer valid today. We saw with the global pandemic of 2020, that people were forced to work from home. This led to adjustments for employees and employer relations, a move to more video conferencing, and a work-life balance affected by working from home. As a result, work became more challenging and that face-to-face that you were so used to no longer existed.

For situations like this, you have to be willing to adapt and change. If you do not, people will leave. You'll also find citations where employees will take up possible side gigs. This is where your employees will take on additional responsibilities outside of their work usually to earn additional income. Generally, employees can make a lot more with their time on side gigs, and this can be a distraction if it spills into regular work life. An example might be a videographer who works full time for you, but at the weekends shoots wedding events for other clients. If the income generated from these side gigs gives more financial stability and fulfillment, then the chances are high that they will leave their job with you.

Finally, competition is another factor to watch out for. If you have a successful business, competitors may try and lure your best employees away from you, using attractive salary and bonus packages. I saw this at Apple every week; companies like Google and Facebook would try and recruit their engineers.

The thought of my best employees leaving me is often scary; that's why I put in effort to ensure they are satisfied, enjoy their work, and are appropriately compensated. You see, I don't mind paying people well if their work generates a consistent ROI.

So if we know it's both time-consuming, stressful, and costs a lot of money to replace people, how do we focus on retaining our best people? How do we make them feel like an integral part of our success and give them opportunities to really focus on what they value? As mentioned before, the first step is to understand people's values.

Earlier in the book, I talked about having each of your employees undertake the values of the determination process. It was created by Dr. John DeMartini. What this will do is give both you and your worker an insight into what your employees truly value in life.

"The more important a value is – the higher it will be on your hierarchy of values and the more discipline and order you will have associated with it. The less important a value is – the lower it will be

on your hierarchy of values and the less discipline and more disorder you have associated with it." - Dr. John DeMartini.

I am sure there are other ways to understand what people love, but this process is something I use whenever I need to decide if I should take on a new venture or challenge. By understanding one's values (what really matters most to people), you are able to gauge whether someone is suitable for your job role or not. Also, if you see that a person is unhappy at work, you'll be more in a position to solve that problem because you will know what they value through the survey process. An example might be if one of your best employees all of a sudden starts to show signs of unhappiness, lower performance levels, or signs of resentment. If you truly understand their values, you'll be able to get to the bottom of their problems. By also having those initial values identified, conversations become a lot more open and honest.

Let's take a common example: salary. If someone is unhappy at work and has money on the top of their values list, you may find that that person does not believe that their efforts are being properly compensated. It's often something as small as that. I know myself; there were days in my corporate life where I could never understand why I was overlooked for promotion. Resentment set in until I had the courage to discuss, and I was open about what I really wanted. Once I had gotten my feelings out in the open, I was able to come to an agreement with my boss for increased pay based on clear and identifiable milestones.

Of course, there may be other external factors for employee discomfort, but you get the idea around values and why it's important to start with them. The more you know about your employees, the better you can meet and exceed their expectations.

Another reason people quit their jobs is because they are simply not thriving and engaged enough to inspire them to keep working. What I mean by this is that they are unfulfilled at the workplace, are not excelling in their career, or are not being challenged with new and exciting opportunities and projects. No one wants to be in a job where they are not being stimulated. I know people that have quit their jobs because they were not promised what was discussed in the interview process in terms of job opportunity.

The following are my best tips for holding on to key employees and reducing turnover in your organization:

Recognizing retention starts with recruiting: It all starts with the end goal of the hire. Set the reasons for hiring. What is the purpose of this new hire and what is the impact they will have on the organization as a whole? If you aimlessly hire for the sake of it, the results will speak for themselves and it will not be pretty. How often have we seen the best soccer players join successful teams only to find that they were surplus talent? Great players will not stay around if they are not wanted or feel that their skills are not being utilized to their full potential. So, before you hire, know the role, purpose, and desired outcome that this new hire will bring. The cherry on top is relaying these goals and objectives in the interview process, so everyone is clear.

Recruit based on your company culture: The company culture refers to the beliefs and behaviors that determine how a company's employees and management interact on a daily basis. You have to find people that fit into your specific culture. You cannot hire an outspoken and aggressively toned employee if your culture is built on a calm, peaceful and productive workforce.

Family: In a family culture, everyone is committed to growing together. The success of the company is attributed to everyone on the team and everyone is rewarded no matter how big or small the contribution. The importance of maintaining what has been passed down from the founders is crucial to the success of the company. Open communication is key inside the business. Everyone knows the importance of work-life balance and getting to know your employees at a deeper level is what makes them thrive. Everyone inside the company is committed to helping one another. Everyone typically knows one another and topics outside of work will come up during the day. The atmosphere is friendly, open, and co-operative.

Flexibility: In this culture, it is more relaxed and flexible in nature. Rules and regulations tend to be less important and strict. I remember I worked for a company in Dublin, Ireland, almost a decade ago, and the managers of the company were less micro managers. They cared more about the work results and had a relaxed and informal dress code. Some people love working in a flexible environment. It blends more into their regular life and gives more freedom and authority for them to work to their own schedule. Often, giving people more control can get more out of your employees. Again, people leave their bosses and not their jobs.

Competition: This work environment is competitive and can be a double-edged sword. On the one hand, it pits workers against each other to see which one performs the best, and ultimately who is fit for promotion and accepts greater responsibility. On the other hand, it can lead to high turnover, stress, and the likelihood that they will do what is right for them and not the company. This workplace is identified by long hours, high turnover, and disgruntled employees if management cannot handle the good and bad aspects of it.

Hierarchy: This environment is based on the chain of command. You report to a boss and that boss reports to a boss and so forth. Communication rarely goes outside of your duties and it is generally hard to find growth opportunities in the company. Decisions take more time to approve and is generally a style that exists in larger, stable companies. The motto here is to get the job done right and by the rules of the hierarchical structure.

For someone who is creative and likes to get things done fast, this style can be frustrating. When I worked at Apple, there were many projects that existed on a yearly basis, and often those projects were put on hold because it used to take so much time before approval was gained from the likes of Tim Cook, Steve Jobs, and the executive team. Your performance was often dictated by how fast your project moved. If you could show signs of participation in a number of finished projects, it would give you bargaining power in your reviews. If your projects were placed on hold or lacked funding, you may often find yourself in a frustrating situation and not as much room to receive promotions or recognition.

To summarize, think about the culture you are trying to build and promote. No matter how good you think a person is on paper, if they are not aligned with the culture, most likely they will not be a good fit and cause disruption for your other team members.

In my first e-commerce business, I named our team "Team Pacquiao," because of the fighting pride that Manny Pacquiao gave as a fighter and leader in his country. Also, my team was primarily based – remotely – out of the Philippines. The values of my team were: take pride in your work, help one another, work hard, and always do what is right for the company. It was definitely a family-style culture.

Managing people is often one of the most difficult parts of running a business. In fact, dealing with other stakeholders like suppliers and customers is also difficult, but something you will get better at with practice. If you are running a large organization, I encourage you to seek more help from people who can relieve some of that pressure. One strategy is building strong mid-level management as they are often the first touchpoint between you and your employees.

As CEO, your job is to steer the ship, be strategic, and keep the vision strong. Having said that, you cannot neglect how your employees are treated. Hiring great managers who align with your vision or by adequately training them to work in a manner that will inspire and motivate staff, you will ensure your employees remain happy, are willing to go above and beyond, and work in harmony with your direct line managers.

If your managers lack personal skills, are poor communicators, and are aggressive and authoritarian in nature, then your employees may not stick around. We are again in quadrant four, which is about systemizing, and if you have managers who are not up to par, you'll have to intervene in more ways than you'll have wanted. This is not how we systemize properly, and you'll find yourself "working in your business" rather than "working on your business."

In order for systems to work, your people need to be successful and willing to follow the vision you've set forth. If you like certain people in your company, build them up to be successful managers. If you do not like to train, go hire the best people to do it.

The second opportunity to retain employees is by showing them how committed you are to their growth by delivering ongoing education and clear paths to career advancement. People are driven by a hierarchy of needs.[66] As one is satisfied, the higher need becomes the motivator. Some people are ambitious to succeed in certain areas of their lives and you need to become aware of it.

Maybe you have introverts on your team who are afraid to ask for help or are seeking additional training but feel they have not earned it yet. By showing that you care and by investing in your people, it gives your employees a sense of worth and they feel they have the potential to keep progressing in their career through additional education and training. The good thing is training and education is tax-deductible. Grant Cardone, a top entrepreneur who spoke at an event my business partners and I created, is constantly stressing the importance of reinvesting in your people.

Finally, the world is changing rapidly. Skills get outdated fast and you must be willing to adapt and confront the obstacles that may impact your business. If I don't know how to tackle a problem, neither will my employees and students.

This was a long section of the book but an important one. Without a strong team, it will be very hard to scale and systemize your organization. I will note that for e-commerce businesses, we usually have remote teams. This makes it even more important to understand your employees and ensure they are happy and inspired in the workplace. Happy hunting. Now, go hire!

WORLDWIDE EXPANSION

When I first saw success with my dog products, I knew I had an audience in the United States. One quick look, I could see in my analytics dashboard that I was building a buyer profile of very passionate 25+ male and female dog lovers. At the time, I was running traffic solely to the US market because if I could successfully crack the US market, I could start selling to the other top countries. Essentially, I was tackling the biggest market first and using it as a testing ground to gather information on who was buying from me. The analytics inside my ads dashboard would give me a decisive result after a few weeks.

Then came my expansion plan, which was as follows: Take the knowledge and data I had acquired, I branched into the next big four countries of Canada, the United Kingdom, Australia, and New Zealand.

Once the systems, currency website converters, communication with suppliers, and customer reviews came in positive, I decided to go to the next tier of countries: Japan, Finland, France, Belgium, Denmark, Taiwan, Austria, Iceland, Germany, Australia, Sweden, Netherlands, Hong Kong, Switzerland, Norway, Ireland, Singapore, and Luxembourg.

It was a this point I knew I had found a great product that resonated with different countries, cultures and languages. I had finally found a product that I could expand worldwide.

Keep in mind, without data, you cannot make decisions like this, and to be really strategic, I always tend to start with the United States with my product testing, which often has the largest number of buyers and conversion rates.

The following are some of the considerations you need to take before branching beyond your own country or going International.

Going International Considerations:

- How does your brand and message translate into a foreign language? This should be done prior to launching your business, but ensure your brand name or products do not translate inappropriately in another language.
- Have you a team to deal with the additional support, timezone challenges, and in general, a greater workload?
- Is there any red tape in the way, what are the laws for other countries that may prevent you from doing business?
- Know your why, what is the purpose of expanding and can you deal with it right now?
- How will you overcome language and cultural differences?
- Prepare to notify International customers with additional shipping information, possible import duties, and any other tariffs they may have to deal with themselves based on doing business with your company.
- Add currency converters on your store to ensure the customer is viewing your product's prices in their home currency.
- Add shipping rates for the countries you are expanding into.

The beauty when it comes to digital marketing is worldwide expansion is not as daunting as it sounds. Literally, the first steps I took when expanding worldwide was duplication of my advertising campaigns, adding additional currency and shipping rates, and communicating to my suppliers on my forecasted future demand.

POSTMORTEM ANALYSIS

We are now going to talk about how to constantly improve the way you run your business, and more specifically, the projects and tasks that you identify as key deliverables and milestones. Remember the 80/20 rule: Twenty percent of the projects that you work on will produce eighty percent of the results. An example might be the holiday season months of November and December that bring the greatest revenue for your store over the entire year. As a result, we conduct postmortems or post-project reviews to determine the effectiveness of a campaign and how to improve it the next time.

A simple post mortem example is a two-day event I perform in January, where we as a team discuss the effectiveness of our performance during the holiday season. We look at performance, sales, and overall success. We also look at what worked well and what didn't, and what are the actions and lessons learned to be better next time.

If you have been part of any type of project, whether it is in school, at home, or in your current business, you'll know that things don't always go as planned. The likelihood is that if you could, you would probably go back and change the way things got done or the way things happened.

Instead, we focus on how we can learn from our mistakes and how we can use it as a way to grow and evolve into better leaders, increase team performance, and ultimately drive the overall success of the business. Similarly, how can we take what worked well and double down on it?

One of the most important things you should set in your calendar is a post-mortem analysis. I know it doesn't sound the most pleasant but trust me, it is going to help you become a better entrepreneur, help your employees, and ultimately help the success of your business overall. A post-mortem meeting is a team gathering that takes place at the end of a project where the group examines the challenges and successes of the endeavor.

One of the biggest mistakes people make is they set a time and date to perform the post-mortem analysis, but once it comes around they make excuses like, "oh, we are too busy," or "we found a better way," or "we cannot remember what happened." The list goes on!

Take the time to follow through and understand that everything does not have to be perfect. It may not seem like a big deal, but trust me, a lot of great information will come out, people will realize they have a voice, and ultimately it will improve the team morale and your company culture.

The biggest realization will be that you, as the owner, will uncover areas of your business that are not running as smoothly as thought, and you will find the pockets of your business that are thriving. You'll soon discover whether it is a people, process, or systems issue. This goes back to the importance of a SWOT analysis I discussed earlier in the book.

Here is a list of the benefits of holding postmortem events:

Improved efficiency: You'll discover better ways to perform tasks by creating standard operating procedures (SOPs). An example might be the team who managed your social media discovering that a social media scheduling app like Hootsuite or Buffer could take them one hour instead of eight hours in a week to meet their objectives.

Increased Team Morale: Have you ever felt like just another faceless employee? Your voice rarely gets heard; you feel like you have no say in the company direction? Well, if you felt that way, there is a good chance that members of your team might be going through that exact same process. By involving your team in a discussion-based analysis like a postmortem, it shows your employees that you value their role, value their feedback, and see them as an integral part of the company's success. As a boss, involving your team does wonders for you, too. It shines you in a different light and can boost your employee's satisfaction and productivity levels.

Work in Harmony: By having group discussions, it shows each individual the importance of his or her role in the greater scheme. It also gives more clarity to your employees on how the business runs and often can lead to more acceptance and empathy. Also, by having your employees involved, they become better listeners and learn how to be more responsive because they now have a better understanding of how things work. Remember, we are in the quadrant of systemization. If we have removed ourselves from the business at this stage, we need to find leaders to emerge from our team.

Sign Off on Projects: If a project is complete, postmortems can be an official and effective way to officially close the project and move onto the next.

Celebrate the Wins: Postmortems should not just deal with what went wrong. If there was an area that was successful, it is important to highlight and celebrate those wins. Life is about balance, and if you focus on the negative too often, you will adopt a negative mindset and so will your team.

Mastermind Principle: The next principle came from one of my favorite books—*Think & Grow Rich*.[67] In this book, the author Napoleon Hill describes the Mastermind Principle as, "The coordination of knowledge and effort between two or more people who work towards a definite purpose in a spirit of harmony...no two minds ever come together without thereby creating a third, invisible, intangible force, which may be likened to a third mind," also known as, the Mastermind. Masterminds have become a common habit of mine through my entrepreneurial journey. I have held my own mastermind events in Miami and Arizona.

Simply put, masterminds involve more people in the same room, and therefore you conjure up far better ideas and a magical spirit of collaboration.

Competitor Analysis: Just like a team of expert TV pundits who will offer post-game analysis to determine what worked well and what didn't, you too can look at the opposing team or opposition to see what they did right and what they did wrong. Sam Walton of Walmart was famous for visiting his competitors' stores to see what sales promotions they had and how he could compete against them in any way, shape, or form. During a postmortem, you can look at all the promotions and offers that your competitors had and what made them work well and vice versa. If you have no sight of your competition, soon you will be out of business because you will be too focused on yourself and not how the industry is evolving.

Training & Systems: By discussing internally, it starts the process of documenting the areas that need to be worked on for the future. By documenting, you can create training or guides that can be used as SOPs so that next time a question comes up in that area, it can be referenced.

So now, let's move to the actual process of conducting a full postmortem analysis.

Postmortem Key Steps:

Prep work: This is the preparation work that happens before the postmortem takes place. This is where you gather everyone's feedback, either through a meeting (whiteboard discussion), or an online survey to gather information on what worked and what didn't. Everyone involved is responsible for filling out their own survey or contribute to the pre-meeting. The advantage of this is you are able to quickly gather hundreds of the different data points before you go into a discussion-based scenario. If you do not complete step one, you will have an inefficient meeting where there is no agenda or structure to how you discuss the key topics.

Synthesize Information: Once step one is finished, you'll have a wide array of information, feedback, advice, and so forth. The goal in step two is to synthesize and organize the points into different categories. Once you categorize the information, decide on the key points and rank them in each department from one to ten (one being the most important).

Set Rules & Timing: If you follow the first two steps, then the actual main meeting is a lot easier to manage and facilitate. The goal of the meeting is to keep the meeting to ninety minutes in order to keep people engaged. If the content and discussion is providing value, I recommend having one more meeting the following day. Also, be prepared to set some rules so that the purpose and agenda is adhered to for maximum efficiency.

Conduct the Meeting: Let your team know that you are thankful for their pre-meeting feedback and you have organized the agenda based on the feedback received. Usually, I divide the meetings up into three sections: What worked well; What did not work well; and Next Steps & Follow Up.

Be sure to note that this meeting is meant as a discussion and feedback exercise and not something that should turn into blame. I recommend having one person take minutes and I encourage you to be impartial by having a facilitator (maybe someone on the team who wasn't involved in the project) chair the meeting. Keep the meeting light, discussion-based, let everyone speak, respect one another, and never get personal.

Here is an example of how the final product should look after the meeting. Everything should be documented, organized, and assigned a directly responsible individual.

Project Name: Q4 Analysis

Meeting Date:10.1.2020

Attendees: John, Jack, Mary, Steve, Megan

Column headings: Issues, Issue Solution, Action Item, Owner, Links, Notes

Once the meeting is over, an action is assigned to each discussion point and someone is responsible for completing it. The goal of a post mortem is to learn from your past experiences, whether good or bad. In the case of my quarter-four analysis example, the expectation would be that the following year's quarter four event leads to greater efficiency, more sales, better processes, and happier employees. Albert Einstein is widely credited with saying, "The definition of insanity is doing the same thing over and over again, but expecting different results." Don't ever repeat the same mistakes in business. Use these meetings as a way to not only improve how your business operates but as a way to involve your employees and make them feel part of the mission at hand.

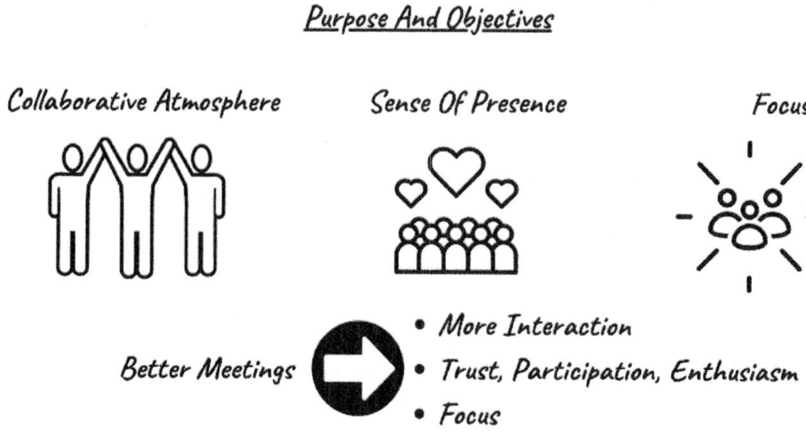

Purpose And Objectives

Figure 71 - The power of involving your team.

BECOMING A LEADER & VISIONARY

Every successful organization, company, or entity has natural born leaders and visionaries that push, inspire, and lead its people towards specifics goals or a final destination.

When Tom Brady joined Tampa Bay at 43, he had a strong vision, but he needed buy in from his coaches, teammates, owners, and fans to win his seventh Super Bowl ring. At the post Super Bowl press conference, all eyes were on Brady and his incredible accomplishments. As questions began from journalists, instead of taking the limelight he said, "Let's bring some other people up here."[68] Brady knows the power of a team that works in harmony towards a common goal and focuses on everyone becoming a better player and person. Winning in a team sport must be a team effort.

Likewise, if you look at any successful company, it has its leaders. Someone carries the momentum and vision of where the company is heading, just like the captain of a ship who takes responsibility and works with the helmsman to ensure everyone on board is safe. A professional helmsman maintains a steady course, properly executes all rudder orders, and communicates to the officer on the bridge using navigational terms relating to the ship's heading and steering.

The same applies to any business. There needs to be someone directing and delegating to a team through both calm and rough water. This person, to me, is the leader or visionary. This person is representing the company culture at the highest level and is someone people can turn to in times of need. They are seen as someone to trust, someone willing to listen to the voices of others, embrace communication and collaboration, support personal development, and inspire others to find their voice.

If you really want to systemize your business and have others take up the roles and responsibilities, you have to work on the core attributes of becoming a truly great leader.

Attributes of Great Leaders

Promote open communication: Communicating effectively is critical to running your business. One question to ask yourself: if you were removed from all company emails and communication channels, would the business run without you?

If there are doubts, I recommended creating a system that allows for people to communicate across departments. In this digital age, most teammates are spread across the world, in different times zone, with various cultural and language differences. By using apps like Slack and Asana, you can centralize communication in one place. Slack will allow you to streamline communication based on your department or project, as mentioned earlier. Once you have built a system that allows people to see what is going on, the next piece is encouraging people to be open and realize they are a valuable asset to the conversations taking place.

Your best feedback often comes from people who have tactical roles. What I mean here is people who are often closest to the product or customer will provide the greatest insights. In the case of customer service, your customer service reps are interacting with customers every day. By encouraging lower-level employees to provide feedback (no matter how small it may be), it is going to allow you and your management to adjust and improve on that particular department.

Encourage professional growth: By involving your employees in the day-to-day operations and by you becoming a role model, you are building confidence and promoting everyone on your team to become better versions of themselves. In the case of the customer service example, if employees feel their opinions are being heard, they will be more inspired to go above and beyond in delivering better customer service and contributing to the company's overall effectiveness. Nobody wants to work for someone who is not open to their personal and professional growth.

When I worked at Apple, there were people who started with zero qualifications but had been with the company for thirty-plus years. They started on the production floor as general operatives and were now in managerial positions because they were pinpointed as leaders and people who wanted to expand and grow. This all came about because Apple knew the importance of encouraging professional growth.

Connect at a deep level: Every human being is different. Some people require more hand-holding, while others want to be left alone and focus on their work. You need to identify which of your employees are which and how best to accommodate their personalities. By having an open one-to-one conversation, you can explain the benefits of open communication and how it will allow everyone to be more efficient in their daily work, and as a result, make everyone's work easier. You have to sell the benefits involved for all. Remember, you are trying to systemize a business that will run without you, and if everyone is singing off a different hymn sheet, you will not be able to remove yourself.

Remain Positive: If everything is burning down around you, you need to be the one who remains calm. A positive attitude is contagious and if you do not possess one, it will trickle down to all levels of your company. I remember in my corporate days; there was once a situation where the entire department was in a frenzy around rumors of potential cuts in departmental spending. This would mean a freeze on hiring and the possibility of temporary workers being let go. The following morning at 9am, the director held a departmental meeting where he reassured everyone that it was going to be OK and he answered any questions from the floor. This was true leadership. It showed people that they were valued and it put the director in a position where he was seen as a trustworthy leader. It's always better to act with a sense of urgency and honesty.

Teach rather than give orders: As a teacher and online educator myself, I know the most effective way to train my staff and to help other e-commerce entrepreneurs succeed is by teaching and involving others rather than giving direct orders. If I email a team member and ask them to create their first-ever Facebook ad, without any guidance or knowledge transfer, number one they are going to feel overwhelmed, and number two, I will most likely be dissatisfied with the finished product, which means I will have to rework it. If you are going to pass responsibility, take time to teach and take time to inspire, showing that not only do you trust them, but you are backing them in their ability to do a great job.

"Tell me and I forget. Teach me and I remember. Involve me and I learn." - Benjamin Franklin

Set expectations and targets: A good leader will set expectations and targets. If for example, a cycling coach is not going to give their cyclists targets and expectations, then they will never make progress or accomplish their goals. The role of that coach is to tell you when to dig deep, when to ride, how much to ride, how hard to ride, what to eat, and all the things that go along with becoming a better cyclist. Just like automating and systemizing your business, you should set expectations around how business performance is measured, who reports to you, how they report, and to what cadence.

Give feedback on performance: Either you or your managers need to give feedback on performance. An employee might feel they are doing a fantastic job until you actually approach them and say that they've had a decline in performance. It's not their fault; it's your fault for not providing a feedback mechanism. Every basketball team in the NBA watches game tape. The coach sits down with their team and watches the last game together. They look at the areas where they did well, the areas where they fell apart, and where they can improve in the next game. This is just like the example I gave about having postmortems in your business—so you can learn from previous mistakes and double down on what worked.

Seek Feedback: Sorry to burst your bubble but it is not all rainbows and unicorns. You may have flaws and bad habits that you are not aware of, and that is perfectly fine. If you are someone who is open to constructive criticism, and you make those needed improvements, you will reach the level required for a visionary leader a lot quicker. I recommend creating two touchpoints per year to evaluate your performance by having honest feedback meetings with your team. If you wish, you can have your employees provide the feedback anonymously. Finally, having a mentor and coach will give you the hard truths. If I am doing something wrong in my life or business, my parents and/or business coaches will be frank and honest with where I am going wrong and what I need to do to fix those issues.

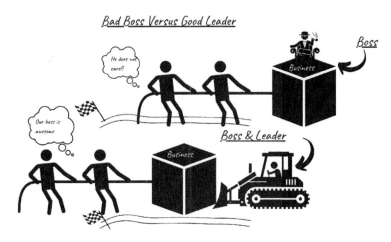

Figure 72 - The difference between a bad boss and a great leader.

BUILDING A BRAND

Building a brand is what truly builds your business into an e-commerce empire. At the beginning of your journey, you might be OK with just making a few online sales, learning the ropes, and getting to know how everything fits together. That's perfectly fine; in fact, it is much better to go this route than not taking any action at all. It is this exact route that I chose because I was so eager to prove to myself that I could make money online.

However, there will come a time where you will realize that to get to the next level; you'll need to turn your store from a general store selling random products to a real brand that people recognize and will continue to buy from year after year. No one wants to buy a business that has no brand equity or identity.

A brand will bring many benefits to your business. First, it will give you an edge over your competitors and it will allow you to charge a premium price. Second, as mentioned many times in this book, it will allow you to have repeat and loyal customers. Third and last, brands are key to selling products and services, but also can be the major deciding factor when you go to sell your business. Investors are more inclined to pay a premium price for a brand that is instantly recognizable and has a passionate and loyal following.

If you consult with a business broker, you'll see how company valuations change based on the company's perceived brand equity. The next bonus I want to give you is a personal video that my broker created for you. It'll teach you what goes into selling an e-commerce business. Go to EcommerceActivated.com/broker.

Branding is a huge topic and too big to cover in this book. The main tip I will give you is to realize that a brand is your identity (logo, color, design, mission, values, culture etc). Set a clear mission and follow through on what your company stands for and serves. It's best to start creating your brand immediately, rather than trying to piece it together a couple of years later. The sooner you brand, the faster the rate of success.

BBB ACCREDITATION

Becoming accredited with the Better Business Bureau (BBB) will help you become more credible and build trust through your website.[69] The BBB helps consumers in the United States, Canada, and Mexico find businesses and charities they can trust. I think it was one of the reasons I was able to sell my store because Investors knew that I had put the necessary time and effort into building a brand and looking after my customers.

How to Get BBB Accredited in Five Steps:
1. Verify that your business meets BBB requirements.
2. Go to BBB.org/become-accredited to get started.
3. Fill out the BBB accreditation application.
4. Wait for BBB application evaluation.
5. Earn accreditation & pay the fee.

I added BBB in section four of my ESF framework. It is yet another asset that is nice to have as part of building a brand and to ultimately systemize and predict the future success of your business. If you cannot yet achieve the BBB accreditation, you can ask your customers to review your site on websites like Trustpilot and more.

PRODUCTIVITY HACKS

In a world of distraction, where social media, news, and our own limiting beliefs, cloud our judgment, it is important to remain productive and clear on the mission at hand. This is an area of focus that is needed when you decide to systemize and outsource the work. You must focus on the areas of your business that produces the highest return. As you gain experience, you'll realize that time is your most precious commodity. As a result, if you are not productive and you tend to lack discipline, you'll find yourself becoming complacent and start looking for the easy way out by focusing on the easier or less valuable company deliverables.

I looked at my iPhone the other day and noticed I was spending far too much time on certain apps on my phone. Those social media apps really know how to suck our attention. I performed some research on ways I could become more productive. I studied books, audios, and podcasts to find ways to become more efficient with my time.

Once I acquired this knowledge, which I found fascinating, I passed the information to my team, not only to have them learn what I learned but to let them know why I would be focusing on those improvements. Because of this commitment, I have already begun to see a vast improvement in the day-to-day company productivity.

The first tip I learned was to actually just say no! If you let others suck your time, you become part of someone else's plans. I was once a person who would say yes to everything and then I realized it was one of the reasons I didn't hit my targets. Ask yourself if a given task is adding to or taking away from your attention to the company mission. The same applies to your employees. Often they may take up a task just to stay busy, but the task may add no value to the company; therefore, it is always wise to tell your employees to quantify the importance of each task they are working on.

The next tip is to batchwork your tasks or focus on one thing at a time. Most people will tell you to multitask but I disagree; I think human beings perform much better when tackling one thing at a time. If for example, you know you need to shoot five pieces of YouTube content per week, then I recommend shooting all of the videos in one day and have them scheduled out to run over the course of the week. Can you imagine how much time you are saving?

I also love to keep my desk clean. It might sound minor, but having a clutter-free desk allows you to remain focused. I like having just my laptop and a piece of paper on my desk. My phone is usually out of sight.

Meetings are another way to stay productive. A meeting will get everyone clear on the current mission at hand. By focusing everyone on one main goal, everyone is committed to achieving it. A Monday morning team meeting is essential to set the intention and a Friday evening meeting to discuss what got done and what didn't and why.

As mentioned earlier in the book, I usually have a digital record of my goals and to-do items. Trello is a fantastic app to manage your daily, weekly, monthly, and yearly activities and goals. I encourage you to train your team to do the same.

Before you leave for work, or before you fall asleep at night, plan the next day's activities: What is needed and how are you going to achieve it? This helps you wake up with purpose and avoids you having to make decisions when you may not be in the right frame of mind. Planning is such a crucial part of having a great day.

I won't go into any more detail but I am sure you have your own ways of staying productive. I cannot stress how important it is if you really want to reach your goals. One final tip: get enough sleep and rest! Mounting evidence suggests that a good night's sleep seriously boosts productivity. One study of 4,188 U.S. workers found "significantly worse productivity, performance, and safety outcomes" among those who slept less and estimated a $1,967 loss in productivity per worker due to poor sleep.[70]

THE FINANCIAL POSITION

Believe it or not, most new business owners do not know the financial state of their company. What I mean is that they do not actively monitor the cash-in versus cash-out on a daily or weekly basis. This becomes important if you are starting with little to no money or looking to scale aggressively by investing back into your business by hiring and creating more infrastructure.

Ask someone like successful serial entrepreneur Grant Cardone what is the first thing he asks for in the morning—it's a financial report of all of his companies' accounts. For people who operate at a high level like Grant, the goal is to multiply your money. In his case, he wants to make money work for him and not just sit in the bank earning tiny amounts of interest.

I recommend you use business credit cards to leverage points and use those points as a way to balance the funds going in and out of your business, especially if you are cash short. One credit card I use regularly is the Amex Business Gold card that gives you triple points on US advertising. I take things a step further by cashing out my points to a brokerage account (Charles Schwab) and therefore turning points into dollars. If you are not in the US, find a card that gives you the most benefits.

To stay "in the black," I highly recommend you to check your financial reporting, your Excel files, cash accounts, or whatever other reports are necessary to get a daily picture of company profit and loss.

Don't be afraid of money. It doesn't go away just because you ignore it. Make money your friend and focus on raising the positive cash balance each day. I promise the more you confront the beast, the more you will be in control. I also recommend you create a specific bank account for your e-commerce business, and separate the expenses from your personal or other business accounts.

MY TOOLBOX

Just like a carpenter or plumber needs the right tools to go to work every day, the same holds true for you and your employees. Having all the brains, resources, and the best people in the world won't help if you do not have an efficient way to maximize its return. A good tool doesn't solve everything but it will improve the way you work.

In this chapter, I am going to give you an overview of some of the key tools I use every day in my business. These are the tools my team and I use to give us an edge, and the more I try to systemize and streamline, the more I am reliant on these tools to help ensure things run smoothly without me. As these tools change, which they may, I will update them in the resources section.

Some questions to ask yourself first are:

- How do you communicate with your team and suppliers?
- Who is doing what and how long does it take to accomplish tasks?
- How do you report accurately and how do you keep track of finances?
- How do you maintain company morale and ensure the vision remains strong?
- Who reports to who and is there an organizational chart?
- What SOPs exist and who is responsible for them?

Let's now dive into the apps and tools that help me when growing and scaling my business.

Firstly, as mentioned earlier, I use an organizational software called Trello as a way to prioritize and assign tasks and projects, both for myself and my team. It's an awesome tool that can be used on your phone or computer. It keeps me accountable for all projects.

I use Slack as a way to communicate with my different departments and team members. Slack integrates with Trello, so communication and productivity are in sync.

I use Skype and Zoom when communicating with suppliers, students, and business partners. I may also use WeChat when working with Chinese suppliers.

I'll use G Suite to handle my emails, storage, forms, SOP's, and presentations.

For reporting, I use the Shopify, Facebook and Google Analytics reporting dashboards, and Excel.

I'll use Canva or Photoshop for images and graphics that I can do myself and are urgent. I will have my designer do ninety-five percent of the other graphic and artistic work.

To manage social media automation I use Hootsuite. This allows me to reduce the number of hours that I spend on social media and I can literally plan a month of content in one day.

For email marketing, I use Klaviyo not only to send customer emails but also to provide automated flows based on actions my customers take and whatever segments they fall into.

For advertising, I use Facebook, Google & YouTube, Twitter, TikTok, Snapchat, Pinterest, and whatever new platform comes up after the writing of this book. You must adapt to what is working and where the market is headed. Who knows, at the time of you reading this book, TikTok and Snapchat might be obsolete.

I also use a company called Criteo to help remarket my products across other high-profile websites. It again helps because it follows my warm traffic around the web, those people that were on the fence but did not buy.

For capturing leads on my website, I use a tool called Wheelio or depending on the brand; I may use Optimonk.

If I am doing in-house fulfillment, I will use Shipstation to help me manage my orders and streamline my fulfillment.

To track taxes in individual states, you can use Taxjar. I used Quickbooks for my accounting when I first started. I have now outsourced this task to a tax accountant as I grew bigger.

For helping with referral marketing, I use Referral Candy or Refersion. Both are awesome ways to allow customers to refer others to your business in exchange for rewards and commissions.

For gathering customer reviews, I use Yotpo or Loox. Loox is what allowed me to drive crazy engagement with photos during the scaling of the dog sneakers.

Google Analytics allows me to track everything that happens on my site. It is a free tool and is very easy to integrate with your e-commerce store.

For print-on-demand companies, I use Shineon, Customcat, Printful, Viralstyle, Gearbubble, Teelaunch, Pillow Profits, and whatever other companies exist that provide new and innovative products.

SMS marketing has become huge over the past few years and it is a great way to sell through text. I use SMS Bump.

If you are selling high-ticket products, Afterpay is a great option to allow customers the flexibility to buy what they want today and pay over time.

Fiverr is an awesome marketplace for helping you outsource tasks for pennies on the dollar. You can also use Freelancer or Freeeup. You can run competitions and get multiple different entries and choose the one you like the best. This is great for tasks such as creating a logo.

I use Clickfunnels when I want to run sales funnels and really maximize my average order value.

Vitals is another great Shopify app that combines 40 different apps in one.

And finally, Dropbox is great for storing large documents and sharing information.

These are just some of the tools I use in my business and very helpful when scaling and growing a company. I may or may not move away from these tools over the course of time, as there is always something better that comes on the market. I am always looking for the next tool to help me get more efficient in my business. For special discounts on these tools, visit the resources section of this book at EcommerceActivated.com/resources.[71]

RAISING CAPITAL

There may come a time when you'll need to raise capital because you are trying to do something beyond your current financial position. Don't worry, you are not the first and you won't be the last. This is actually a good sign because it shows you are not afraid to expand and take your business to new levels. If we are not growing, we are fading, and we never want to contract our business, but rather we want to expand it.

You may want to hire more people, so you can remove yourself from the day-to-day operations, grow into new markets, diversify your product range, buy inventory to carry you through a busy season, or create your own manufacturing base—whatever the reason it is important you way up the pros and cons.

Here are some questions to ask:
- Do you know why you want the capital?
- Do you want to give up an equity stake?
- What are the repayment terms?
- How much will the loan cost?

- What is the contingency plan?

The following are options available so you can raise capital and gain strategic partnerships to help you finance and grow:

- Partners - Family, Friends, Mentors, Business Professionals.
- Paypal - https://www.paypal.com/workingcapital/.[72]
- Kabbage - https://www.kabbage.com/.[73]
- Stripe Funding Circle - https://stripe.com/works-with/fundingcircle.[74]
- Kickstarter - https://www.kickstarter.com.[75]
- Indiegogo - https://www.indiegogo.com.[76]
- Ideas.me - https://www.idea.me/.[77]
- Shopify Capital - https://www.shopify.com/capital.[78]

Regarding business partners, I am not a financial expert, so I will tell you to speak to a financial advisor because I have heard many stories about entrepreneurs who worked so hard to build their business from the ground up, only to have it ruined by finances and/or bad business partners. Whenever you move to acquire knowledge, the first step is always finding someone who has done what you are looking to achieve. Choose your circle wisely.

WORKING WITH PARTNERS

There are a lot of entrepreneurs who like to have complete control of their business and, as a result, want to keep one hundred percent ownership of the company. Other entrepreneurs, especially those who want to remove themselves from the operations to focus on other ventures, will give up equity stake by bringing in experts in exchange for equity share and profits splits. I also know entrepreneurs who start businesses with friends and family members, and therefore I think this is an important section in which we deal with the harsh truths of making a business partnership work.

We have all heard of someone who has had a bad business partnership. Even look at marriage as an example, which is essentially a partnership of two people — one in three marriages fail in the US.[79] I think people often rush into a partnership, not fully understanding one another and not being open and honest with how the partnership should run. When this happens, it has the potential to unravel in a way that leads to legal consequences. One way to avoid becoming another statistic is by focusing on setting very clear and agreeable partnership rules.

Seven Tips for Making A Business Partnership Work:

Share the same vision: Do you and the potential partner share the same values and vision for the company? What would have had to happen in the business for both of you to say this was a job well done?

Complement each other: You want to find a partner that complements your skills. Let's say you love computers and working on the technology. You really enjoy coding, making funnels, all of the technical aspects of e-commerce. You don't really like to be on camera and prefer working in the background. The ideal partner would complement your skills by being someone who loves being on camera, passionate about marketing and sales and is all about creating brand awareness. Now, both of you have specialized skills, and those skills work congruently to add value on the front and back end of the business.

Proven track record: Does the person you are going into business with have a track record of success? What knowledge can they bring to the table and what makes them an expert? Are they vetted as someone who is trustworthy and a person with integrity and authenticity? Take the time to do your research before you make any decisions.

Define roles: You may agree on the vision and the end goal, but if you and your partner(s) are not clear on the individual roles, you'll have lost before you've even begun. By being upfront with very clear and specific duties and responsibilities, everyone is clear on each other's roles to the success of the partnership. Most of the time, if the roles are not defined, then arguments and resentment will begin before you even attempt to build the shared vision. By creating clear roles and responsibilities, you'll also see how they flow naturally into the organizational chart hierarchy.

Business structures: How do you want the partnership to be structured? There are plenty of options, limited liability partnership, S-Corp, C-Corp, etc. Each has its advantages and disadvantages in terms of risk, liability, and tax. Speak to an advisor or attorney to find the best structure for you.

Put it in writing: It's all amazing and exciting to share a glass of champagne and toast success, but unless you get everything down on paper and signed, none of it is legally binding. Put time into creating a professional contract and have everyone agree and sign on the partnership details.

Be honest: Most partnerships come to an end if partners are not 100 percent clear on the vision and where the company is heading. By having frank and open discussions early, it helps deal with the issues early on. If you feel you are no longer inspired by the partnership, or you feel someone else has lost their passion or is not doing their part, having open and honest communication is necessary before it spills down into the lower chain of commands.

BENEFITS GRANTS & SUBSIDIES

Who loves free money? Most business owners are unaware of the grants, subsidies, and benefits available to support their business, whether at a local or domestic level. Even if you are making enough money, you should never turn down help or any type of grant in your state or country. A simple Google search will tell you what local funding opportunities and benefits are available for your business.

2020 was a rough year for everyone, so much so that governments around the world gave stimulus checks and relief to their citizens and business owners. Times might be good for you right now, but that doesn't mean that the money or help won't be used in the future. It's important to build those relationships now and invest the time to find out what is available out there. Put the ego aside and grab that free aid.

An example in Ireland is the Enterprise Ireland board.[80] Enterprise Ireland is the government organization responsible for the development and growth of Irish enterprises in world markets. They work in partnership with Irish enterprises to help them start, grow, innovate, and win export sales in global markets. There will be an equivalent in your country.

ASSETS THAT ADD VALUE

I spoke earlier about building a business the right way, with an eye on long-term success, and making it attractive to investors if you ever decide to sell it down the line. One mistake people make is they do not build assets in their business. In this chapter, I am going to show you how you can do it. I went through the process and it helped me tremendously when I went to sell my store.

The goal should always be to build something from nothing; something that has value and will help the company in the short, medium and long-term.

Too many people take shortcuts and end up having nothing when it is all said and done. What I mean is they will see some success with initial sales, but because of poor management and short-sightedness, there will be nothing left of value in the end. Perhaps, they didn't keep an eye on finances, or they never kept looking for new products to sell, or they didn't build an email list.

An asset in my eyes, is anything that benefits or adds value to a business, whether tangible or intangible. So, as you saw in the previous quadrants, we were starting to gain momentum as we tested more products and started to find what customers really wanted to buy. Along with this momentum comes the need to grow and evolve.

Trust me; I wish I knew about the importance of building assets sooner. I got a little excited in my first six months of business, especially when I was making sales as I slept.

As Charles Darwin says, "it's not the strongest that survive but the ones that can best adapt to change." Now imagine something happens in your business, whether due to internal or external factors—How quickly can you adapt?

Throughout this chapter, we are going to talk about building assets and why you should begin as quickly as possible, no matter how small they may be at first. It is something that a lot of people fail to do or at least leave it very late.

Building assets is something that your entire company has to do together and hold each other accountable to achieve—from the CEO on down.

While generating sales is awesome and fun, you have to think long-term and you must, as I keep mentioning, start with this question: What is the long-term goal for this new business?

Some questions you need to ask yourself:

- What does my business look like with $100,000 in monthly sales?
- Who do I need to hire?
- How will I manage customer support?
- How do I finance scaling?
- Where will my business be located?
- What is the organizational chart going to look like?
- What is the procedure for finding human capital?

I break assets into four types:

- Fixed Assets
- Monetary Assets
- Digital Assets
- Physical Assets

Fixed Assets: Let's start with fixed assets. The good thing with e-commerce is that you can run your business remotely in the initial early stages of growth, for the most part. This is one of the other reasons why so many people have decided to start an e-commerce business. I know people running six and seven-figure stores from their parent's basement.

If you've read the book *Made in America* by Sam Walton, founder of Walmart, you'll know that they too started with a drop-ship model. (Shipping directly from the manufacturer to end customer)

The first phase of your business will usually be drop-shipping from a supplier. A customer buys from your store and your supplier ships the product directly to your customer.

Essentially, you don't hold any inventory and you push complex supply chain responsibilities onto the supplier. It's much better this way and frees up a lot of time and capital in the early stages of growth.

This means you do not need the traditional expenses of having a large warehouse, rent, forklifts, machinery, packaging materials, warehouse workers, and what not.

Having said that, your supplier can be seen as an asset in an indirect way. Finding great suppliers is hard and when you find the right one, they are golden. So, treat them like an integral part of your business.

Through experience and trial and error, I have found some of the most talented and hardworking suppliers in the marketplace and know most on a first-name basis. If you go to my website or resources section, I will be able to share some of my connections with you.

As you scale though, plan for growth and expansion because along with a lot of revenue comes the need to build a real organization.

When you do, ask yourself:
- Where are you going to have your office located?
- What are the expenses?
- How can you cut costs?
- Can you leverage local tax laws?

Look around you to maybe a family member, partner, or friend. Try and strategically think about where you can locate an office or warehouse that can handle growth.

My friend Jonathan has his e-commerce office in Miami, which is a fantastic location as it has a massive shipping port for imports and exports, good tax laws, and on the East Coast of the United States.

Bear in mind that if your buildings are rented or leased, they are registered under liabilities in your chart of accounts.

Another idea when launching your business is to find partners that complement you. Let's say you are really good at marketing but terrible at logistics. Well, why not partner with someone you know who owns a considerable amount of assets but lacks the knowledge to launch a business.

I'm sure they would want to put their assets, land, or buildings to good use. Make sure with every partnership that there is an equal benefit for both partners.

Monetary Assets: The next asset is monetary. Just like any business, it needs capital. Having cash on hand to meet the weekly expenses is key. Luckily with our business model, we do not have to buy inventory upfront. We only pay for our products once the orders are made in our store. You can also work deals with your suppliers if cash is tight.

It's also incredibly important to separate your personal and business finances. It becomes important for your accounting and of course, paying taxes at the end of the year.

The IRS (if you are in the USA) will need their piece of the pie. I recommend consulting with your local accountant.

A good book I recommend is *Profit First* by Mike Michalowicz. His book is quite interesting as he talks about taking profit first in your business and then allocating what's left to various accounts.

What I like to do is daily reporting on my profit and loss statement. That's right; I want to know at all times where my money is coming in and going out. There are many ways to do this, with good old-fashioned Excel or through various online apps that can sync to your e-commerce store.

Cash is, of course, an asset. Be frugal with your finances and only spend money on things that add value to your company and bottom line. Most businesses run lean for a few years.

In my case, I would much prefer to spend available cash on acquiring more customers and top talent than on fancy equipment and the latest technology that does not produce a return on investment.

What you will notice later is this: As you scale, you will require more capital. So, think long-term and think about how you can get your hands on more capital and credit.

Digital Assets: Digital assets are important, and you should start creating them from day one. There is no doubt that we are living in a digital world where most if not all data is now stored online.

Since e-commerce is online, it is not surprising that there are a lot of systems, processes, and protocols that you need to implement and be held accountable for managing.

People are only as good as the training and information they are given. Employing a top-level college graduate is only beneficial if you adequately train them and provide them with a suitable onboarding process.

As you start and scale a business, people will come and go. In fact, you will fire more people than you think. It is the nature of the business. Some people are just not suitable or lack the drive and passion for what you are trying to achieve.

Therefore, it is important that you have your existing employees (and you) focus on a documentation process. If someone quit in the morning, how fast could someone new in that specific role take the reins.

It is going to happen! And don't stress; people come and go in and out of your life. Often the people that you think are suitable for your business never end up being a good fit.

One great app that most businesses use is Google Workspace. It has a number of different apps like Google Slides, Google Docs, and Google Drive as a way to manage your documentation and standard operating procedures (SOPs).

What it allows you to do is keep all of your digital assets in one location, which can be easily shared amongst team members freely.

Here are some examples of digital assets:

- **Email list:** The money is in the list. A large email list is what investors like to see, and this almost "free" traffic is going to carry you over during those poor-performing ad days. Data suggests that, on average, businesses can earn $44 for every dollar spent on email marketing, and the average conversion rate for landing page traffic sent through email is 6.05 percent. Start by adding a pop-up to capture emails on your website. Nurture your subscriber through a sequence of emails until they become a buyer. Do not be afraid to email your list.[81]

- **Company org chart:** Communication is key! How do you ensure communication and a chain of command amongst your team? Start creating an org chart, so everyone knows their role and who they report to.

- **Company onboarding process:** How fast can you take new hires from knowing nothing about your company to value-adding team players who crush every single deliverable. Empower people through the best documentation and onboarding process. Another great tip is to have some of your best employees write the company documentation; once complete, have input from the rest of the team in ensuring it is updated monthly or whenever needed.

- **Brand guidelines:** How do you want your brand to be represented. Stay consistent by ensuring your employees know the mission, brand ethos, and specific branding whether its color, font, or tone.

- **Mission statement:** Your mission statement is also a type of asset. It is unique to you. How do you want people to feel when they think about your brand?

- **Customer FAQ:** You are going to have questions from prospective buyers. How do you efficiently and effectively give them the information they need. Often having a FAQ on your site leads to a reduced number of customer emails and a higher customer satisfaction rate.

- **Privacy policy:** This is important for consumer protection.

- **Refund policy:** Customers may not purchase unless they know your refund policy.

- **Terms of service:** Another important legal page needed on your site.

- **Product pricing:** Product pricing is another important document you need. How does pricing change during promotions? Who keeps track of it? What is the impact on profit margins?

- **Inventory stock list:** How accurate are you forecasting future demand. Will you have enough inventory at your supplier, or if you are doing in-house fulfillment, how soon will you have to replenish your stock?

- **Customer service templates:** Be efficient by typing up email responses to the most common questions that require the same response. The goal should be to have a consistent theme, for example, in the way you correspond with your customers. A common customer query is, "Where is my order?" Instead of having your customers receive different responses, why not automate and have a consistent message that aligns with company standards. By automating this process, the response can be copied from a document and tailored slightly depending on the specifics. Not only are you delivering consistent and clear messages for the best customer experience, but you are also getting more output from the same number of hours from your customer support team.

- **Company & store how to's:** Other important documents are the "how to" procedures? You can add video links to the documents through the loom software. This helps your teammates search Google Drive for the SOPs that will allow them to perform various tasks. This is useful because you may have remote workers and your language may not be their native language, so video reduces that language barrier.

- **Product videos:** Another great idea is taking customer reviews, company videos, or videos of your products and storing them in your drive so they can be repurposed for marketing.

- **Product descriptions:** Product descriptions are also key as they act as the selling force behind the product. Have someone on your team who loves to write, or hire someone who knows about SEO and how to bring organic traffic using keywords.

- **Design files:** I don't know how many times I have looked for old designs but failed to locate them. If you are working with designers, ensure they load their final files to your database and not theirs. It is your asset not theirs. Down the line, if one design becomes extremely valuable, that designer might request they be paid a royalty, so be sure you own the asset files.

- **Product PDFs:** Some products need PDF's. Designing a great PDF can help sell your product, especially if it requires training or is a high-ticket item.

- **Company branding:** Another great digital asset is your brand guidelines. Sharing it with staff allows you to ensure the company is represented how you want.

- **Presentations:** You, or someone at your company, may be giving presentations at events or online so be sure to record it. By doing this, down the line investors or people interested in your company can see the story of your company play out over time. People want to see a story, and they are investing in the person and their track record in most cases.

- **Social media pages:** This is huge. When I launched my dog products, I built a Facebook dog page with over one hundred thousand dog lovers. This allowed me to attract millions of impressions to my site and build a brand by positioning me as a leader in the dog apparel space.

- **Investor docs:** If you plan on selling your business, investors will want to see a number of different documents. They range from profit and loss to income statements to trademarks and other intellectual property. Start preparing and updating as you go through each year.

These were just some examples of digital assets. You can assign the management of these tasks to someone who loves systems and documentation. Most likely, this would be the responsibility of the Chief Operating Officer to delegate.

Again, this is why it is important to understand people's values. People will gladly work on the things that they are inspired by and will tend to drift and avoid responsibility on items that do not align with their highest values.

Every month digital assets need to be updated or as soon as a major change occurs.

By creating more digital assets like SOPs, you become more reliant on systems and less reliant on people.

Physical assets: The last assets are physical assets. As mentioned before, our model of e-commerce does not require us to buy or store inventory upfront. As we decide to expand our business and perhaps take control of our own inventory and shipping process, we will take on more physical assets.

Any physical asset is something you can see or touch—tables, chairs, computers etc. Don't be afraid to buy used if you are on a budget. Or, if you are buying new, you can leverage credit cards—though proceed with caution—to gain points for business expenses. When I bought my laptops, cameras, and displays, it was all bought through American Express. As a side note, my advertising spend gives me triple points on every dollar I spend, which allows me to acquire massive amounts of points that can be used to travel for free and so forth.

So why am I telling you to start building assets? Because e-commerce moves quickly. With digital marketing, you can basically scale as aggressively as you like. While a traditional brick and mortar shop will only ever have the sales relative to its physical store traffic, an e-commerce store can push the boundaries to all corners of the Earth and when you scale, you must be in a good position asset-wise.

Summary:
- Start building company assets from day one.
- Company assets can be fixed, digital, physical, or financial.
- Everyone on your team needs to be part of the asset building.

- Create SOPs for every task in your company.
- Documentation and systems are used to create a blueprint for how the business is run.
- Become more reliant on systems and less reliant on people.
- If you decide to sell your company in years to come, company assets will need to be accounted for in detail.

BUILDING A COMPANY PLAYBOOK

"How does this process work?" I asked my virtual assistant. She had just asked for time off last week, which I agreed to, but I was only now realizing that I would be the one covering for her. You see, I completely forgot to find her replacement and now I was playing catch up before she left for the weekend.

Stephanie was the head of product fulfillment, and we had a backlog of orders going into the weekend. The sweat began to form on my forehead. As you have already read, if there is one thing that I obsess over in my business, it is my complete focus towards utter customer satisfaction. When it comes to product fulfillment, I do not want any delayed shipments. If I say a product will arrive in five days, I want it to be one day early.

"Oh, it's very easy," she said. "Let's jump on a quick video call." We jumped on the call and to my dismay, it was anything but easy. You see, it might have been easy for her; she had managed that role for over a year. As we went through the screen share, I knew it was going to be anything but easy.

Then I remembered back to my corporate days, where everything had a system and process, with a directly responsible individual (DRI) and a backup person. I knew I had deviated from what I had learned over the years. I was running too fast to know that my business had zero processes and systems.

It was time to change. I needed processes. I needed systems. I needed documentation that outlined how my entire business ran. And finally, I needed a system for cover in case someone was sick or on vacation.

I managed to get through that weekend of order fulfillment; it wasn't pretty but I pushed through. The following Monday morning I had a meeting with my team. We needed to document and systemize everything to avoid issues like this happening in the future. It was at that moment; we went on a spree of document creation that told us how things got done, why they got done, who did what, and who was the backup cover in their absence.

The documents are known as standard operating procedures (SOPs). "A standard operating procedure is a set of instructions that describes all the relevant steps and activities of a process or procedure. Standard operating procedures are essential to an organization to deliver consistent, measured, high-quality responses to complex and unpredictable events." – IBM[82]

Since we are in quadrant four of ESF, it is where we take everything you and your team have learned thus far and document it. We also plan for the future, acquire knowledge, and document it for different scenarios that may arise in the future. We also look back at the things we may have missed and overlooked in our post mortem analysis.

One thing I want you to get from this chapter is that any business (traditional or online) is essentially a bunch of systems. You may not need to know them all, but it's important you are at least aware of the impact one system has on the next.

If tomorrow, Facebook changed the way they track sales, would you be able to adjust your Facebook marketing in line with their new standards? Or a more generic and simple analogy is building with Legos. How does each block of your business fit together to build the finished product?

When creating SOPs it is important to note that it is not final documentation but something that is continuously refined over time so that others can edit, improve, learn and build upon, without having to repeatedly train or make assumptions on how the business operates.

Now you may be saying, Damien, this has nothing to do with e-commerce. Why do I need to care about systems and boring documentation? Well, it does. Just like any real business, you need to have systems, processes, technology, and people all working together in sync.

If you are just starting, chances are you are wearing multiple hats in the business and find the day-to-day running of your business overwhelming. In quadrant three, we talked about scaling and how overwhelming but rewarding it can get. If you have gone through a large scale, you'll know how busy it can get. Imagine if you could document it so that next time you are prepared and you are in a position to be proactive rather than reactive.

One of the reasons we read is to acquire knowledge so that we can become better at what we do. The goal is to not always learn from a person's successes but learn from their mistakes. The same applies to your business. My goal for you is to alleviate some of that strain by building a plan of record or blueprint at which others can take up some of that responsibility.

If you have no record, then how do you expect the business to make sales and continue to function. If you have no playbook, no marketing plan, no sales strategies, then you are essentially running your business without structure and formality.

Coming from a corporate background gave me a headstart in my entrepreneurial career. I worked for seven years in a company obsessed with documentation. As a result, when I launched my first e-commerce store, I immediately started to document and record everything I did. Why? Well, because I knew at some point I would either no longer want to keep doing tasks I was uninspired by, or I would become far too busy with more important high-priority tasks.

This obsession with building systems and documentation was one of the reasons I was able to sell one of my main stores to hungry investors after building it from the ground up. The buyer loved how I documented every single part of the business as if it could run without my existence. I had also retained my day one employees up until that point, and they were happy to move to the new owner as a part of the agreement.

You have to remember that when people buy businesses, they are buying more than the brand! They are buying the intellectual property, the people, the systems, the email list, the customers, future forecasted revenue and much more. Just like any successful business like Apple or Amazon, they have documents, rules, procedures, mission statements, customer service scripts, etc and so should you.

The ultimate goal of quadrant four is to semi remove yourself from the business. Essentially, you want to become more of a leader and visionary and less of an operator and worker.

How do you remove yourself from the business? One way is to document, systemize, and structure it so that it can run efficiently without you being present in the day-to-day business.

Questions you need to ask yourself before designing a playbook/SOP?

- How do your customers see your company and how do you want to portray your brand?
- How well do you service your customers and clients?
- How do you hire and bring on new employees when they join?
- How do you launch your marketing and sales campaigns?
- What are your company's privacy, refund, and terms of service policies?
- If you went on a week vacation, would your team run the business without your guidance?

These are just some of the many questions that need answering. In short, what is your documentation process for success across the business? How can you make your business as predictable as possible?

There are a few advantages to having a company playbook:

- You can onboard new hires very quickly.
- You save time, resources, and capital.

- You become more efficient and predictable in how you run your organization.
- If you decide to sell or attract funding, investors will be delighted to see you invested in building a company playbook.
- You set a standard for excellence.
- You can pivot easily.
- It gives you, the CEO and founder, leverage to work on other things.
- Once you design the initial playbook, it can be updated by employees and refined as the business changes.
- You are impartial by involving everyone in the documentation process.
- You get input from all the team members, which fosters culture, growth, and empowerment.

I suggest building a number of different playbooks:

Marketing Playbook: This will list everything you do to attract and drive customers to your business. It might be all of the organic marketing strategies like social media management and all of the paid marketing like Facebook, Google Ads and so forth.

Sales Playbook: It might be the sales scripts that you use for live website chat.

Company Playbook: This is a guide to your company —what it does and why. It usually includes a company overview, company history, what you do for your customers, how you engage with your customers, your mission and value statements and how you operate. It can also include the brand guidelines.

Operations Playbook: This details how you run your organization and it should include sub-categories like fulfilment where you show how you ship your products to your customers via your supply chain. A playbook can be created on a Google Doc or Microsoft word document starting off. In the document I would include the following information. Below is an example of a Facebook ads playbook that would fall under the category Sales & Marketing.

Playbook Name: Facebook Ads
    Department: Marketing
    Date Document Created: 1/1/2020
    Date Last Updated: 12/05/2020
    Revision Made: Added CBO campaigns
    Extractor: Joe Bloggs
    Document Writer: Damien Coughlan
    Status: Live
    Version: V2

Purpose: To easily create, launch, and manage Facebook ads for the customer acquisition and scaling of the business. By having a Facebook ads playbook, the company is able to test new products faster, leverage the correct audiences and pixel data already built, and therefore increase profit margins and remove top-level management from the daily process. Through time, we learn what ads work best in our business, why not document it, and refine it rather than reinvent the wheel every time you launch a new ad.

Resources: Resource Document Number 1: How to launch a Facebook ad in 10 steps. Resource Document Number 2: How to scale Facebook ads and the different types of scaling. References: e.g ., a list to all our Facebook targeting and audiences.

Playbook backlog: This is to be used when a new enhancement has been introduced by Facebook and the documents need to be updated.

Video Resources: Different videos showing a screenshare of document number 1 and 2 above.

Final Check: Has a member of the team approved the playbook and has someone new tried following the steps inside the procedures. If so, is it pushed to live and is it now used throughout the company.

Now, this is just a rough example; I will include some more detailed examples on my site. I highly recommend you to start listing all of your company tasks and setting a priority against each one so you can start the process of creating a standard operating procedure for each.

You will typically have 5 phases to creating a Playbook:

Phase 1: Extraction
- Identify why this information is needed to help the business.
- Identify who has knowledge of the particular business process, such as customer service.
- What particular information is needed, is it partial or complete?

- Decide how you want to extract the information from the subject matter expert: Video or screen share, Google doc or Word doc, face-to-face or old school pen and paper?
- Pick a time and date at which the extraction should take place.

Phase 2: Recording

- For some businesses, recording live is a perfect opportunity to get the best footage. It could be while the subject matter expert is performing their role.
- For others, they prefer quietness and it is usually done in an interview style process.

Phase 3: Documentation

- Once you extract the information and record it, you must now document and edit it so that it makes sense to the person who is acquiring the information.
- I use Google Docs, Trello, video links, PDF's, infographics, and much more, depending on the nature of the content.

Phase 4: Review

- The review process is where the documentation is reviewed for completeness and release to the company. It will serve as a plan of record once it moves from draft to a live plan of record. As soon as the document is approved, it should be uploaded into your organization's drive or database and distributed to those who need it.

Phase 5: Updated

- The only constant is change. No playbook ever remains the same. Each time an update is needed, the document should be updated and renamed to a new version.
- It is important to make a copy and rename the new version so you have a plan of record of the changes made.
- You can list the specific changes made on each document and the author.

The main lesson you need to grab here is that if you have a process that is currently undocumented in your business, it is time to document it and make it available to everyone who needs it. If you ask your team right now, "How do you run social media for the week?" they should have a document they can hand to you describing the entire process.

Summary:

- An SOP is a set of step-by-step instructions compiled by an organization to help workers carry out complex routine operations. Standard operating procedures get down to specifics of how a task is to be accomplished.
- It helps you document the business so that you have control over each business process.
- The more structure and systemization in your business, the better it will function.
- Business is like building with Legos; each department connects with the other.

- Employees come and go; with SOPs you can hire and train people better and faster.
- With SOPs you can have more formality, predictability, and synchronization in your team and business operations.
- A SOP should be created for every process within each department of your organization.
- Involve subject matter experts (SMEs) in the creation of documents.
- There are a few key steps to effective SOP creation. Extraction, Recording, Documentation, Review, Updates.
- SOPs are most effective when you can combine a video showing a process in action with actionable steps, for example, launching a Facebook ad.

Finally, a company has three types of people who work in the business: Technicians (workers), managers, and the entrepreneur or CEO. Do your best to ensure that everyone is in agreement with the way documents, processes, and operating manuals are to be used. An SOP is useless unless it has the buy-in from everyone involved.

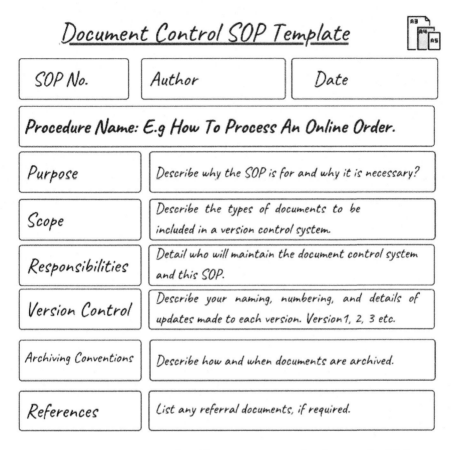

Figure 73 - An example of how to structure the design of a SOP.

INVEST IN AUTOMATION

Going back to my story of our family farm transformation. It would not work as well as it did if we did not have automation in place. Automation not only frees up your time but is also a lot less prone to human error. Your employees will also thank you, as it makes their life easier—especially for mundane and repetitive low-value, high-volume tasks.

For example, with Facebook ads, you don't want to be at your desk for twenty-four hours a day monitoring ad spend. You can set up automated conditional triggers that can make adjustments to your ads based on the metrics you define. I have seen people lose a lot of money by failing to create cost per acquisition (CPA) limits, for example, on their manual bidding ads. Look at your current business and write down every single task that you need to perform each week.

Identify the importance of each task and estimate the total amount of time it takes to complete, then find ways to automate and streamline if possible. If you don't feel like documenting the processes, hire someone to do a complete audit on your business and find the areas that need to be automated.

Everyone has heard of the saying, "there's an app for that!" A simple Google search will reveal a host of apps and tools to help you automate your business and life. The world is changing how we know it: We are moving into the era of artificial intelligence, autonomous driving, virtual reality, renewable energy, high-speed Internet, cryptocurrency, and blockchain. Keep those innovations in mind when thinking about the future of your business.

SELLING YOUR STORE

As mentioned throughout this book (and if you follow me on social media @damiencoughlan), I am always looking to build a brand asset whenever I take on a new opportunity.

The reason is that at the end of the day, I want to own something that is a sellable asset. After all, we are in the business of making money while also providing value in the marketplace.

Trust me; there are people and businesses out there that will snap your hand off for the right business. Everything from high-paid doctors who want to diversify their income streams to competitors that may want to buy you out.

At the beginning of the book, I spoke about starting with the end in mind. You have to know where you are going and to really understand what needs to get done on a daily, weekly, monthly, and yearly timeframe.

If I decide that I want to build an e-commerce business that can be sold in twelve to twenty-four months, then I need to perform activities that are conducive to that notion.

When I built my second store, I wasn't just building a website that sold products; I was building a brand that brought together communities, social media, a mission statement, products, data, and a returning customer into one idea.

Everything I did on a daily basis was an action that was geared toward increasing the brand equity of my business.

In this section, I am going to explain the process that I took in selling one of my e-commerce stores. What you will notice is I wasn't just selling my website—I was selling a brand.

I hope this section will give you the drive to start or pivot from just selling products to actually building a brand for long-term success.

Please note, it will be your decision whether to sell your business. Some people choose not to, but I was a first-time entrepreneur, and it was one of those things that I wanted to do. Yes, I sometimes regret that I didn't take it further, but I was also learning another valuable skill, which was to go with your gut instinct.

First, you'll need to think about the assets that make up a successful e-commerce business. Let's list out some of the components of a sellable asset, some of which we covered earlier:

- Website.
- Inventory.
- Customers.
- Email Subscribers.
- Social Media Followers.
- Employees.
- Standard Operating Procedures.
- Systems.
- Knowledge.
- Suppliers.
- Data.
- Domain.
- Intellectual Property.
- Supply Chain Management.

Every one of these items has to align with the bigger picture. Your employees must know what the vision is for the company, the products must represent the brand, the systems must help the employees, and the suppliers must ship top-quality products.

The following is a rough outline of the steps I took to sell the store.

Step 1: Identify a platform to attract buyers. There are a couple of ways you can sell your store.

Private: You can simply reach out to the people you think might be interested. A good way to find such people is in the big e-commerce groups where other sellers are members.

Platform Exchange: Platforms like Shopify have their own Exchange platform and they provide an easy way for you to sell your store. Since its launch, Exchange has attracted thousands of buyers searching for e-commerce businesses of all sizes.

Broker: Find a broker who has experience in your niche. A broker is a person or firm who arranges transactions between a buyer and a seller for a commission when the deal is executed. In my case, I paid a $1,500 retainer and qualified for a discounted commission structure: Eleven percent on the first $250,000 of any deal, ten percent on $250,000 to $500,000, and nine percent on $500,000 and up. I personally wanted to be removed from the process, as I still had a company to run and employees to support. My broker had a list of ten thousand potential buyers in his database.

Step 2: Clean up the current website.

Step 3: Manage Inventory.

Step 4: Financial Analysis.

- o Last three years of sales revenue.
- o Percent of growth per year.
- o Active wholesale accounts.
- o Number of customers, orders, and conversion percentage.

o Value of inventory on hand.

o Number of unique designs we owned.

o Monthly operating costs.

Step 5: Price your asset.

Step 6: Start selling.

Step 7: Negotiate.

Step 8: Communicate with your team.

Step 9: Letter of Intent.

Step 10: Due diligence process.

Step 11: Purchase agreement.

Step 12: Funds in escrow.

Step 13: Transfer of assets.

Step 14: Three Month Handover Period.

If you'd like help with selling your store, simply reach out to me on email or social media and I'll walk you through the strategies that I just listed here. I also have another free bonus for you at the following link EcommerceActivated.com/broker from my personal broker.

BUILDING YOUR EMPIRE CLOSING THOUGHTS

Summary: As you can see, this book was about more than just e-commerce. It was a deep insight into the world of entrepreneurship and how it looks like from idea generation right through to the systemization of your business. Building businesses is fun, but eventually, we all want to move to bigger and better things and more challenging projects. Your first business is a stepping-stone to the next and so forth.

This section in particular, was about building an empire. You cannot do it alone. Behind every great man is a great woman and vice versa. Behind every great entrepreneur is a great team. Behind every great team is a series of processes, systems and a common culture. If any of these interconnected assets fail, you cannot remove yourself from the daily operations of the business.

The reason we become entrepreneurs is because we have the creativity and mindset to think big and far. You cannot expand if you are concentrated on low-value, non-income producing activities. You must learn to delegate and outsource. Of course, you might have to wear multiple hats starting out, but quadrant four is where you want to end up.

You must make a decision to launch your business (quadrant one), you must find a great product to sell (quadrant two), and you must scale with people, processes, and technology (quadrant three). Once you have gone through these three phases, it then puts you in a position to take everything you have learned and map it out and delegate, so you can repeat the process in finding or launching the next successful product, but this time with you as an advisor/leader rather than the tactical operator (quadrant four).

This video link is an awesome interview with a friend of mine that goes into detail on how he structures and systemizes his operations for scale with people, processes, and technology. Access at: EcommerceActivated.com/systemize.

E-Commerce Success Framework

Quadrant 1 - Start	Quadrant 3 - Scale
• Learning	• Optimization
• Mindset & Focus	• Capital
• Planning	• People
Quadrant 2 - Sell	Quadrant 4 - Systemize
• Testing	• Systems
• Sales	• Processes
• Data	• Technology

Figure 74 - E-Commerce Success Framework.

Action Steps:

- Reaching level four of the quadrant is the final stage and is all about removing yourself from the tactical deliverables of the business. Are there currently tasks that you are performing that can be delegated so that you can concentrate on more pressing and important issues? Or would you like to completely remove yourself from the daily operations?

- Automation is great when it works and you know where to put the machine; what areas of your business need automation?

- Who are the key people operators in your business and which ones have the potential to become managers and leaders?

- Sit down with your employees to discover what they truly value and want.
- Start creating assets that add value to your business which ultimately leads to you building a valuable brand over time.
- Document the key processes in your business so you have a plan of record that anyone in the business can follow, execute and cover in times of need.

FINISH WHAT YOU STARTED

In the very first chapter of this book, we talked about starting with the end in mind. This is where you set the goals and objectives based on the end result. An example might be as follows: *In twelve months, your end goal is to generate $100,000 in sales in your e-commerce business.*

The importance of starting with the end in mind is that it allows you to work backwards to determine what it's going to take you to accomplish your goal.

Once you set the target or end goal, you need to work backwards to figure out the steps needed to achieve it. Now, you won't know all the steps at the beginning, but you'll get a high-level overview of where to start and what type of budget or resources you'll need.

While $100,000 in sales may seem like a giant goal, the truth is, it isn't. When you break it down into smaller pieces, it becomes much easier to comprehend. The hard part is the limiting belief that people experience in the early stages of entrepreneurship and business.

And if we're honest, $100,000 is easily obtained through the proper strategies of paid and organic traffic. Once you've identified the target, you have to set the wheels in motion and become committed.

Often the hardest thing is to get traction and take those initial baby steps. It may take a little extra effort to move the rock, but once it gets rolling, it becomes unstoppable.

Along your journey, you are going to get distracted. I know I did. Trust me, writing this book in Colombia on a very strict lockdown with major uncertainty has been challenging. But I see the vision. I see how this book can help thousands of people begin their e-commerce journey. I see the impact it can have on people whose businesses were affected because of the global pandemic of 2020 and how they can now move their business online.

I often wanted to quit and just take the easy way out, and just put my feet up and watch the news and fall into the trap of becoming a consumer rather than a producer. In troubled or challenging circumstances, it's important you step up to the plate. For me, I found the best time to write was early in the morning. The same applies when running my e-commerce stores. My mind is at its freshest in the early hours, and it is a fantastic way to start the day and get those tasks that you usually procrastinate out of the way.

Set aside a time each day if you are on a tight schedule. Most people who launch their business with me have family duties or additional work commitments.

You have to make it a priority in life. If you set the goal and you write it down, and you believe in it one hundred percent, there is a very strong chance that you will achieve it.

One of the biggest reasons people fail and give up is because they quit too early. There are a lot of distractions in today's world and it can be difficult to focus. Again, it goes back to remembering why you started and keeping the target you have in your mind.

If someone comes to you with a business idea, ignore it if it does not align with your vision. You have to be selfish. That does not mean you have to be totally cut off from the world but set clear boundaries.

You are also going to want to manage your resources and keep good people. That is why this quadrant four is so important because it teaches you how to systemize your business and remove yourself from a lot of the heavy lifting. If you think you can do everything yourself, you are mistaken.

Burnout is real and eventually, all those late nights of trying things yourself will catch up. Slow and steady wins the race. Find the right people to help you on your journey. Invest in yourself and find good mentors. In my first few years, I came across some difficult challenges and did not know what to do. After speaking to my mentor, those challenges all of a sudden didn't appear so big. He broke each one of them down for me and gave me a solid game plan on how to crush and overcome it.

I also want you to know that it is OK not to seek perfection. Quit trying to make everything perfect; this is one sure way you will not finish what you started.

Enjoy the process. It is a learning process, and it will challenge you. Every challenge can help make you a better person. Follow it with an open mind and don't feel as if you are not growing even if you are not seeing initial results. Again, track your achievements and progress and you'll be blown away by the things you've achieved.

One of the biggest reasons I recommend e-commerce as a business model is it teaches you pretty much everything you need to master in order to make money online. When you learn online skills, you become extremely valuable to the marketplace, and you can brand out into many other business models if you choose to do so. There may be billions of people that have social media accounts but a tiny percentage of people actually know how to run paid online advertising. We are moving to a digital world and if people do not adapt, they will get left behind.

What I've been able to do is not only build my own ecommerce brands but help others do the same. Being an expert (someone who has dedicated years of learning in the space) allows me to work with other companies to get their online stores up and running in the most effortless way possible.

The people who go through my mentorship from start to finish get equipped with knowledge, confidence, and experience to grow their business from start to finish.

It is a marathon, not a sprint and that is why I built my framework into four sections. Again, quadrant one is start, quadrant two is sell, quadrant three is scale, and quadrant four is systemise. I designed it in such a way because these are the major milestones to e-commerce success.

Realize that every day will bring new challenges. As I type this chapter, my student Seamus texted me to tell me that his advertising account got shut down. To him, it was a catastrophe; to me, it was just a minor setback. Throughout my years of experience, there are workarounds for everything and by tomorrow, Seamus will have had his appeal ruled in his favor to start back advertising. Sometimes we are at the mercy of others, especially billion-dollar companies who may inadvertently restrict you from advertising for no apparent reason. Have faith, take a deep breath, appeal the case and you will be ready to go again.

One of the best books I've ever read was *Think and Grow Rich* and in it, the author talks about stopping "three feet from gold."[83]

You may be closer to the finish line than you think. Too often, people give up. Building a business is hard; that is why so many people will settle for the average nine-to-five job, but I promise that you are capable of achieving anything you set your mind to. After reading this book, take that bit of fire inside you and write down on a piece of paper your top three goals for launching your e-commerce business. It will give you a sense of reality and something to pursue.

In this final chapter, I want you to finish what you came to do. If you have already launched your store but have not seen success, start connecting with people, join my online community, reach out to me, and ask me questions.

My mission is to help as many people around the world realize their goal and true potential of building a legitimate online business. E-commerce is the future, and it is time you activated your very own e-commerce business.

HOW TO GET MORE HELP

YOUR FREE TICKET

If there's one thing that I love to do, along with building my own successful businesses, it is to inspire and teach others how to replicate my success.

Along with the bonus videos that I have included throughout this book, I have also included a special and exclusive one-hour VIP training for those of you who have purchased my book.

I welcome you to attend this free one-hour training which goes into more details on the strategies I share inside this book.

Go to EcommerceActivated.com/ticket to watch your free training now. I can't guarantee the training will be up forever, so take advantage of it while it exists. This particular training is the perfect complementary asset to this book. Visit EcommerceActivated.com/ticket now.

HOW TO ACCESS YOUR BONUSES?

I've sprinkled throughout this book a number of free bonuses. These are training videos hosted on our website to accompany the content in the book. You'll see the links to the videos included throughout the chapters; however, here is a list of each one mentioned in the book for quick reference below.

How to Launch A Successful E-Commerce Business (Case Study)

How one of my students launched their online business with e-commerce and grew to over six figures. This is a particularly powerful story and shows you how anyone can launch a successful online business with zero experience and little to no startup costs.

Access at: EcommerceActivated.com/start

How to Find Viral E-Commerce Products

Watch me over the shoulder as I show you how I perform product research at a high level. Product research is required to find those "pockets of gold" that will help you discover what products are selling in the marketplace and what people are actually searching for.

Access at: EcommerceActivated.com/sell

How to Scale with Digital Marketing

This video breaks down the system that is digital marketing and how you can replicate it to either start or scale your business online. This is a fantastic overview of how big social networks operate and how they leverage data.

Access at: EcommerceActivated.com/scale

Systemizing Your Business at A High level

This is an awesome interview with a friend of mine that goes into detail on how he structures and systemizes his operations for scale with people, processes, and technology.

Access at: EcommerceActivated.com/systemize.

Client Results

If you are curious about some of the results and happy customers who have implemented our strategies, I've compiled a list of screenshots and videos celebrating their wins. Feel free to check these out to inspire you towards what's possible.

Access at: EcommerceActivated.com/success.

Broker Video

In this video, my personal broker, who helped me sell one of my stores gives a really valuable presentation where he outlines the process of how to sell your store and what to expect.

Access at: EcommerceActivated.com/broker.[84]

What's Working Now

My latest strategies today on what is working in the industry and how you can take advantage and implement in your business.

Access at: EcommerceActivated.com/ticket.[85]

SPEAK TO US

If you would like help implementing the strategies and secrets in this book and to help you start or scale your e-commerce business, I invite you to speak with us. You can go right now to EcommerceActivated.com/speak.[86]

There will be a short application asking a few simple questions that allows us to find out more about you and your business or business idea. (This allows us to review your answers and be prepared for the call)

Simply answer the questions and on the following page, you'll see a calendar with available dates and times for you to select and book your call.

Once you book your call, the confirmation page will have instructions on how to best prepare for your call. Please review carefully.

Watch the video as it gives you an insight into what it is like working with us. You can also check some of the case studies from our clients.

Once on the call, my team will take a look at where you are at and some of the issues or challenges you are facing, and if we can help or not.

If we can help, we will show you what it looks like to work with us to grow your business; you can then decide if it is a good fit for you or not.

No pressure, regardless, you are going to get a lot of advice, clarity, and an actionable plan to move your business or idea forward.

Go to EcommerceActivated.com/speak to book your call today.

ABOUT THE AUTHOR

 Damien Coughlan was born and raised in Ireland on a family farm in the beautiful county of Cork. Growing up on the farm with his parents, two brothers, and two sisters taught him a lot about entrepreneurship and what hard work, determination, and focus can bring.

Damien has a marketing degree and an e-commerce master's degree from the Cork Institute of Technology and University College Cork, respectively. Damien spent ten years in the corporate world working for some of the biggest companies in the world, most notably Apple, where he was a business analyst based out of Silicon Valley, California, USA.

Damien turned to entrepreneurship in 2016, where he launched his first online business selling dog products. He instantly became a success and started to teach others how to leverage the power of e-commerce and social media.

Damien's inspiration is his father, Gerard, and mother, Mary. One of Damien's missions is to help educate thousands of people online and help businesses transition from brick and mortar to online.

You can visit him online at damiencoughlan.com and on social media @damiencoughlan. You can also open your cell phone camera and scan the below codes. It will automatically send you to the QR code destination.

Website

Facebook Group

Instagram

Twitter

YouTube

Facebook

END NOTES

¹ Statista, "Statista," 2021. [Online]. Available: https://www.statista.com/statistics/379046/worldwide-retail-e-commerce-sales/.

² Wikipedia, https://en.wikipedia.org/wiki/Retail_apocalypse.

³ "Facebook Audience Insights," Facebook, [Online]. Available: https://www.facebook.com/business/insights/tools/audience-insights.

⁴ "Shopify Themes," [Online]. Available: https://themes.shopify.com/.

⁵ J. Biggs, "Tech Crunch," 2018. [Online]. Available: https://techcrunch.com/2018/08/17/movado-group-acquires-watch-startup-mvmt/.

⁶ E.-C. Damien's reviews, "E-Commerce Activated," [Online]. Available: http://ecommerceactivated.com/success.

⁷ "Oberlo," [Online]. Available: https://oberlo.com/

⁸ "Dropified," [Online]. Available: https://dropified.com/.

⁹ Blendjet, https://blendjet.com/.

¹⁰ "Dollar Fulfillment," [Online]. Available: https://dollarfulfillment.com/.

¹¹ A. S. Humphrey, "Wikipedia," [Online]. Available: https://en.wikipedia.org/wiki/Albert_S._Humphrey.

[12] A. M. a. J. C. George Doran, "CCE.Bard.EDU," 1981. [Online]. Available: https://cce.bard.edu/files/Setting-Goals.pdf.

[13] D. J. DeMartini, The Values Factor: The Secret to Creating an Inspired and Fulfilling Life, 2013.

[14] Shopify, "Shopify," 2021. [Online]. Available: https://www.shopify.com/future-of-commerce/2021.

[15] E.-C. Start Bonus, "E-Commerce Activated," [Online]. Available: http://ecommerceactivated.com/start.

[16] M. Schmidt, "Discover Magazine," 2019. [Online]. Available: https://www.discovermagazine.com/planet-earth/dogs-and-their-owners-share-similar-personality-traits.

[17] 2017-2018 U.S. Pet Ownership & Demographics Sourcebook , "Avma," 2018. [Online]. Available: https://www.avma.org/resources-tools/reports-statistics/us-pet-ownership-statistics.

[18] "Pet Food Industry," 2016. [Online]. Available: https://www.petfoodindustry.com/articles/5695-report---say-pets-are-part-of-the-family.

[19] "Google Trends," [Online]. Available: https://trends.google.com/trends.

[20] "Similar Web Tool," [Online]. https://www.similarweb.com/

[21] "Fashionnova Clothing," [Online]. Available: https://fashionnova.com/.

[22] "Pinterest," [Online]. Available: https://www.pinterest.com/.

[23] "ASD Marketweek," [Online]. Available: https://asdonline.com/.

[24] "Teespring Company," [Online]. Available: https://teespring.com/.

[25] "CustomCat Company," [Online]. Available: https://customcat.com/.

[26] "Gearbubble Company," [Online]. Available: https://gearbubble.com/.

[27] "Teelaunch Company," [Online]. Available: https://teelaunch.com/.

[28] "Pillow Profits Company," [Online]. Available: https://pillowprofits.com/.

[29] "Viralstyle Company," [Online]. Available: https://viralstyle.com/.

[30] "Facebook Ad Library," [Online]. Available: https://www.facebook.com/ads/library.

[31] "Youtube," [Online]. Available: https://www.youtube.com/intl/en-GB/about/press/.

[32] S. Walton, Book, "Made in America", 1992.

[33] "Sem Rush," [Online]. Available: https://www.semrush.com/.

[34] E.-C. Sell Bonus Training, "E-Commerce Activated," [Online]. Available: http://ecommerceactivated.com/sell.

[35] "Shopify," [Online]. Available: https://www.shopify.com/.

[36] "Retail Dive," [Online]. Available: https://www.retaildive.com/news/wal-mart-snags-shoescom-domain-for-9m/440773/.

[37] "Lean Domain Search," [Online]. Available: https://leandomainsearch.com/.

[38] G. d'Aboville, "Klaviyo," [Online]. Available: https://www.klaviyo.com/blog/exit-popups.

[39] "USPTO," [Online]. Available: https://www.namecheckr.com/.

[40] "Name Checkr," [Online]. Available: https://www.uspto.gov/.

[41] "Shopify Image Resizer," [Online]. Available: https://www.shopify.com/tools/image-resizer.

[42] "Remove Bg," [Online]. Available: https://remove.bg/.

[43] "GtMetrix," [Online]. Available: https://www.gtmetrix.com/.

[44] "Investopedia," [Online]. Available: https://www.investopedia.com/financial-edge/1012/how-much-americans-spend-on-halloween.aspx.

[45] "Adobe Analytics," [Online]. Available: https://blog.adobe.com/en/publish/2020/12/01/cyber-week-online-shopping.html#gs.xlwqva.

[46] "Forbes," [Online]. Available: https://www.forbes.com/sites/abrambrown/2020/08/06/tiktoks-highest-earning-stars-teen-queens-addison-rae-and-charli-damelio-rule/?sh=56d0abad5087.

[47] A. S. R. Out, "Bnc Tv," [Online]. Available: https://bnc.tv/black-content-based-instagram-page-sells-for-85m-owner-of-page-is-not-black/#:~:text=The%20owner%20of%20the%20Black,IMGN%20Media%20for%20%2485%20million..

[48] J. Orlowski, Director, *The Social Dilema*. [Film]. 2020.

[49] E.-C. Scale Bonus Training, "E-Commerce Activated," [Online]. Available: http://ecommerceactivated.com/scale.

[50] "Facebook Ads Manager," [Online]. Available: https://www.facebook.com/business/tools/ads-manager.

[51] "The Guardian," [Online]. Available: https://www.theguardian.com/technology/2012/apr/09/facebook-buys-instagram-mark-zuckerberg.

[52] "Google Ads," [Online]. Available: https://ads.google.com/.

[53] G. Roumeliotis, "Reuters," [Online]. Available: https://www.reuters.com/article/us-tiktok-cfius-exclusive-idUSKBN1XB4IL.

[54] TikTok, "TikTok Business," [Online]. Available: https://www.tiktok.com/business/en.

[55] @katieaka, "Twitter Blog," [Online]. Available: https://blog.twitter.com/en_us/a/2016/new-research-the-value-of-influencers-on-twitter.html.

[56] "Facebook Pixel," [Online]. Available: https://www.facebook.com/business/learn/facebook-ads-pixel.

[57] V. Beat, "Hubspot," [Online]. Available: https://blog.hubspot.com/blog/tabid/6307/bid/25110/5-steps-to-using-twitter-for-ecommerce-marketing.aspx.

[58] M. Farah, "Mo Farah," [Online]. Available: https://en.wikipedia.org/wiki/Mo_Farah.

[59] "Monetate," [Online]. Available: https://monetate.com/blog/2020-ecommerce-stats/.

[60] "Shopify," [Online]. Available: https://www.shopify.com/enterprise/site-performance-page-speed-ecommerce#:~:text=Through%20client%20experiments%2C%20web%20performance,the%20opposite%20is%20true%20too..

[61] "Klaviyo," [Online]. Available: www.Klaviyo.com.

[62] "Cone Comm," [Online]. Available: https://www.conecomm.com/news-blog/cone-releases-first-cause-consumer-behavior-study.

[63] N. Shacklock, "Linked In," [Online]. Available: https://www.linkedin.com/pulse/decoy-effect-how-businesses-tricking-your-mind-nic-shacklock?articleId=6622416310326427648.

[64] "Sumo," [Online]. Available: https://sumo.com/stories/ecommerce-upselling.

[65] L. W. J. Cohen, "CNBC," [Online]. Available: https://www.cnbc.com/2019/07/16/third-of-us-workers-considered-quitting-their-job-in-last-3-months.html#:~:text=More%20than%203.5%20million%20Americans,replace%20the%20workers%20they%20lose..

[66] A. Maslow, "Maslow's hierarchy of needs," "A theory of Human Motivation" in Psychological Review.

[67] N. Hill, Think And Grow Rich, The Ralston Society, 1937.

[68] "Forbes," [Online]. Available: https://www.forbes.com/sites/hillennevins/2021/01/25/shine-a-light-tom-brady-mlqh/?sh=6386c9b02296.

[69] "BBB," [Online]. Available: https://www.bbb.org/.

[70] M. R. P. Rosekind, K. B. B. Gregory, M. M. P. Mallis, S. L. M. Brandt, B. P. Seal and D. P. Lerner, "The Cost of Poor Sleep: Workplace Productivity Loss and Associated Costs," Journal of Occupational and Environmental Medicine:.

[71] The resources section of this book. EcommerceActivated.com/resources.

[72] "Paypal Working Capital," [Online]. Available: https://www.paypal.com/workingcapital/.

[73] "Kabbage Funding," [Online]. Available: https://www.kabbage.com/.

[74] "Stripe Funding Circle," [Online]. Available: https://stripe.com/works-with/fundingcircle.

[75] "Kick Starter," [Online]. Available: https://www.kickstarter.com/.

[76] "Indiegogo," [Online]. Available: https://www.indiegogo.com/.

[77] "Idea. Me," [Online]. Available: https://www.idea.me/.

[78] Shopify, "Shopify Capital," [Online]. Available: https://www.shopify.com/capital.

[79] "WF Lawyers," [Online]. Available: https://www.wf-lawyers.com/divorce-statistics-and-facts/.

[80] "Enterprise Ireland," [Online]. Available: https://www.enterprise-ireland.com/en/.

[81] "Campaign Monitor," [Online]. Available: https://www.campaignmonitor.com/resources/knowledge-base/how-

do-you-calculate-email-marketing-roi/#:~:text=When%20it%20comes%20to%20customer,on%20an%20email%20marketing%20campaign..

[82] "IBM," [Online]. Available: https://www.ibm.com/support/knowledgecenter/SS3NGB_1.6.0/ioc/use_sopconfig.html.

[83] "Think and Grow Rich," [Online]. Available: https://en.wikipedia.org/wiki/Think_and_Grow_Rich.

[84] E.-C. Broker Bonus, "E-Commerce Activated," [Online]. Available: http://ecommerceactivated.com/broker.

[85] E.-C. Call Training, "E-Commerce Activated," [Online]. Available: http://ecommerceactivated.com/ticket.

[86] E.-C. Call Bonues, "E-Commerce Activated," [Online]. Available: http://ecommerceactivated.com/speak.

Printed in Great Britain
by Amazon

61885707R00224